THE ANIMAL RIGHTS CRUSADE

The Growth of a Moral Protest·

James M. Jasper and Dorothy Nelkin

THE FREE PRESS
A Division of Macmillan, Inc.
NEW YORK

Maxwell Macmillan Canada
TORONTO

Maxwell Macmillan International
NEW YORK   OXFORD   SINGAPORE   SYDNEY

The Free Press
A Division of Macmillan, Inc.
866 Third Avenue, New York, N.Y. 10022

Maxwell Macmillan Canada, Inc.
1200 Eglinton Avenue East
Suite 200
Don Mills, Ontario M3C 3N1

Macmillan, Inc. is part of the Maxwell Communication
Group of Companies.

Printed in the United States of America

printing number
1 2 3 4 5 6 7 8 9 10

Library of Congress Cataloging-in-Publication Data

Jasper, James M.
    The animal rights crusade : the growth of a moral protest / James
M. Jasper and Dorothy Nelkin.
        p.   cm.
    Includes index.
    ISBN 0-02-916195-9
    1. Animal rights.   2. Social movements.   I. Nelkin, Dorothy.
II. Title.
HV4708.J37   1992
179' .3—dc20   91-26015
                                                                   CIP

For
James Dudley Jasper
and
Erica Epstein

Contents

Acknowledgments

Our research has relied on the cooperation of many people. Animal rights activists and supporters as well as scientists and others targeted by them helped us by submitting to extended interviews, opening their files for our perusal, and sending us detailed information. We have cited our many informants throughout the book. Julie Van Ness of the Argus Archives was especially helpful in guiding us through that collection. John Deats, Betty Ann Kevles, Roy Henrickson, Stephen Hilgartner, Mary Phillips, and Evelyn Walters graciously gave us access to their files and sent us materials. In addition, we developed our material and our sense of the movement from several years of observations at meetings, demonstrations, and animal rights events, and from reading the voluminous literature disseminated by the animal rights groups. With the help of graduate students at New York University (Ralph Chipman, Cynthia Gordon, Kelli Henry, Joan Lambe, David Starr, and Stella Zambarloukos), we surveyed participants at two demonstrations—one in New York City and one in California. In addition, we engaged friends, colleagues, and students—too many to name—in innumerable discussions and debates, as we tried to define the social meaning of the movement and to sort out our own ideas.

Several people provided invaluable services. Mary Bernstein was a tremendously resourceful research assistant, checking facts and quotations, calling strangers on the phone with odd questions, and patiently reconstructing references from minimal clues. Jane Poulsen, Tamara Dumanovsky, and Julie Newman also provided excellent assistance for briefer periods. We received useful comments on portions of early drafts from Susan Abrams, Sandra Bressler, Lee Clarke, Jonathan Cobb, Elliot Katz, John McCarthy, Mark Nelkin,

Andrew Rowan, Mark Sagoff, Neil Smelser, Joyce Tischler, and Alan Wolfe. Finally, we wish to thank our editor, Joyce Seltzer, for her patience, insight, and tenacity. Our research was supported by the National Science Foundation program on Ethics and Values Studies, grant number DIR-8820241. The views expressed in this book are those of the authors and do not necessarily reflect the view of the foundation.

Acronyms

AAAS	American Association for the Advancement of Science
AAVS	American Anti-Vivisection Society
AFAAR	American Fund for Alternatives to Animal Research
AFAR	Attorneys for Animal Rights
ALDF	Animal Legal Defense Fund
ALF	Animal Liberation Front
AMA	American Medical Association
ARM	Animal Rights Mobilization
ASPCA	American Society for the Prevention of Cruelty to Animals
CASH	Committee to Abolish Sport Hunting
CBRA	California Biomedical Research Association
CEASE	Coalition to End Animal Suffering in Experiments
CFAAR	Coalition for Animals and Animal Research, formerly AFAAR
CITES	Convention on International Trade in Endangered Species of Wild Fauna and Flora
CLEAR	Citizens for Life, Education, and Research
DELTA	Dedication and Everlasting Love to Animals
FACT	Food Animal Concerns Trust
FARM	Farm Animal Reform Movement
FBR	Foundation for Biomedical Research
FDA	Food and Drug Administration
FOA	Friends of Animals

HARE	Humans Against Rabbit Exploitation
HFA	Humane Farming Association
HSUS	Humane Society of the United States
IDA	In Defense of Animals
iiFAR	Incurably Ill for Animal Research
IPPL	International Primate Protection League
LD_{50}	Lethal Dose fifty percent
NEAVS	New England Anti-Vivisection Society
NIDA	National Institute on Drug Abuse
NIH	National Institutes of Health
NYU	New York University
PAWS	Performing Animal Welfare Society
PETA	People for the Ethical Treatment of Animals
RSPCA	Royal Society for the Prevention of Cruelty to Animals
SACA	Student Action Corps for Animals
SAV	Society Against Vivisection
SCAW	Scientists' Center for Animal Welfare
SPCA	Society for the Prevention of Cruelty to Animals
SUPRESS	Students United Protesting Research on Sentient Subjects
TSU	Trans-Species Unlimited (since 1990, Animal Rights Mobilization
USDA	United States Department of Agriculture

ONE

A Moral Crusade

On a warm spring day in May 1980, Henry Spira was on Manhattan's posh Fifth Avenue with a flatbed truck filled with white rabbits. With him were three hundred more demonstrators, many of them dressed in bunny suits. On the sidewalk in front of the headquarters of the cosmetics giant Revlon, they were protesting that company's extensive use of white rabbits to test the safety of new products. The demonstrators were angry about procedures in which substances were placed in rabbits' eyes to test if these ingredients caused redness, swelling, or cloudiness. Many demonstrators had been drawn to the protest by full-page advertisements in the *New York Times* and other papers that asked, "How many rabbits does Revlon blind for beauty's sake?"

After a friend left him a cat in 1973, Spira, a burly man in his early fifties, had become increasingly outraged over humans' treatment of animals, wondering about "the appropriateness of cuddling one animal while sticking a knife and fork into others." He grew more and more critical of such common practices as wearing furs and leather and eating meat. For more than a year he had talked to Revlon officials, hoping to persuade them to contribute several hundred thousand dollars to help develop alternative tests that did not use live animals. When Revlon officials listened politely but then ignored him, he put together a coalition of four hundred animal groups, mostly humane societies operating spay clinics and offering cats and dogs for adoption. And he gathered funds for the newspaper ads. He felt public opinion would be on his side: "I think there are very few people on the street who'll say, 'Yeah, go around and blind rabbits to produce another mascara.'"[1]

Following the May rally, public protests continued alongside Spira's private negotiations, and in December of 1980 Revlon capitulated, announcing that it would provide Rockefeller University $750,000 for research on alternative tests. Soon other companies followed Revlon's lead; by 1987 many had ended live animal testing; and the cosmetics industry claimed to have contributed about five million dollars to alternatives research.

Four years after the Revlon demonstration, another effort to liberate animals unfolded in the laboratories of the University of Pennsylvania Medical School. On Memorial Day weekend in 1984, five members of the Animal Liberation Front (ALF) surreptitiously entered the deserted research lab of Thomas Gennarelli, who headed a team of researchers studying the effects of severe head injuries. Underway for fourteen years, these experiments currently involved severe shocks and injuries—similar to whiplash in car accidents— to the heads of baboons. The intruders destroyed equipment worth $20,000 and removed sixty hours of videotapes made to document the experiments.

The members of the ALF shared Henry Spira's goal of eliminating any use of animals for human needs, but they felt a stronger sense of urgency that compelled them to break the law. In most of their break-ins—Pennsylvania was one of more than one hundred entries—the ALF has liberated animals rather than videotapes. Its members value animal lives so highly that they feel a moral obligation to act to save them, even to damage property in doing so. Violence against property, they claim, is justified to stop violence against living beings (the animals they liberate). As one activist put it, "Property laws are artificial constructs. We feel we answer to a higher law."[2]

Perhaps the most important result of the Memorial Day break-in is what then happened to the videotapes. The ALF, an illegal group designated as a "terrorist" organization by the FBI, passed the tapes to another animal rights group, People for the Ethical Treatment of Animals (PETA). PETA edited the tapes into a twenty-minute film called *Unnecessary Fuss,* which portrayed bantering among researchers and joking about the injured animals—"mocking them," as animal activists put it. It also appeared that the animals were not fully anesthetized. Scientists were painted as callous, even sadistic, and so brutal that discussion with them about their methods would be useless: direct action against such research was the only appropriate response. The film proved a powerful instrument for PETA in its efforts to recruit new and committed members to an emerging protest movement.

The Revlon and University of Pennsylvania incidents are just two among thousands of recent animal rights protests, lawsuits, break-ins, and other actions that have targeted scientific laboratories, cosmetic and pharmaceutical firms, slaughterhouses and butchers, fur ranchers and retailers, rodeos and circuses, hunters and trappers, carriage drivers, and even zoos. Since the late 1970s, new animal "rights" organizations have rejuvenated the older and larger animal welfare movement, and together they are reshaping public awareness of animals. As many as ten or fifteen million Americans send money to animal protection groups, which have proliferated: by 1990, there were several thousand animal welfare and several hundred animal rights organizations in the United States. Some focus on particular animals (The Beaver Defenders, Bat Conservation International); others have a religious bent (Life for God's Stray Animals, Jews for Animal Rights); some are organized around tactics (the Animal Legal Defense Fund); others protest particular uses or abuses of animals (Students United Protesting Research Experiments on Sentient Subjects); still others represent links with related causes (Feminists for Animal Rights). The pull of these groups was evident in June 1990, when 30,000 people participated in a march on Washington for animal rights, with slogans such as "Fur Is Dead," "No Tax Dollars for Torture," and "Blinding Bunnies Is Not Beautiful."

Renewed concerns about animals have generated a powerful social movement driven by a simple moral position: animals are similar enough to humans to deserve serious moral consideration. They are sentient beings entitled to dignified lives, and they should be treated as ends, not as means. Protestors ask how we can love our pets, yet experiment on identical animals in laboratories; how we can cuddle one animal, yet eat another. They have themselves mostly given up meat, dairy products, and eggs; they refuse to wear leather shoes or belts; they do not patronize the products of certain corporations; and many will not wear wool—let alone fur—garments. While some would allow occasional animal research if subjects are fully sedated and the benefits outweigh the harm, others say this concession violates the inherent right of animals to a full life independent of human goals. Movement leaders often use the morally charged language of good and evil, and their political actions and rhetorical style often display an absolutism that discourages discussion or negotiation with those who disagree.

The new movement has exploded into Americans' awareness. Animal rights has been the cover story of magazines as diverse as *Newsweek, U.S. News and World Report, New York Magazine,* the *Atlantic Monthly,* the *New Republic,* the *Village Voice,* the *Progressive,* and the lawyers' weekly *National Law Journal;* its issues have been featured in network television series like *L.A. Law, MacGyver,* and *Designing Women;* it has been examined in major news programs such as *48 Hours.* Despite a tendency to focus on secretive and sensationalist ALF commandos, most media coverage has been sympathetic to the ideas of the movement. Typically, the activists are portrayed as eccentric, but their positions are treated with respect. Comic strips such as *Doonesbury* and *Bloom County* have favorably portrayed animal activists and their issues. *Saturday Night Live* at least recognized the controversy over fur coats in a skit titled, "They're Better Off Dead." Celebrities such as Bob Barker, Doris Day, Casey Kasem, River Phoenix, and several of *The Golden Girls* have given their support to the cause.

Consumer goods have followed suit. One Barbie Doll is an "animal loving" Barbie, marketed as an animal rights volunteer—even as real-life activists attack the mink stole sold by the Spiegel Company for other Barbie Dolls. Vegetarian food is sold for the dogs of those with strict animal rights sensibilities. Public opinion polls show a slippage of support for scientific research using animals, even when it generates information about human health. Activists have delivered a crippling blow to the American fur industry—from which it may never recover. Animal protection is not only one of today's fastest-growing protest movements, it is one of the most effective.

The social roots of this movement lie in the changed relationship between humans and their fellow creatures that resulted from urbanization and industrialization in Western societies, as city dwellers began to encounter animals only as family pets, and less and less as instruments of labor and production. Animals have accompanied men and women throughout their history, some as members of the family to be cherished, others as tools to be used. But in modern times the balance between these attitudes—one sentimental, the other instrumental—has been questioned, as more and more people insist that all animals be treated as though they were partners— "companion animals"—rather than objects.

In the United States, the first societies to prevent cruelty to animals were founded in the 1860s as part of the more general humanitarian impulse of the time. While these societies persisted, further expansion of this animal welfare movement took place in the 1950s, with the founding of such organizations as the Humane Society of the United States. Most of these groups concentrated on problems associated with the growing number of pets: overpopulation and frequent abandonment, the issue of shelters, and the frequency of brutality and cruelty. These humane societies and welfare organizations saw animal cruelty coming from poorly educated or abusive individuals, not from the systematic activities of institutions.

A new ideological agenda for animal protection emerged dramatically in the late 1970s, combining ideas from several sources. It retained the animal welfare tradition's concern for animals as sentient beings that should be protected from unnecessary cruelty. But animal activists added a new language of "rights" as the basis for demanding animal liberation. In the individualist culture of America, "rights talk" is often the only way to express moral values and demands. Rights—whether of patients, women, fetuses, or animals—are accepted as a moral trump card that cannot be disputed. Justified in terms of tradition, nature, or fundamental moral principles, rights are considered non-negotiable. Protestors compare animal rights to human rights, and the charge of "speciesism" takes its place alongside racism and sexism. Wildlife traffickers are engaged in a "monkey slave trade," laboratories become "torture chambers," and animal testing is a "holocaust."

The moral vision of animal rightists is partly drawn from other recent movements, especially feminism and environmentalism. At the core of these ideologies is a critique of "instrumentalism," the confusion of ends and means said to prevail in contemporary society. According to this critique, instrumental attitudes reduce nature and women, as well as other humans—all with inherent value as ends in themselves—to the status of things and tools. At the same time, instrumentalism promotes technologies, markets, and bureaucracies—all intended to be the means for attaining the good life—to the status of ends. Uneasiness with instrumental attitudes is widespread: many people feel that there is something wrong with basing all decisions on economic values; that science lacks a human face; that consumer society creates artificial needs rather than satisfying real ones; that humans are treated like cogs in a machine.

Recent protest movements—ranging from Christian fundamentalists to radical feminists—insist that policies and decisions be guided by moral values and social needs, not by profits, technological feasibility, or bureaucratic inertia. Just as environmentalists question the exploitation of nature for commercial purposes, so animal rights advocates demand the end of animal exploitation for human gain. Animals, like human beings or nature, should be treated as ends rather than as means. This view grounded the mistreatment of animals in institutions rather than blaming misguided individuals. Rather than searching for individual scientists who inflicted unusual pain on their animal subjects, activists condemned all research using live animals, thereby attacking the heart of biomedical science. Instead of criticizing the occasional circus for its cruelty in training animals, they rejected any use of animals to entertain people as exploitation and humiliation. Here was a new view of the relationship between animals and human institutions, one that often condemned the very essence of those institutions. The appeal of this critique helps explain the transformation of animal protection into a radical animal rights movement.

But a fuller explanation lies in common cultural beliefs and implicit understandings about animals in our society, since the treatment of other species often reflects a culture's moral concerns. Animals were the first subject of paintings—on the walls of caves—and the first metaphors in human thought—for example, as symbols of tribes and families. They may have been the first objects to be worshiped, perceived as embodiments of spirits. Animals exhibit enough diversity of behavior and attributes to provide an extensive vocabulary for our own thinking. Throughout recorded history, men and women have found that animals were "good to think with," a rich source of symbols that humans could use to impose order on the world. They are blank slates onto which people have projected their beliefs about the state of nature, about "natural" forms of hierarchy and social organization, about language and rationality, and about moral behavior. Lessons are drawn from the supposed behavior of tortoises and hares, from the social organization of ants and grasshoppers, from the territoriality of lions and wolves.

We also project onto animals the characteristics of humans—sensitivity to pain, emotional bonds such as love and loyalty, the ability to plan and communicate. People have long endowed animals with human characteristics—crafty foxes, greedy pigs, lazy cats. Conversely, they use animals to characterize humans—people chatter like magpies, work like mules, and squirrel things away. We speak of male chauvinist pigs; we complain that Uncle Pete hogs the sports section. We use expressions like rat's nest, rat race, dirty rat, and smelling a rat. The sloth was even unlucky enough to be named after one of the seven deadly sins. But we can also romanticize animals, projecting onto them traits that make them better than people: a goodness, innocence, and purity rarely found in human company. Animals often come to represent the best in human nature, those qualities we cherish and try to protect.

If animals share so many human characteristics, what are the essential differences? The distinction between humans and other animals is the key issue in the growing number of disputes over animal protection. "A life is a life is a life," whether human or nonhuman, is a common refrain in animal rights rhetoric. Ironically, science itself has helped to blur the boundaries between humans and other animals. Evolutionary biology, after all, is controversial among Christian fundamentalists precisely because it violates the long assumed distinction between man and the animal world. While religious movements like creationists struggle to maintain boundaries, believing Man was created in God's image, animal rightists have taken biologists literally, denying moral distinctions between species as the "effluvium of a discredited metaphysics."[3]

For most people, the boundaries between animals and humans are intuitively clear. A human life is simply worth more than a non-human life, and while animals deserve some moral consideration, they are not to be exempt from human use. Such distinctions, however, remain matters of belief, not of evidence; they are affected by cultural preferences, personal values, and moral sentiments—traits not entirely open to rational persuasion. Rhetoric that compares animal suffering with the holocaust, that equates speciesism with racism, has emotive power for those who blur the boundaries between humans and other species. For others, these metaphors appear outlandish, threatening, dangerously defying accepted categories. The conflict between animal advocates and animal users is far more than a matter of contrasting tastes or interests. Opposing world views, concepts of identity, ideas of community, are all at stake. The animal rights controversy is about the treatment of animals, but it is also about our definition of ourselves and of a moral society. For this reason, it cannot be easily resolved.

Animal rights is a moral crusade. Its adherents act upon explicit moral beliefs and values to pursue a social order consistent with their principles. Their fervent moral vision crowds out other concerns. Most moral crusades focus on single issues: some focus on abortion; others on drunken driving; still others on the evils of pornography. Their members—moral missionaries—often insist they have no broader partisan agenda. They are less interested in material benefits for themselves than in correcting perceived injustices. Animals are a perfect cause for such a crusade: seen as innocent victims whose mistreatment demands immediate redress, they are an appealing lightning rod for moral concerns.

The symbolic importance of animals in this crusade underscores the importance of ideas in inspiring social movements, shaping their tactics, and enhancing or limiting their effects. To organize a crusade, movement leaders appeal to the moral sentiments of like-minded citizens, inciting their anger with emotive rhetoric and strategies ranging from colorful public rallies to clandestine break-ins that free animals from laboratories. The language of moral crusades is sometimes shrill, self-righteous, and uncompromising, for bedrock principles are non-negotiable. In the strident style of Old Testament prophets, scolding and condemning their society, organizers point to evils that surround them and to catastrophes that will befall society in the absence of reform. Extreme and even illegal strategies and tactics are seen as justified in order to stop widespread immoral practices. Their sense of moral urgency encourages believers to ignore laws and conventional political processes, and they organize themselves into groups structured for quick action, not participatory debate. Proselytizing and interventionist in their style, such crusades frequently appear dangerous to those who do not share their judgmental and uncompromising views.

Yet animal protection groups vary widely in their aims and thus in their shrillness. Contrasting goals, tactics, and philosophical positions bring forth different organizations that form a continuum from reformist to radical. However, they tend to cluster into three kinds of groups that we label welfarist, pragmatist, and fundamentalist. In the humane tradition of the ASPCA, animal *welfarists* accept most current uses of animals, but seek to minimize their suffering and pain. They view animals as distinct from humans, but as objects entitled to compassion. Their reformist position, advocated through public education and lobbying for protective legislation, has long enjoyed wide public support and continues to do so. Welfarist groups like the SPCAs and the Humane Society of the United States existed before the animal rights movement appeared, and remain the largest, most powerful organizations.

In the late 1970s, however, more radical groups formed on the fringes of the animal welfare movement, redefining the issue of animal welfare as one of animal rights. Some of these new advocates organized around the well-articulated and widely disseminated utilitarian perspective of philosopher Peter Singer. Because animals could feel pain and pleasure, Singer argued that they deserved moral consideration, and he demanded drastic reduction in their use. The *pragmatist* groups feel that certain species deserve greater consideration than others, and would allow humans to use animals when the benefits deriving from their use outweigh their suffering. They seek to reduce animal use through legal actions, political protest, and negotiation. Henry Spira is a prominent example of a pragmatist.

Some of these new advocates, however, demanded the immediate abolition of all exploitation of animals, on the grounds that animals have inherent, inviolable rights. These more extreme animal rights *fundamentalists* believe that people should never use animals for their own pleasures or interests, regardless of the benefits. Some see even the ownership of pets as a distortion of the animals' natural lives. Insisting that increased understanding of head injuries does not justify harming baboons, the Animal Liberation Front expresses the fundamentalists' position, as well as their compelling sense of urgency. Although far less numerous than pragmatist or welfarist organizations, these groups set the tone of the new animal rights movement. And they are growing in size and wealth.

These distinctions are not absolute or rigid. Some activists, for example, believe in full animal rights, but pursue their goals with pragmatic strategies. Many shift their language and tactics depending on the issue or political arena. And all are tempted to indulge in fundamentalist rhetoric that simplifies the moral issues and demonizes opponents. But these three labels are useful to highlight important differences and tensions within a movement often described in monolithic terms. For the movement itself is divided over many issues: whether the same attention should be given to helping wild animals and domestic ones, whether insects or reptiles should be championed as fervently as furry mammals, and, especially, whether destructive tactics are acceptable.

Nevertheless, welfarists, pragmatists, and fundamentalists cooperate on specific issues, and their interests as well as rhetoric often merge. Together, they form a remarkably powerful animal protection movement, in which the pragmatists and fundamentalists represent the radical wing—the animal rights crusade. These crusaders would like to challenge Americans to rethink their fundamental beliefs about themselves and their connection to the world around them. They wonder if the boundaries we have drawn between ourselves and other animals are as rigid as we suppose. They would force us to extend the rights we promote for humans to other species. They want nothing short of a moral revolution that would change our food and clothing, our science and health care, our entire relationship to the natural world.

TWO

Moral Sentiments

Animal rights activists call their pets "companion animals," implying a relationship based more on friendship and equality than on domination and obedience. Their language reflects two moral intuitions: that animals are like humans in essential ways, and that they must not be exploited instrumentally simply to fulfill human goals.[1] Animals, in their view, not only feel pain, but have the capacity to live "full" and "happy" lives. They can communicate, express their emotions, and return our gaze. Such similarities, protestors believe, give animals unassailable rights and impose on humans corresponding obligations. Though animals are not themselves moral agents—they cannot, after all, reciprocate moral responsibility—we must take them into account in making our own decisions. Like children, they are vulnerable, innocent, incapable of demanding their own rights, but nevertheless to be respected and protected.

This way of regarding animals is part of a tradition of sentimental anthropomorphism, which is centuries old but has gained new momentum in the last quarter of the twentieth century. It portrays animals as partners to humans in intimate emotional relationships, valued for their own sake and not merely regarded as useful tools, metaphors, or totems which we might use in pursuit of our own ends.[2] If animals have inherent worth, activists argue, then men and women must no longer treat them as resources, as mere means for human pleasures. These arguments against using animals as instruments have changed traditional concerns for animal welfare into an aggressive movement of animal rights activists.

Anthropomorphism, always present in the animal welfare tradition, has today combined with a critique of instrumentalism to spur and energize the movement for animal rights. Drawing on the ideologies of recent political movements such as feminism and environmentalism, animal rightists attack the goals of profit, bureaucratic self-interest, and technological development they feel are crowding our moral values. They hark back to Jeremy Bentham, who said that animals, "on account of their interests having been neglected by the insensibility of the ancient jurists, stand degraded into the class of *things*."[3]

How have so many people today come to regard the animal kingdom in these terms? To comprehend the animal rights vision, we need to explore the idea of anthropomorphism: the attribution of human characteristics to nonhuman entities, especially animals. Humans have always projected their own feelings and intentions onto animals, for we have no way of understanding creatures that are both very familiar yet utterly alien.

Anthropomorphic projections break down the boundaries that humans perceive between themselves and other animals. Animal rightists believe that animals share traits such as the ability to plan a life, to have intentions and to carry them out, or to be loyal and loving. They say that, "A life is a life is a life . . . It's alive and that's all that matters," and that, "A rat is a pig is a dog is a boy." Taking this belief to its extreme, one activist could even claim that "it is obvious that the life of a healthy chimpanzee must be granted a greater value than the life of a human who is a hopelessly retarded infant orphan."[4] How are such beliefs possible?

Most societies in the past (and many today) have held two distinct attitudes toward animals. The first is an intimate, familial view, marked by emotional attachment and sympathy: as part of the family, pets are kept in the house, given names, and often highly prized. In contrast, in the instrumental view of animals, they are resources to be exploited for human benefit or pleasure: to be hunted, eaten, milked, worked, and even tortured for human amusement. René Descartes expressed this view when he claimed that animals were like inanimate machines, incapable of feeling pain. Through most of human history, these seemingly opposed attitudes have peacefully coexisted.

Historically, animals were "subjected *and* worshipped, bred *and* sacrificed. Today the vestiges of this dualism remain among those who live intimately with, and depend upon, animals. A peasant becomes fond of his pig and is glad to salt away its pork."[5] Yet those who could afford the luxury of pets (the English word dates only from the sixteenth century, indicating the relative newness of the practice) have often distinguished between categories of animals, regarding some as household pets and others as inanimate resources. Those who pampered their pets were capable of atrocious cruelty toward other animals. While British gentry lavished attention on their hounds, they used them to hunt other species. While Spanish aristocrats treasured their riding horses, they sacrificed other horses to the bulls. Exceptional were those individuals, such as Saint Francis of Assisi, who expressed a spiritual concern for *all* animals.

The balance between sentimental and instrumental attitudes shifted, however, with the industrialization of the West. As people retreated emotionally into a private life centered around the immediate family and distinct from the workplace, they slowly lost contact with animals as anything other than family pets. By the nineteenth century, British and Americans were obsessed with pets, and found many similarities between animals and humans. Partly from observation and partly from projection of their own feelings, they attributed to animals feelings such as love and affection, obedience and loyalty, trustworthiness and valor. A novel and sentimental form of anthropomorphism spread, as Victorians saw pets as objects of pure affection. Such perceptions of animals as thinking and feeling creatures were necessarily matters of subjective interpretation: science could demonstrate little beyond the experience of pain in animals. Thus, where some people saw in animals a broad spectrum of human characteristics, others saw very few. This divergence remains true today.

If humans vary in their tendency to anthropomorphize animals, animals differ in their susceptibility to such treatment. The animal traits that encourage anthropomorphism include the ability to express pain and suffering in ways reminiscent of humans: through whines, whimpers, and cries, or by spilling red blood. Species that are related to humans through evolution, that look like humans, that have "cute" faces like those of human infants, or that seem capable of complex mental states are likely to arouse anthropomorphic sympathy. Fur is a big advantage over scales. Similarly, with their eyes large in proportion to their heads, and their heads large in proportion to their bodies, many animals resemble children. Size, longevity, and the lack of any repugnant habits help to arouse sentimental feelings. It is easier to project one's thoughts and feelings onto a cat, dog, or ape than onto a tree frog, mosquito, or bat.[6]

Certain anthropomorphic beliefs distinguish animal rights from animal welfare groups. Rightists, both the pragmatic and the fundamentalist groups, for example, emphasize the cognitive as well as emotional life of animals. While the welfare movement focuses on the animals' ability to feel pain and have emotions, fundamentalists insist that animals have a full, conscious life to lead, so that humans cannot morally justify cutting that life short, even painlessly. It is not enough that cattle be slaughtered painlessly, they should not be raised for human use at all. It is not enough that chickens range free: they should not even be used for their eggs. Welfarists and some pragmatists resist such extreme beliefs: How do we know what a full life is for an animal? Do dogs derive more pleasure from being trained to obey humans than from running wild? Do animals plan their lives? The varying answers to such questions has been a source of tension even within the animal protection movement.

Changes in beliefs about animals extend back to the growth of towns and mercantile values in the midst of the aristocratic, agrarian societies of sixteenth- and seventeenth-century Europe. A new urban middle class appeared, and by the nineteenth century it had changed daily life in Western Europe. The "civilizing process" that discouraged the new bourgeoisie from spitting on the floor, wiping their noses on their sleeves, and eating with their hands, represented an increased concern for the feelings and sensibilities of others.[7]

The keystone of bourgeois emotional life was a new image of family, home, and especially children—an image and valuation that laid the foundation for a new perception of animals. Previously, the idea of family had coincided with the household, including servants, retainers, and others not related by blood. There had been little private space in such households: people passed through the chambers where others slept, and several generations would share a single sleeping chamber, if not a bed. Rising bourgeois concern for the sensibilities of individuals required greater intimacy and privacy for the nuclear family, and unrelated members of the household were pushed into separate floors or wings of merchants' homes. A new gentleness appeared in family relations.

Within the emerging bourgeois family, children were increasingly viewed as vulnerable beings in need of protection. In previous centuries, small children had been seen as simply small adults, but childhood now became a special stage of life. The mothers and nannies who cared for children began to see them as cute and lovable creatures to be cuddled and cherished. At the same time, moralists, priests, and philosophers wrote about children as intellectually and morally fragile, in need of discipline and training, in need of education. As children became the focus of moral concern in Western Europe, sensitivity to all vulnerable creatures became a recognized virtue.

Heightened emotional bonds within the middle-class family—its sentimentalization—provided the base for changing attitudes toward animals, as they increasingly became part of the family. As urbanization removed many people from their direct dependence on animals as a resource, except as a means of transportation, close experience with animals other than pets declined. The bourgeois wife in town had fewer chickens to feed or cows to milk, so that her appreciation of animals came from her pet dogs. By 1700, people were naming their pets, often with human names (especially in England); pets appeared regularly in paintings; and some even received legacies when their owners died. When pets died, they (unlike farm animals) were never eaten; often they were buried in style, with epitaphs written by their owners.[8] As the family home and its members became privatized and idealized, so did the family pet.

This new attitude toward animals had a distinct basis in social class, as Robert Darnton's description of "The Great Cat Massacre" dramatically suggests.[9] The massacre occurred in the 1730s at a Paris printing shop where the wife of the master printer was "impassioned" of several pet cats. They were fed at the table with the family, while the printer's apprentices ate table scraps—the cat food of the time— in the kitchen. In symbolic rebellion, the apprentices and workers captured sackfuls of pet and stray cats, held a mock trial, and hanged them all. Torturing cats was an old European tradition: a favorite pastime at many holidays was to set cats on fire, largely to hear their terrible "caterwauling." The apprentices' action dramatized the conflict between the traditional view of animals and the emerging sensibility of the wealthy classes. The new moral sensitivity began in the rising middle class, but quickly conquered much of the aristocracy, and eventually—although not widely until the twentieth century— the laboring classes. In each case, its apostles were mainly women, priests, and the occasional philosopher who articulated the changing beliefs.

Before the nineteenth century, only a few individuals had expressed a heightened moral sensibility toward animals. Margaret Cavendish, Duchess of Newcastle, wrote extensively in the 1650s and 1660s about the human tendency to tyrannize other species.

Considered highly eccentric by her peers, she criticized the hunting of song birds and claimed that "the groans of a dying beast strike my soul."[10] In the eighteenth century, pastors and poets such as Alexander Pope, John Gay, and William Blake attacked cruelty to animals, reinterpreting the biblical acknowledgement of man's dominion over nature to mean thoughtful stewardship rather than ruthless exploitation. As the age of democratic revolutions ushered in new standards of respect and dignity for the rights of individuals, new attention was paid to the treatment of animals. In the often-quoted words of Jeremy Bentham in 1789, the question to ask about animals, ". . . is not Can they *reason*? nor Can they *talk*? but, Can they *suffer*?" Here was a new criterion, one that placed humans and animals in the same circle rather than drawing a boundary between them.

Science of the eighteenth and nineteenth centuries further fueled concern about animals by blurring traditional boundaries. Theological assumptions had long guided scientific thought, and theories about the "fixity of species" drew clear distinctions between man and the animal world. But in the eighteenth century, naturalists like the Comte de Buffon—who thought the orangutan to be the missing link between humans and other species—began to speculate about the possibility of evolution, as they tried to explain the development of increasingly complex forms of life. These thoughts culminated in Darwin's controversial theory of natural selection. The different mental powers and moral senses of animals and humans, Darwin concluded, were of degree and not of kind, and he wrote *The Expression of Emotion in Man and Animals* to demonstrate their common physiological source. Many of his contemporaries resisted the new science, for denying any qualitative gulf between humans and other animals seemed to challenge the overarching design and ultimate purpose of God. Louis Agassiz, for example, insisted that the essential characteristics of every species must be distinct and immutable, though he accepted the idea of evolutionary change. However, Victorian culture soon absorbed Darwinian ideas. For many animal lovers in Britain and the United States, the theory of evolution raised other questions: If humans and brute creatures shared common ancestors, could their intelligence and their ability to feel pain be so different?[11]

The nineteenth-century expansion of industry and cities in Britain and America accelerated the spread of bourgeois moral sensibilities, including sympathy for animals, across all social classes. The realities of nature had little bearing on the lives of those in cities, who were free to project onto nature a pleasant, pastoral image that overlooked its cruelties and dangers. They could forget the violent, precarious lives of animals in the wild and exaggerate their innocence and goodness. The romanticization of nature was largely a reaction to industrial society and the passing of rural life. Nature in towns and cities had been domesticated, reduced to a few tame, symbolic replicas: household pets, the garden and lawn of the suburban house, and the landscape paintings that became a staple image in every bourgeois parlor.[12]

As the family and the home came to represent a "haven in a heartless world," a refuge from the cutthroat pressures of a market society, pets were part of that haven. Pet ownership became a fad in Victorian Britain among all social classes, though the kind of lives pets led depended on the wealth of their owners. The pet-products industry so familiar to us today had its origins in Britain of the 1840s. Wealthy middle class families, perhaps as badges of status, might spend hundreds of pounds sterling on a purebred dog, and they purchased special dog food, combs and brushes, brass collars, and even gold and silver ornaments for their pets.[13]

By the end of the nineteenth century, the British and American middle classes had learned to see in their pets a range of feelings and responses not so different from those of humans. But they often romanticized animals as innocent and pure: animals were similar to humans, yet in some ways better. They needed protection, and were a worthy object for compassion. Even while servants were treated as inanimate and the poor lived in vicious conditions, animals and children became the focus of reform movements.

———

The trends that gave birth to the nineteenth-century humane movement are far stronger in contemporary America. More people now live in cities or suburbs, far removed from conditions where animals are a natural presence and resource. By 1980, barely a quarter of Americans were classified by the Census as residing in rural areas or small towns (under 2,500). And fewer than 3 percent of employed Americans worked in agriculture, the industry most likely to retain traditional attitudes toward animals.[14] As middle-class lifestyles and values have expanded, so too have bourgeois compassion and emotional sensitivity to animals.

Today most homes in the United States contain pets, with pet ownership at its highest point ever. There are over one hundred million pet dogs and cats in this country, found in about 60 percent of households. Americans have half a billion pets, including fish and other species. Animals are appealing because they offer straightforward companionship in a world where relationships with humans are often painful and complex. Pets appear innocent, grateful, forgiving, and steady in their love. They may provide behavioral surprises, but few emotional ones—almost the opposite of human friends and lovers. Pets offer a kind of social relationship that human beings often fail to provide.

Today's burgeoning pet-products industry testifies to Americans' affection for their pets. The patterns of pampering reflect both contemporary prosperity—more people have more cash to spend on pets—and current ideas about what is necessary and desirable for a high quality of life. As humans adopt new products and professional services, they believe their pets deserve them as well. Even the indulgent Victorians would be shocked to see psychiatric services for pets, the new profession of animal dentistry, or expensive animal surgery. Dogs have root canals, hip replacements, plastic surgery, acupuncture, and radiation treatment; one California schnauzer even received a pacemaker. Boston's Angell Memorial Animal Hospital has a blood bank for cats and dogs, and in 1989 held a donor drive. There are attorneys to help clients with estate planning for pets. One New York artist does a thriving business in pet portraits, at $1,500 each. Another designs furniture for animals, with a dog's bed starting at $5,000. Dog clothing is no longer limited to knit sweaters; there are mink stoles, bow ties, raincoats, and even nail polish.

Pet foods—a $7 billion industry—also reflect anthropomorphic projection of human tastes: "Canine Quencher" is a bottled water for dogs; "Frosty Paws" is an ice-cream substitute to please dogs without adding pounds; "Poached Salmon Dinner" and "Catviar" are for the upper class cat. And, of course, there are low-cholesterol foods. Eukanuba is the "first New Age dog food, a high-powered nibble for high-powered dogs on the move." But the extreme in projecting human preferences onto pets may be the vegetarian food marketed for that ultimate carnivore, the dog. "For Fido, broccoli and yogurt" is recommended by a veterinarian who practices holistic medicine. "Our pets can benefit from the same holistic care that we are learning to give to ourselves."[15]

Perceptions of animals among urban Americans in the 1980s has been marked by these distinctly anthropomorphic attitudes and values in contrast to the utilitarian sentiments which once prevailed (and still do in rural areas).[16] People treat their cats and dogs as if they were human members of the family. One survey found that 99 percent of owners talk to their pets; 80 percent say that, at times, their pets are their closest friends; half keep photos of pets in their wallets or on their desks; one quarter celebrate their pets' birthdays; and more than half share their beds with their pets.[17] They interpret the responses of their pets—their facial expressions, sounds, and body movements—in human terms. Pet owners can go overboard in their anthropomorphism, assuming human qualities that extend well beyond provable evidence. Saying that animals feel pain is not controversial; feeding them vegetarian food and dressing them like children is. While animals often benefit from the protection and indulgent treatment that follows extreme anthropomorphism, imposing human traits on an animal can even be harmful. One woman gave her dog an ulcer and "reduced it to a nervous wreck by spoon-feeding it while it was forced to sit on a chair at the dinner table."[18]

The attention lavished on pets has affected not only the marketplace but also scientific research, which has given new credibility to anthropomorphic beliefs. Animal–human relationships are a growing field of scientific investigation: in 1981 the University of Pennsylvania held a conference on the human–companion animal bond attended by 400 scientists from around the world; 1,000 attended a Boston conference in 1986. They discussed, for example, the role of companion animals in the treatment of disturbed children, the elderly, and people trying to deal with life crises. Others have found that watching an aquarium or petting a dog can reduce anxieties, even lower blood pressure.[19] These experiences and observations have helped to "humanize" animals.

So, too, has research on animal communication and intelligence. Scientists who work on animal behavior argue for a kind of equality of intelligence across species, in that "every animal is the smartest" in its own ecological niche.[20] Koko the gorilla has learned human sign language, and primate studies have promoted both "the anthropomorphizing of the animal and the animalizing of the human being."[21] Other species communicate in ways scientists are only beginning to appreciate fully, providing insights into their thought processes. Whales sing each other complex songs that last up to thirty minutes and incorporate individual innovations. Musician Paul Winter began working to save whales around 1970 because he saw an "obvious intelligence" behind their haunting songs, and "found out that these wonderful creatures were being exterminated for lipstick and dog food."[22]

The ultimate anthropomorphism, in which creatures combine human and nonhuman traits or humans and animals exchange roles, is a common theme in popular culture—for example, in films like *Planet of the Apes*. Children's fantasy worlds are populated by surprising creatures like Eeyore and Piglet, Mr. Toad, Big Bird, Smurfs, and Teenage Mutant Ninja Turtles. Teddy bears and human dolls mingle as playmates. In a popular comic strip, a six-year-old boy named Calvin has a constant companion named Hobbes—to Calvin an articulate, living tiger, to others a silent stuffed animal. Children learn to converse, to play, and to try out social roles through interaction with imaginary animals.

Because artists frequently express new intuitions before others are fully aware of them, works of the imagination lend insight into emerging attitudes toward animals. Some artists project their anthropomorphic sentiments in political ways. Sue Coe's "Porkopolis" is a series of paintings portraying the lives of pigs from their origins in horrid factory farms to their slaughter in nightmarish assembly lines. Susan Boulet paints portraits that blend features of animals and of humans. A short story by Amy Hempel depicts animal rights sensibilities, as a widow who adores her cats begins to hear voices describing the slaughter of animals around the world, voices that become so persistent that they destroy her.[23] Another writer, Desmond Stewart, tells a story in which a species from outer space lands on Earth and uses humans as we now use other species. In his story, some humans are bred as food; others as work animals; others as pets; some are hunted; others are deployed to search out prey. The story ends with the cooking of a young woman according to an old human recipe for a lobster; her attempts to escape are dismissed as "reflex action."[24] Creative artists push the limits of sensibility, language, and understanding.

The conditions of modern urban life which sustain anthropomorphic sentiments have persisted, even accelerated, in recent decades. The pervasiveness of pet ownership, research into animal cognition, portraits of personified animals in cartoons, children's books, science fiction, and movies—all serve to reinforce romanticized and anthropomorphic sentiments about animals. These trends, however, are insufficient by themselves to explain the sudden growth of the animal rights movement.

Also critical to the development of the contemporary animal rights movement were ideas articulated in the 1960s and 1970s, as growing political disaffection condemned the instrumental attitudes driving the major institutions of American society. The generations of middle class children raised after World War II, never threatened with severe economic hardship or domestic war, developed special concerns for environmental quality, participation in workplace decisions, and the accountability of government institutions, and the postwar expansion of higher education gave them the intellectual tools with which to articulate their values. They criticized the confusion of technical means with moral ends, the reliance on balancing costs and benefits, the use of technical feasibility as the main criterion for social and policy choices. Efficiency, they claimed, had become the only criterion that counted in modern society. This instrumentalism, they feared, minimized the importance of moral considerations.[25]

Several protest movements formed around this anti-instrumental position and its emphasis on moral values rather than material gains. In the 1960s, the New Left brought attention to the instrumental and denigrating uses of humans by corporations and the state. The sins of Stalinism, which made citizens mere tools of the state, were as horrible as those of capitalism, and the New Left questioned the Old Left's concern with economic growth and production. Inspired by this critique, environmentalists, feminists, and antinuclear and peace activists soon attacked instrumental attitudes toward nature and women. These protestors associated instrumental reasoning with capitalist priorities, guided by profit more than by human needs; or with bureaucratic preoccupation with smoothly functioning organizations more than with the quality of life of employees. They sometimes implicated political parties as pursuing parochial goals and being distant from the voters who supported them. They often implicated science as the very essence of instrumentalism, creating knowledge with little regard to its social and moral consequences.

Nineteenth-century Romantics had attacked the pursuit of progress as the destruction of nature, and their views have become a significant part of the discourse of protest since the 1960s. The ideology and rhetoric developed by earlier social movements provided a set of beliefs about society and a language that animal rights activists could draw upon as they sought to replace exploitative attitudes toward animals with an ethos of care and sympathy. The emerging vision challenged the view of nature as a store of raw materials, as inputs for productive economic activity. The new vision—"Limits to Growth," "Small is Beautiful,"—saw nature as a fragile web of interconnections that linked humans to the rest of the universe, and caused many to question their own treatment of the environment. Animal rights protestors believe that, "Human beings must live in harmony with nature in order to survive." They express suspicion of large bureaucracies, unfettered profits, and never ending economic growth. They believe that technology is "out of control." In contrast to the humane tradition motivated by compassion for individual animals, the anti-instrumental rhetoric of the 1960s and 1970s suggested that the abuse of animals was the modus operandi of many major social and commercial institutions.

Reinforcing the critique of instrumentalism which set humane against technocratic values was the rhetoric of "rights" that burgeoned in the 1970s. Inspired by the civil rights movement and emboldened by increased channels of participation available in the 1970s, women, ethnic and racial groups, and the mentally or physically handicapped demanded rights to full economic and political participation. Special-interest groups such as tenants, gun owners, pornographers, and creationists couched their demands to pursue particular activities in the moral language of rights. Discussions about the care of patients and the treatment of research subjects proliferated, in recognition that the social goals of science were infringing on individual rights.[26] Around the world, human rights were widely discussed, especially during the Carter administration. Many animal rights activists, seeing animals as yet another oppressed and invisible group, seized upon the language of rights to express their aims and agenda. They called upon the popular rhetoric of rights to empower their own crusade.

During the 1980s, the critique of instrumentalism also gained from the popularity of the so-called New Age philosophies. The New Age movement, which includes ritual healing and human potential groups, derives primarily from Eastern mystical religions organized around holistic philosophies. Its sympathizers believe in an energy that flows through the universe, linking past with present, the individual with the universe, and living with nonliving entities. They believe one must live one's life in accordance with this flow, not against it, building up good rather than bad "karma." The New Age discourse includes ideas about spiritual responsibility, the creation of an alternative moral order, and a rejection of instrumental relationships. As one New Age commentator expressed his concern for animals: "Our disregard for animal life and animal welfare contributes to our gang warfare problem in urban areas. Our youth have not learned respect for life in general."[27]

The New Age social mission includes promoting consumer choices that recognize the interdependence between humans and the natural world. New Age magazines are filled with "alternative" products. They ask the buyer to think about how an object was produced and what effect it will have on the world. How many pesticides drained into the ground to grow a broccoli? What will happen to the plastic container after it is discarded? Increasingly, attention has turned to the effects of products on animals: were rabbits blinded to test a shampoo? Did animals suffer to make this meal? Hoping to sensitize consumers to the implications of their choices for animals, animal rights groups have found a convenient ally in the New Age movement. The publications—not to mention the philosophies—of these two movements support each other. If the humane tradition fostered a sensitivity to the suffering of animals, and the critique of instrumentalism added awareness of the institutional structures behind this suffering, the New Age movement contributed consumerist strategies for changing institutional practices. The sentiments of these groups converged with the moral rhetoric of rights to yield a worldview congenial to the animal rights movement.

New Age philosophies and anti-instrumental movements reflect a cluster of concerns that have appeared often in the last 200 years: holistic health, a romantic view of nature, and the sentimentalization of animals. The American, Sylvester Graham, combined them in the 1830s, building a philosophical system around temperance, celibacy, and especially vegetarianism (he created the graham cracker). An outbreak of similar ideas occurred in Weimar Germany and proved useful to the rise of the Nazis. There were 679 animal protection societies in Germany in the early 1930s, and many philosophical treatises projecting their views. In August 1933, Hermann Göring, then chairman of the Prussian ministerial cabinet and later the author of the "final solution" of the Jewish question, issued an order prohibiting the vivisection of animals in Prussian territory. "To the Germans," he declared in a public broadcast, "animals are not merely creatures in the organic sense, but creatures who lead their own lives and who are endowed with perceptive faculties, who feel pain and experience joy. . . . An absolute and permanent prohibition of vivisection is not only a necessary law to protect animals . . . but it is also a law for humanity itself."[28] Any person engaged in such practices would be "removed to a concentration camp." Bavaria soon issued similar prohibitions, and in 1934 the national government prohibited unnecessary torment of animals.[29] In Nazi eyes, biomedical science was a heavily Jewish—that is, polluted—profession, while, in contrast, animals were symbols of nature and purity. Naturally, opponents of animal rights love to point to this strange episode, while animal activists are infuriated by the association.[30]

Today, holistic healing, anti-instrumentalism, and concern for animals hardly take the perverse form they did in Germany. But animal rights is part of a broad tendency for political movements to contrast their views with the instrumentalism of formal organizations.[31] It represents a search for bedrock moral principles in a world that many find so bureaucratized that there is little room for individual moral choices.

The role of emerging moral and political sentiments in sparking the animal rights movement reveals a process common to many protest movements. All complex societies contain diverse and often conflicting moral sentiments and values that serve as guides to acceptable behavior. As transformations of social institutions and common practices generate new political sentiments, certain people are quicker than others to question dominant values. This may be because they engage more fully in the new practices—for instance, living in towns rather than on farms. Perhaps their occupations encourage them to analyze or challenge existing beliefs, as with artists and philosophers. Or they may feel alienated or oppressed by the dominant institutions of society, as do many women. It is through social movements that such groups find a new source of personal meaning and a way to articulate and disseminate their new moral vision.

The present animal rights movement grew out of the transformations from rural to urban life, from farms to factories, and from the use of animals as tools to their role as pets. Changing social situations like these have always shaped the moral visions underlying protest movements. The civil rights movement, for example, arose in the 1950s after many Southern blacks had moved from rural areas to cities, where preachers were more likely to offer "an emphasis on the everyday demands of the social gospel" rather than a "stress on 'otherworldly rewards'."[32] Biblical stories of Moses leading his people out of slavery helped inspire the emerging movement. Promising actions at the Federal level—most notably *Brown V. Topeka Board of Education in 1954*—helped draw this vision in an integrationist direction, as opposed to the earlier separatism of Marcus Garvey and, later, black nationalists.[33] Similarly, in the antinuclear movement, large numbers of young people were inspired by ecological and feminist critiques of bureaucracy, centralization, and state control to join local opponents of nuclear plants. Higher education, affluent childhoods, and occupations outside industrial production allowed them to pursue quality-of-life issues such as participation and democracy. As changing social practices generate new moral sentiments, goals once unimaginable can be formulated. These sentiments are an essential backdrop to any social movement.

The growth of cities and suburbs has deprived most Americans of instrumental contacts with animals, and the spread of pet owning has encouraged sentimentalism. Animals are widely perceived as similar to humans, yet romanticized as more innocent and pure. Science has contributed to a blurring of boundaries between humans and other species by acknowledging the complex mental life of many mammals. Thus, humane and sentimental impulses have deep roots in modern Western history. Animal rights claims emerged from this tradition, combining compassion with new political sentiments of the last thirty years—the distrust of instrumentalism, the rhetoric of rights, and the philosophy of the New Age. Together, these ideas explain why today's activists could imagine demands for animals far beyond those envisioned by the humane tradition of the nineteenth century.

THREE

The Birth of a Movement

In 1976, the moral sensibilities of thousands of New York City cat lovers were assaulted when they heard that painful experiments were taking place on the sexual behavior of these favored house pets. Henry Spira helped to mobilize these sensibilities in a protest that marked the beginning of contemporary animal rights activism. The groups that began to emerge at this time used dramatic and expressive public actions to implement their ideological positions. They were fervent in their language, their tactics, and their methods of attracting new recruits to the cause of animal rights.

Spira's activities began after his participation in a New York University continuing education course on "animal liberation" taught by philosopher Peter Singer. The course galvanized students who had been interested in the treatment of animals but lacked an ideological frame of reference and spur to action. Spira had spent much of his life writing about oppression and attacking large organizations, including the FBI and a corrupt trade union. He was sensitive to many forms of political oppression, and through contact with Singer he gradually came to link his concern for human justice to his feelings for animals: "Animal liberation was the logical extension of what my life was all about—identifying with the powerless and the vulnerable, the victims, dominated and oppressed."[1] He was stirred by Singer's arguments, viewing them as unsentimental, rational, and defensible, a sound basis for a program of protest and action.

But what to do? Spira, a veteran of labor and civil rights battles, rejected the lobbying and educational strategies of the welfare tradition. He knew that "power concedes nothing without a struggle." What the movement needed, he reasoned, was a specific target, a focused, achievable goal and a single, well-publicized victory. Spira, with a handful of other New Yorkers of similar bent, began to review scientific abstracts and grant proposals for a likely target (proposals for all federally funded grants are available to the public). They learned of experiments on cats underway at the American Museum of Natural History in Manhattan, funded by the National Institutes of Health (NIH). Since 1959, two experimental psychologists in the Museum's Department of Animal Behavior had been studying the neurological bases of sexual behavior through experiments on cats deprived of various sensations and brain functions. The experiments involved a number of unattractive procedures such as removing parts of the brain, severing nerves in the penis, and destroying the sense of smell. *Science* magazine laconically commented, "To those not inured to the practices of experimental psychology, it sounds like no picnic."[2]

For Spira, bent on organizing a successful action, here was an ideal target. Located in New York City, a protest against the popular museum would attract broad public interest and media attention. Taxpayers were likely to be shocked to find that their tax dollars went to support the mutilation of cats in order to observe their sexual performance. As Spira described it, the exposé was likely to mobilize moral outrage.

By the spring of 1976, Spira had mobilized members of several local animal protection organizations to help him organize demonstrations at the museum. Volunteer labor, not massive funds, was enough to launch this campaign. Spira attacked the experiments as sadistic, greedy, "a way of getting government grants in exchange for animal blood and agony." He rejected the instrumental use of animals:

> Neither cats, nor you, nor I, are sex machines to be mechanically and artificially rearranged. We, like other animals, are intricate symphonies with feelings, interests, and preferences; our love involves compassion, tenderness and caring. . . . The theme is liberation and freedom not manipulation and oppression.[3]

In a series of articles for *Our Town,* a free weekly publication (whose sympathetic publisher had ten cats at home and ten at his office), Spira wrote that the experiments were cruel, ethically unacceptable, and unlikely to lead to new knowledge. He found scientists, such as Andrew Rowan, who were willing to support the claim that the research had no scientific legitimacy or demonstrable practical value. In a variety of media, he publicized his demand that the laboratory be closed, and he organized a letter-writing campaign against NIH, Congress, and the Museum.

Museum officials refused to talk to the activists, but were deluged with letters in the summer of 1976: 400 in June, 650 in July, and 1,500 in August.[4] There were also bomb threats, picketing, harassment of museum scientists, and letters to museum donors and trustees. Flooded with mail, 121 members of Congress asked NIH to examine its funding of such research. One congressman, New York's Ed Koch, seizing upon a visible issue, visited the lab and recorded his skepticism in the *Congressional Record:* "I said to this professor, 'Now tell me, after you have taken a deranged male cat with brain lesions and you place it in a room and you find that it is going to mount a rabbit instead of a female cat, what have you got?' There was no response. I said 'How much has this cost the government?' She said '$435,000.'"[5] This account prompted the Department of Health, Education and Welfare to conduct a modest investigation.

Spira's efforts to garner media attention were successful. During several small demonstrations (the largest with 100 people), in front of the museum, activists waved placards saying "Curiosity kills cats" and "Castrate the Scientists." Press headlines ranged from passive criticism—"Museum ends its silence"—to hostile description—"Cats tortured in vicious experiments." Scientists and museum officials, in response, offered their own defense in terms of academic freedom and autonomous scientific inquiry—countering the moral demands of the protestors with their own moral absolutes. The director of the museum defended the institution's "freedom to study whatever it chooses without regard to its demonstrable value."[6] This failed to convince a skeptical press. An editorialist, Roger Simon, responded in an article called "Cutting up Cats to Study Sex—What Fun!": "I am not against the cutting up of animals if it might do some good to somebody some day. But before I blinded cats for 14 years, I would like somebody to tell me that there might be some 'demonstrable practical value' somewhere down the road."[7]

The research was stopped. One reason for the museum's capitulation was that experimental programs are anomalies in museums, where most research involves the assembly and study of collections. Tension over a new staff position had already sparked doubts as to whether the museum should have an experimental program. Because of the weak political position of the lab within the organizational structure of the museum, administrators were unwilling to support it when it became controversial. Another reason was the vulnerability of the research itself, which had few obvious or practical scientific implications. As important was the fact that the museum was unaccustomed to such public interference and simply did not know how to respond. The funding agency, eager to avoid controversy, gave little support; the museum's public relations department paid little attention. There were no precedents to follow. By December 1977, after one-and-a-half years of protest, the administration dismantled the cat laboratory, and in 1980, after a series of reviews, it abolished the whole department.

The Museum of Natural History protest was one of the first visible expressions of the new "animal rights" sentiments in action. Spira criticized instrumentalism in science, arguing that "animals are not things. They have feelings. Their life means as much to them as my life means to me or yours means to you. Pleasure and pain are as vivid to them as they are to you and me."[8] Spira's success in ending these experiments made the more traditional humane movements look passive and sentimental, suggesting that victory required a rigorous philosophy as well as more militant action. In Spira's words, "It showed that we could win, and we were determined to use this first victory as a stepping stone to larger things."[9]

The museum victory was indeed only the beginning. During the late 1970s and early 1980s, animal rights groups began appearing everywhere: groups to preserve ospreys or beavers, groups to support high school students opposed to dissection, groups to enlist the support of major religious denominations for animal rights, groups to arrange for the adoption of liberated farm animals. It was a curious paradox that as the Reagan years encouraged the pursuit of self-interest, and poverty and inequality became more visible, so many people increasingly turned their attentions to the plight of animals.

———

Of the many new organizations devoted to animal rights, People for the Ethical Treatment of Animals (PETA) is one of the most successful. Its story and the background of its two founders, Ingrid Newkirk and Alex Pacheco, suggest how the current animal rights movement integrated elements of the animal welfare tradition dating to the nineteenth century with the environmental ideology of the 1970s. Newkirk, born in Britain but raised in India, recalls making toys for the orphans at Mother Teresa's home in Old Delhi. Her first shock of concern for animals came from seeing an ox-cart driver cruelly abuse his animal. Her feelings were reinforced when she moved to the United States. A distaste for the mistreatment of animals appears in her account of her Maryland neighbors, "a rowdy bunch who ate squirrel pie and occasionally shot over the fence when they'd had one too many jiggers of rye."[10] After a brief stint as a stockbroker, Newkirk began working in animal shelters. In 1976 she became Director of Cruelty Investigations for the Washington Humane Society / SPCA.

At the same time, Alex Pacheco was in college reading Peter Singer's *Animal Liberation,* and he soon decided to interrupt his studies. He shipped out on the *Sea Shepherd,* a ship supported by environmentalists to harass illegal whalers. When he returned to the States in 1980, he met Newkirk. He gave her a copy of *Animal Liberation* and teased her for continuing to eat meat. The same year, they founded PETA.[11]

In May 1981, Pacheco volunteered to work in the Silver Spring, Maryland, laboratory of Edward Taub, whose neurological research involved severing nerves in the limbs of monkeys. Pacheco claims to have chosen the lab from a list of research facilities simply because it was near his home, although it had also been the subject of humane society investigations and allegations several years before. What he saw in the lab was "filth caked on the wires of the cages, faeces piled in the bottom of the cages, urine and rust encrusting every surface. There, amid this rotting stench, sat sixteen crab-eating macaques and one rhesus monkey, their lives limited to metal boxes just 17 3 / 4 inches wide."[12] The monkeys gnawed and attacked their numb limbs, which they no longer recognized as their own.

Pacheco began to keep a diary and take photographs of laboratory conditions. He then brought five sympathetic veterinarians and primatologists to the lab who testified to the substandard facilities. In September, with their affidavits and his documentation, he convinced the local police to search the lab and seize the monkeys on the grounds of a state anticruelty statute. In November, Taub was found guilty on six counts of cruelty and fined $500. The finding was later overturned on the grounds that the state law did not cover federally funded research, but the National Institutes of Health nonetheless discontinued Taub's funding.

The Taub case was a cornerstone not only for PETA but for the emerging animal rights movement. Although PETA did not achieve the conviction it wanted, the case provided a clear message: a re-spected scientist, head of his own research institute, could be law-fully stopped. The publicity given to the case from 1981 to 1983 inspired the formation of animal rights groups around the country, and encouraged activists to examine scientific experiments being car-ried out in their vicinity. Along with the University of Pennsylvania videotapes taken in 1984, the Taub case turned the attention of the emerging animal rights movement to scientific research.

Through *Unnecessary Fuss* (the film made from the Pennsylvania tapes) and a slide show on Taub's lab, PETA gained enough public-ity—including coverage on the Phil Donahue Show—to build animal rights' first successful direct mail campaign. Its membership grew ex-ponentially throughout the 1980s, reaching 8,000 members in 1984, 84,000 in 1987, and 300,000 in 1990. PETA's expansion reflects the rapid growth of the entire animal rights movement during this pe-riod. Although less wealthy than the large welfare organizations, PETA today is probably the richest of the new animal rights groups. Its 1989 budget was $6.5 million, enough to employ a staff of 65. Almost all its revenues came from contributions and membership dues, for PETA's endowment remains small. PETA is anxious to show that contributions are well spent, claiming that 83 percent go directly to helping animals rather than to expanding PETA or enrich-ing employees, and that only three staff members made salaries over $30,000 in 1989.[13] Newkirk herself drew no salary, and Pacheco only $21,000.[14] PETA uses such figures to convince potential con-tributors that it is a more effective defender of animals, and a more visible one, than reformist welfare organizations.

Despite its success, or perhaps because of it, PETA is controver-sial. Other protectionists have accused it of "taking over" the New England Anti-Vivisection Society by packing a meeting with its own supporters, many flown in from Washington. In 1987, members of the animal protection community received an anonymous letter de-nouncing PETA for "no elections, closed decision-making, and rigid hierarchy." It claimed "Newkirk will not tolerate any actions or thoughts which challenge her power over others," and said, "PETA is on a Sherman's march through the animal liberation movement, a warpath where anything goes if it's 'for the animals' in their view."[15] According to these critics, PETA neglects the nuances of operating animal protection groups fairly and openly.

Other organizations were appearing around the country in the early 1980s. On the West Coast, Elliot Katz was a relative latecomer to the animal rights movement. Trained as a veterinarian, Katz left his Brooklyn practice in 1973 to "find himself" in the therapeutic counterculture of California's Esalen and Big Sur area, where he built a home and moved through a series of therapies. In 1982, while he was living in San Francisco and practicing Zen Buddhism, he picked up a pamphlet at a meditation center from Buddhists Concerned for Animals. Responding to his inquiry, the group sent him a copy of *Animal Liberation,* and he was moved: "I gradually learned more and more, and this took me back to my early roots as an animal lover."[16] As a veterinarian, Katz claims, he had "tried to put the needs of animals above the—sometimes selfish—desires of owners," for he "saw the pets as individuals, not just as property."[17] Singer's philosophical treatise had found fertile soil.

Within months, Katz founded Californians for Responsible Research, which soon became In Defense of Animals (IDA). He chose to concentrate on scientific research because he had witnessed what he considered its horrors in his own veterinary school years. He feels that the true purpose of veterinary medicine, helping animals, is often twisted to less noble ends. Katz began monitoring research activities at the University of California at Berkeley, and Berkeley has remained his favorite target (he calls it "Berkeley-gate").

Katz has mastered the art of pugnacious disruption. At an Optical Society award dinner for a Berkeley psychologist, Katz grabbed the microphone in order to denounce the researcher. In other public discussions he has called the chief Berkeley veterinarian, Roy Henrickson, a "prick," "asshole," and "pimp."[18] Katz's experiences at Berkeley convinced him that cordial negotiation would be fruitless, at least there. He lost almost all respect for those conducting research on live animals: "If it's okay to torture animals, it's okay to lie to the public."[19]

Katz is typical of many members of the movement in his concern for vulnerable creatures. He recalls a great love of animals as a child, claiming to "identify more with individuals of other species."[20] Like Spira, he identifies with the downtrodden: "I have always been concerned with justice and with letting people into the system who are excluded."[21] Before his interest in animal rights he had founded "City Celebration," an organization to promote the cultures of ethnic minorities and sponsor activities for senior citizens and the handicapped.

The biomedical researchers whom he attacks detest Katz, and even within the movement he has a reputation for being "difficult."

He admits, "I don't work well with people. I'm abrasive, lose my temper; I'm not very political."[22] But he claims to have mellowed, attributing his early style to the outrage of a new convert: "When you see unjust things that outrage you, you want to correct them immediately; and when you're new to a movement, you want to do everything at once."[23]

Like PETA, In Defense of Animals relies on direct mail fundraising. Robert Parker and Associates, a direct mail consultant for left-liberal causes ranging from the Democratic Caucus and the JFK Library to Central America and Greenpeace, was willing to take on IDA without demanding a fee up front. IDA grew, and when Parker went out of business, IDA was able to manage its own fundraising, using direct mail lists from environmental and other animal rights groups. Its campaign was very successful, attracting ten thousand new members a year in the late 1980s. By 1989, contributions averaged around twenty dollars per member, with 25,000 supporters giving at least twice per year, and another 50,000 giving once every year or two.[24] Katz, whose own salary from IDA was $44,000 in 1989, attributes the success of his direct mail efforts to the visibility of his attacks on Berkeley researchers.

IDA's success enabled it to expand its activities beyond the San Francisco Bay area. Although retaining its local focus on Berkeley research and other Bay Area animal protection activities, it has also hired coordinators for specific campaigns elsewhere. At Emory University in Atlanta, Georgia, IDA sponsored a 1988 building occupation to "Save the Yerkes Chimps," a reference to experiments at the Yerkes Regional Primate Research Center. The occupation was short-lived and had little effect, but it allowed photos to be taken of banners hanging from the building which helped to further publicize the cause—and IDA. Despite IDA's angry tone, its actions have remained nonviolent: lawsuits, civil disobedience, and disruptions.

Another group has gone much further. In March 1979, the Animal Liberation Front (ALF), a British import, broke into its first North American lab, liberating two dogs, two guinea pigs, and a cat from the New York University Medical Center. Since then, it has completed over one hundred clandestine operations in North America (including the University of Pennsylvania break-in), in the process freeing some five thousand animals and causing several million dollars worth of damages.[25] The ALF operates as a loose network of cells of activists who launch occasional night raids. Media attention has highlighted laboratory raids, but a list of California incidents

compiled by the state for 1988 indicates that only one fifth of suspected ALF actions hit research facilities. Other targets include ranches, meat markets, butchers, taxidermists, fur retailers, and Kentucky Fried Chicken outlets. Good figures on the number of raids
are difficult to obtain, however, since the ALF does not always take
credit for its actions and since self-organized groups or individuals
occasionally claim to be part of the ALF—an attribution problem
faced with all clandestine organizations.

ALF actions are carefully planned, often for months before they
occur. Veterinarians are lined up to care for liberated animals, and
foster homes are arranged for them. Activists often come from other
regions, so that they can disperse more thoroughly afterward. They
leave few clues behind. The law enforcement community takes the
ALF quite seriously, and the California Attorney General declared it
a terrorist organization in 1986. An arson investigator in the state
fire marshal's office said, "They're a slick group. They're clever and
sophisticated. They know what they're doing."[26] The result of their
extensive planning is that only a handful of members have been arrested or convicted. Secret organizations do not publish financial reports, but the ALF has a Support Group with 10,000 paying members that markets T-shirts commemorating major ALF break-ins,
including one that boasts of $5,300,000 damages at the University
of California at Davis. The ALF also maintains close ties with animal
rights groups such as PETA, which may defray some ALF expenses,
but its middle-class members presumably pay much of their own
way.

After a raid on the University of Oregon in October 1986, the
ALF issued a statement explaining its motives. The action, which
freed 200 cats, rabbits, rats, and hamsters and caused $50,000 in
damages, "was, first and foremost, a mission of mercy; a nonviolent
direct action carried out solely on behalf of the animals which were
rescued." But it was also "an act of outright retribution" against the
researchers, "an expression of total rage and anger. . . . With this
liberation, it was also our intention to demonstrate our unwillingness
to accept the status quo of animal use and exploitation in principle,
even when carried out in accordance with established requirements
of the law."

With its dramatic military tactics, the ALF has shaped the popular image of animal activists far out of proportion to its small size,
so that many perceive the entire movement as dangerous, destructive, and terrorist. Almost every magazine reporter writing on the

movement recounts interviews of ALF members with the same cloak-and-dagger details: the reporter is blindfolded and taken to a van or safe house; activists wear ski masks and use simple pseudonyms. The comic strip *Bloom County* has adopted this image, and grasped its ironies. In a series of strips, the "Mary Kay Commandos," clothed entirely in pink (even their Uzis), tried to keep rabbits in labs for cosmetics testing, against the efforts of the "Animal Liberation Guerrilla Front," wearing black masks. Both groups carried machine guns and—this being the world of comic strips—used them frequently. One character said about his liberation, "Ah. Nabbed from sadists by terrorists. . . . Sort of a dream come true, ya know?"[27]

While the ALF is a fundamentalist group, using illegal means and rejecting existing animal protection laws, the Animal Legal Defense Fund works within the legal structure to promote animal liberation. The founder and one of the main forces behind the ALDF is Joyce Tischler, a New Yorker transplanted to California's Marin County, who has worked on legal protection for animals since the mid-1970s. At Queens College in New York, she was one of several "cat people" who cared for the strays that lived on the campus. (Two others, Jolene Marion and Esther Dukes, became animal rights lawyers, practicing in New York.) Tischler was already interested in animal rights when she graduated from law school in 1977, having published a law review article synthesizing the environmental ideas of law professor Christopher Stone with Peter Singer's concept of animal liberation.[28] While working in a law firm, she helped organize an informal study group of pro–animal rights lawyers (six attended the first meeting) and took two pro bono cases involving animals. One was a negligence suit against United Airlines for the improper handling and resulting death of a pug being shipped. The other, which achieved wide visibility, was an effort to stop the U.S. Navy from shooting wild burros at its China Lake facility in the Mojave Desert.[29]

In 1979, Tischler and her study group organized Attorneys for Animal Rights (AFAR); and, in 1981, she began working full time on animal issues with the help of a $6,000 grant from the Animal Protection Institute in Sacramento. Hoping to avoid the political rivalries of existing animal protection groups, she wanted to create an independent organization. A mailing to the membership list of another animal group brought $5,000, and AFAR limped along until 1984. That year, it began a concerted direct mail campaign, and changed its name to the Animal Legal Defense Fund. The name was expected to be more appealing because it avoided the words "attorneys" and "rights." By 1990, ALDF had 40,000 members and was able to hire a full-time office manager and a secretary, and was hoping to hire an additional staff attorney. In addition to its national office, the ALDF has local chapters in several large cities, but they are financially independent. Over 320 lawyers contribute time to working for animals through the ALDF.

The ALDF favors litigation likely to have a wide effect, as assessed by its Project and Litigation Review Committee. It allocates its energies equally to wildlife (both domestic and international), factory farming, scientific research, and companion animals. Wildlife issues are the easiest to win, due to environmental regulations and rights of standing in courts (allowing people to sue on behalf of animals), and to the fact that no one "owns" wild animals as they do pets and farm animals. In the late 1980s, the ALDF sued the United States Department of Agriculture (USDA), demanding better enforcement of the 1985 amendments to the Animal Welfare Act (the USDA had delayed issuing the new regulations); blocked the import of Bangladesh monkeys; protected high school students refusing to perform dissections; tried to outlaw leg-hold traps; and defended people arrested during demonstrations. The ALDF has also tried to stop hunts by challenging the composition of state wildlife commissions, and it has promoted the idea of an "animal bill of rights."

The ALDF prefers negotiation, and many targeted organizations may find it easier to talk with a legal organization than to other animal rights groups. Yet Tischler is ready to sue when negotiations fail, saying that, "I do not want an image that I'm easily won over or cowed by the other side. After all, what we're all about litigation."[30] For example, the Louisiana Pacific timber company had been allowing an annual bear hunt on its California forests because the bears were destroying trees. In 1989, the ALDF argued that the company could inexpensively distribute buckets of nutritional feed through the woods so that bears would eat that instead of the trees, and provided evidence from a Washington State study to that effect. When the company took no action, the ALDF sued.

Animal rights activists form a continuum from Tischler's pragmatism to the ALF's fundamentalism. People like Henry Spira and Joyce Tischler are willing to negotiate with those who use animals. Tischler's work within a legal framework depends on negotiation as well as litigation. Spira first aims at private communication with his targets, but if he fails, he can attack them as uncooperative and try to coerce them publicly through media pressure and demonstrations.

In contrast, IDA and PETA place less faith in negotiation except as a public relations gambit, for they generally see their foes as untrustworthy. The ALF goes further; its illegal sabotage and animal liberations leave no room for discussion. For them, their foes are inherently evil. Indeed, the contrast between the ALDF, working within the legal system while trying to change it, and the ALF, angrily breaking laws, is striking. Although the ALDF defends participants in civil disobedience, Tischler fears the ALF's violent tactics could destroy the animal rights movement by undermining public support. She points to Britain, where she feels underground tactics have given the movement a bad name. She notes that many people have come to associate the entire movement with violence and extremists, and hopes the prominent animal rights and welfare organizations will dissociate themselves from ALF tactics.

These four prominent organizations—PETA, IDA, the ALF, and the ALDF—represent the new generation of animal rights organizations that appeared in the early 1980s. They employ diverse tactics, yet share a strong, explicit ideology. And they share an operating style. Though most animal rights groups claim to be grassroots, they usually consist of a small number of highly dedicated believers who have devoted their lives to this cause. Relying on direct mail fundraising to obtain the financial help of many relatively passive supporters, these believers carry out highly visible actions.

The early 1980s saw an explosion in the number of animal rights organizations, and an equally rapid growth in traditional welfare groups. At first, most rights groups were small; but after 1984, individual recruits began joining in record numbers. Fewer new groups formed after 1985, and the consolidation of national organizations such as PETA accounted for most of the increase in recruits.[31] Reasonable estimates suggest that, by the end of the 1980s, the United States had several hundred animal rights groups and several thousand animal welfare groups (mostly local humane societies).[32] Together, all the welfare groups may have ten to fifteen million members, and in a private poll one in five Americans claimed to have contributed to animal protection organizations.[33] A relatively small percentage of these support animal rights organizations—a rough guess would be perhaps 500,000 to a million people.

One measure of the intense interest in the movement is the number of paperback copies of Peter Singer's *Animal Liberation* in print. This book is a kind of Bible to the movement, and many groups give it to all new members. Distribution of the book began to increase markedly in 1985, when about 70,000 copies were in print. By 1988, that figure had increased to over 250,000. Then, distribution fell off, possibly in anticipation of the revised edition, which appeared in hardcover in 1990.[34]

Older animal protection groups also made impressive gains in membership during the 1980s. The Humane Society of the United States, in existence since 1954, added around 15,000 new members each year from 1978 to 1984. In contrast, for the next four years, it added 100,000 members each year, to reach a total size of over half a million by 1988.[35] Even the New England Anti-Vivisection Society, with a stable membership around 9,000 from 1980 to 1985, began growing after 1985, to reach 12,000 in 1990.[36]

Who are the new recruits? The diversity of members and the lack of a comprehensive survey prevent definitive answers, but some facts are available. Both animal rights and animal protection activists and sympathizers are more likely to live in cities than in the country. Most have more education than the average American. Interviews with 270 protestors at a New York City demonstration in 1988 found that more than 50 percent had college degrees.[37] A 1985 poll by the magazine, *Animals' Agenda,* found that 84 percent of its readers had degrees—compared to under 20 percent nationally.[38] Activists and sympathizers are also more likely to be women than men (60 to 70 percent of animal protectionists are women). They are unlikely to have occupations dealing directly with animals in ways other than as pets.[39]

Supporters of animal rights are also strikingly nonreligious. Sixty-five percent of the readers responding to the *Animals' Agenda* poll claimed to be atheists or agnostics. This contrasts sharply with the general population, where—according to a 1984 Gallup poll—90 percent profess a belief in God, 70 percent belong to a church, and 60 percent attend services at least once a month.

Perhaps the most widely shared trait among animal advocates is that they own pets, often adopting animals that would have been sent to a pound to be "put down." The New York interviews mentioned above found that almost all the activists had had pets at some time: 98 percent either had pets or had grown up with them. Eighty percent currently had an animal in the household, and 72 percent had more than one—high figures for those living in cramped New York apartments. Two-thirds of the protestors were single, and many of them lived only with their pets, presumably developing strong emotional bonds with them. A staff member of an animal rights group described why she was at the protest: "I pictured my cat being tormented and tortured and dissected alive in a laboratory, and I couldn't take it any more."[40] Animal rightists exhibit the strong anthropomorphic tendencies discussed in Chapter 2 of this book, and are inclined to push these moral sentiments further than most Americans.

Some of the movement's leaders learned pro-animal values from their parents. Christine Stevens, Founder of the Animal Welfare Institute, was the daughter of a scientist concerned about animal experimentation. Steve Sapontzis' mother was a vegetarian. Nedim Buyukmihci, president of the Association of Veterinarians for Animal Rights, was raised at a wildlife sanctuary founded by his mother, a nature writer. Concern for animals had been part of their early life and experience.

The fact that more women than men are active in animal protection causes is partly due to available time. Despite their increasing participation in the workplace, women are still less likely to be employed full time than men (in 1984, 54 percent of the adult women in the United States were in the labor force, and 76 percent of the men), providing women more time for animal activism. But their involvement in this issue also reflects the persistence of traditional gender expectations: women are expected to be able to express their emotions; they are supposed to be sensitive to the feelings of others; and they are asked to be gentle rather than aggressive.[41] While differences among individuals are immense, women remain more likely than men to exhibit compassion for the helpless, including animals. They have also been prominent members of other recent social movements, attracted by the anti-instrumental positions of environmental, antinuclear, and peace groups.

Young people are also attracted to new causes. Henry Spira is aware of this potential pool of recruits: "Since we aim at lasting change, our Coalition must connect with young people while they are still sorting out their values. We must challenge the inconsistency to which they are very sensitive: Be kind to cats and dogs who are part of the household; but eat other animals, and murder and dissect animals for course requirements."[42] The potential influence of students is clear from their success in the tuna boycott to save dolphins, and from the publicity about high school students who refuse to dissect animals in biology classes.

Pro-animal values are not always related to other political preferences. Many people with liberal and left leanings perceive the animal protection movement as right-wing; those from the Right perceive it as a leftist movement. The confusion reflects reality: intuitions about anthropomorphism and instrumentalism need not line up with conventional political beliefs. The early humane and welfare movements were dominated by social elites and many participants were politically conservative. Later animal rights activists borrowed a moral vocabulary from the fetal rights and anti-abortion movements, whose members are mostly conservatives. But activists also appropriate anticapitalist language from the Left; an advertisement against Perdue chickens, for example, employs a socialist rhetoric denouncing labor exploitation.

In Congress, protectionism cuts across party lines. Republican as well as Democratic legislators have actively promoted animal causes. Republican Senator Robert Dole was the main sponsor of the 1985 amendments to the Animal Welfare Act. PETA has honored Robert K. Dornan, a conservative congressman whose rating by the liberal Americans for Democratic Action in 1988 was an absolute zero, and whose rating on environmental issues by the League of Conservation Voters was only 13 out of 100.

Despite this complexity, the majority of participants in the recent American animal rights crusade identify themselves as politically liberal or leftist, reflecting the political context in which the movement emerged. The most articulate critiques of instrumentalism in the 1970s and 80s came from the Left. The prominent movements to which animal rightists compare themselves—civil rights, feminism, ecology—attract left-liberal members. In the New York interviews, people claimed to have supported diverse human rights causes: Amnesty International, Palestinian rights, civil rights, anti-apartheid struggles, women's liberation, and gay rights. And 65 percent identified themselves as liberal, progressive, or radical left. The *Animals' Agenda* had similar results when it polled its readers, with 34 percent labeling themselves liberal and 32 percent labeling themselves radical. Nonetheless, one-quarter of both samples were middle of the road or conservative.[43] Whereas welfare societies show a mix of conservatives and liberals, rights groups tend to include primarily younger, left-liberal members.

Yet classifying pro-animal protestors as left or right politically misses the point, for their moral sentiment are largely independent of traditional political cleavages. Most moral crusades focus on a narrowly defined set of issues—in this case, the treatment of animals—with little regard to their implications for other ideological questions. Thus, for example, in opposing pornography, feminist and conservative crusaders overlook their other differences to further their common cause. Similarly, the animal protection movement is open to allies wherever it finds them. Saving animals is the single goal, to which all other ideologies and identities are subordinate.[44] The result is that in the traditional sense of "liberal"—that of a tolerant, live-and-let-live attitude toward other humans—many animal protestors are not liberal at all. The fundamentalist belief that they possess the Truth makes them quite intolerant.

Radicals typically help a protest movement by attracting extensive media coverage and swelling the ranks of new recruits, and the high-profile actions that began with the cat sex protest attracted many new converts to animal protection. Most joined the traditional welfare societies still oriented toward compassionate reforms of existing animal uses. But others, reflecting a younger generation's ambivalence about science and technology, sought more radical changes in the way Americans view and treat animals. Though radicalization inevitably caused tension among organizations, the actions of groups like the ALF and PETA drew attention to animal issues and thereby boosted the membership of welfare societies as well as the rights groups. Such unanticipated gains muted criticism of the new militancy by the conventional humane societies. As a result, the radical groups have generated the moralistic language and sense of outrage that has increasingly come to characterize the campaign for animal rights.

FOUR

Moral Militancy

In a brochure distributed by an animal rights group called Trans-Species Unlimited, its founder, George Cave, describes his "vast numbing rage" at the treatment of animals: "rage at the researchers responsible for inflicting tortures, rage at our society for condoning and even encouraging such ruthless exploitation, rage at the failure of our movement to put an end to these atrocities, and rage at myself for succumbing all too often to feelings of desperation and hopelessness in the face of the holocaust of animal suffering."[1]

The growth of the animal rights movement depends on the production of such rage. Cave's own anger had developed out of his philosophical thinking. After receiving a Ph.D. in philosophy during a dismal period for the academic job market, and being offered only a job teaching writing at Penn State, Cave decided to abandon his academic career for full-time activism and to found an animal rights group more aggressive than existing animal welfare organizations. In 1981, Cave and his companion, Dana Stuchell, organized Trans-Species Unlimited (the name indicating an effort to remove moral boundaries between species). His goal was to promote change by drawing members of the general public into direct action on behalf of animals. Cave recalls no special childhood experiences with animals, claiming that a philosophical sense of justice, more than pity, propelled his activism: "Like other arbitrary and capricious sources of motivation, empathy, sympathy, or love of animals (call it what you will) is *intrinsically* discriminatory . . . I always knew that if I stopped eating animals it would be because I was convinced that it was *wrong,* not because I had had a pet horse or rabbit as a child." He admits, however, that pet owning can propel people into the movement: "How one comes to the realization that it is wrong can, and often does, involve contact with an individual animal."[2] Both heart and mind, he believes, are necessary for mobilizing a social movement.

Cave's feelings came out of an abstract philosophical position, but for most protestors, rage is provoked when movement organizers appeal to sentiments about particular subjects. Some recruits are angered by furs because their moral sensibilities condemn frivolous luxury. Others feel the same way about cosmetics. Still others, skeptical of science, are shocked by scientific experiments. As activists learned how to build on these feelings effectively with gruesome photographs, philosophical arguments, and emotional slogans, the movement attracted recruits morally and passionately committed to radical action on behalf of animals. Certain in their moral beliefs, the new animal rights groups that proliferated in the 1980s have become more militant in their tactics and far broader in their concerns than the traditional welfare groups. But the hubris of self-righteousness has proven to be both a source of strength and a potentially fatal flaw. The same moral confidence that attracts so many recruits makes others wary of the new movement, and the same confident rhetoric that inspires devotion to the cause may encourage an overly simple division of the world into good and evil. The beliefs that provide strength to movement members may make it harder for them to communicate with nonmembers.

The moral militancy of the movement derives from its concentration on a single issue of such overwhelming importance to advocates that it crowds out other political concerns. As a result, many animal rights activists define themselves as nonpolitical, rejecting politics as constant negotiation over the interests of human groups. They see themselves, instead, as pursuing a pure, moral agenda. As one activist puts it: "If there's something that sets the animal protection movement apart from other social change movements it is its pronounced distaste for 'politics.' We seem to think—when we think at all about these topics—that we are . . . free to pursue social change outside the larger political context in which most issues are eventually resolved."[3] Yet politics cannot be avoided if activists are to change society.

Even within the movement, political conflicts are unavoidable. As groups have proliferated, so too have the strains; fundamentalists and pragmatists struggle over what species are most important to protect, what abuses of animals are the worst, and what tactics are acceptable.

———————

Animal rights activists act as moral entrepreneurs, igniting and then building on moral outrage. They appeal to widespread beliefs about the similarities between humans and animals, the love of pets as part of the family, and anxieties about encroaching instrumentalism. And they use shocking images of common practices that violate deeply held sentiments about decency and justice to convert people to the cause.

Shocking visual images are perhaps their most powerful tool. Monkeys in restraining devices, furry raccoons in steel traps, kittens with their eyes sewn shut, and other images of constrained mammals appeal to anthropomorphic sympathies. People's worst fears of a science and a technology out of control seem justified by photographs of animals probed with scientific devices—rats with syringes down their throats, cats with electrodes planted on their heads. A bright patch of red blood on a black and white poster catches the eye.

The animal rights literature contrasts such images of "tormented" animals with "happy" animals: puppies and kittens cuddled by their owners, chimpanzees frolicking in sanctuaries. Animals appear innocent, trusting, and helpless. Good and evil face each other on opposite pages of glossy magazines, in full color; each makes the other seem more extreme.[4] If loving care of pets is portrayed as natural, the instrumental use of animals appears unnatural, and the ancient juxtaposition of sentimental and instrumental attitudes seems inconceivable. If there are no clear boundaries between humans and animals, then exploitation of animals seems wrong.

Most moral shocks inform the viewer about what others—scientific researchers, circus trainers, cosmetics companies—do to animals. Some, like New Age consumer efforts, try to shock viewers into thinking about their own actions—their own contribution to animal cruelty. Where did the hamburger in the neat styrofoam container come from? What was the original animal like? How did it live and how did it die? "Meat's no treat for those you eat!" What animal died to make your fur? "Are you wearing my mother on your back?" We are forced to think of animals, not as commodities, but as living beings with a point of view that we are invited to share.

Moral shocks are recruiting tools for protest movements, but the power of a shocking image is not by itself sufficient to build a movement. Membership generally requires time for activities, discretionary income to contribute, and a conviction that participation can make a difference. But shocks can be so persuasive that even people with no prior political experience become "converts." Moral crusades are often filled with recruits who have not been in other movements; the anti-abortion movement is one example.[5] Of Trans-Species demonstrators in New York, only one third claim that activism in other causes helped involve them in animal issues.[6] For most activists, moral shocks appeal directly to longstanding feelings they have about the importance of animals, enough to involve them in organized protest for the first time.

Movement activists often talk about their "conversion." A woman running the February 1989 meeting of Trans-Species opened the meeting with her own mea culpa: "I was brought up in the Judaeo-Christian philosophy, that animals were put here for our use." She described her disillusionment with two friends. She first found out that a boyfriend was a vivisector, "more concerned about where the next grant was coming from than about curing cancer." Then she was troubled by a weekend host who hunted deer with bow and arrows. At this time, several books about animal abuses profoundly affected her, and she gave up eating meat. As she found groups of like-minded people, she began to link animal abuse to world starvation and the destruction of the ozone layer. She became a missionary for animal rights.

Giving witness to one's conversion was a collective ritual at meetings of Trans-Species Unlimited, one of the few animal rights groups to hold regular public meetings. Because each witness learned how to tell her story by listening to those of previous converts, the stories came to sound similar. Most referred to loving animals as a child; to sympathy but also frustration with environmental and other movements; to disturbing experiences that shocked them; to reading *Animal Liberation*; to learning to give up meat; to finding an organization that helped them act upon their budding ideology. They spoke of heroes—many of them authors of recent books on animal abuses—as well as villains. For some, Gandhi and Schweitzer functioned as heroes. Common conversion stories bond participants together; they are an important mechanism for building a sense of solidarity and they reinforce a conviction that protestors possess the truth in an abusive and ignorant world.

———

Moral truth inspires missionary zeal. Those who believe they know the truth are often loud and shrill in their attacks. Fundamentalists hurl venomous labels at those who abuse animals. Scientists are "sadists," meat-eaters are "cannibals," factory farmers are "fascists," and furriers are "criminals." But even those who simply disagree with the fundamentalists—including some welfarists and pragmatists—become targets. At a public forum, Michael W. Fox of the Humane Society of the United States was asked whether there were any circumstances in which he would accept animal experimentation. He replied, "Just to ask that question indicates you are a speciesist and probably a sexist and a racist."[7] Such labeling inevitably precludes further dialogue.

The smug zeal of moral crusades is familiar. Seeing the moral world in black and white, many activists, especially those drawn into activism for the first time, are politically naïve and dismissive of majority sensibilities. In addition to saying that "A rat is a pig is a dog is a boy," PETA's Ingrid Newkirk declared in a controversial statement in 1983: "Six million people died in concentration camps, but six billion broiler chickens will die this year in slaughterhouses."[8] Others compare the plight of today's animals with that of African-American slaves before the Civil War.[9] Those willing to grant moral rights to chickens easily make comparisons that offend mainstream tastes.

Moral certainty inspires calm confidence even in the most trying of circumstances. An ALF member spoke about her participation in a lab break-in: "I wasn't really nervous. I've gotten philosophical about break-ins: either you get caught or you don't. But even if I got caught, it would still draw attention to Morrison's experiments with cats and his role against the animal right movement."[10] Like the martyrs of old, sure of their beliefs, she could look placidly on the prospect of arrest and even imprisonment, since she was working for a higher cause for which personal sacrifice was necessary.

But the confidence of moral certainty can yield arrogance as well as fortitude. The moral urgency of the animal rights movement is often combined with an impatience and indifference to democratic process. At Trans-Species meetings, discussion and debate were often discouraged. The board member running the April 1989 meeting curtailed discussion from the floor; the meetings were "to mobilize our core of activists who attend every month. . . . We do need your ideas, but we must restrict questions to make the most of our time. This may seem harsh, but it's in the best interests of the animals." When disagreement flared, Trans-Species leaders cut it off. They maintained clear authority, and made little effort to achieve internal consensus. "The best interests of the animals" was a trump card with the moral authority to end discussion.

Like many animal rights groups, Trans-Species also exhibited a

gendered division of labor. In the late 1980s, the most visible leaders—the national president, the New York chapter president—were
men, while the surrounding staff—the national president's partner,
the New York staff—were mostly women. Rank-and-file participants
were predominantly women. While women did most of the talking
at New York meetings, there was sustained, reverent applause when
the chapter president appeared. It might be expected that a movement with more women than men would make special efforts to have
women in visible positions. The environmental, antinuclear, and
peace movements have made such an effort, but the leaders of Trans-
Species did not think this way.[11] Privately, women active in animal
rights often trade complaints of patronizing, condescending attitudes
on the part of some of their male collaborators.

   Rage over animal abuses can also play into racist and xenophobic stereotypes. At meetings and demonstrations, occasional comments can be heard about Asian immigrants thought to eat dogs;
Latin American immigrants believed to engage in practices like cock-
and bull-fighting; Jews whose religious values were supposed to encourage exploitation of animals; and gays who support AIDS research that uses animal subjects. Apparently spurred by a mailing
from In Defense of Animals, a Pittsburgh resident wrote to Chancel-
lor Chang-Lin Tien of the University of California at Berkeley in
1990. Speaking of a Berkeley professor: "This lowest form of human
garbage should not be allowed to breathe air that normal humans
breathe, but rather crawl back underneath the rock from which he
obviously emerged. . . . Why do you permit a torture and mutilation specialist in your midst?" She continues: "Could it be, perhaps,
that you condone such profound cruelty to animals and sadistic types
such as DeValois due to your Asian background? It is no secret that
Asians have no respect for animal life; therefore, I certainly do not
expect compassion from you." Murky passions are shaken loose by
such deep rage, and a certain number of animal activists turn to an
invective that betrays their own misanthropic feelings.

   The movement has also stirred anti-Semitic statements, possibly
because of the large number of Jews in the sciences and the fur business. Jewish researchers receive explicit hate mail, such as one letter
Taub received: "Bastard, too bad the Nazis didn't get you."[12] In response to his article in the *New England Journal of Medicine* supporting animal research, philosopher Carl Cohen received anti-
Semitic letters.[13] So, too, have many furriers. An anonymous letter
to the President of U.S. Surgical reads: "How dare you filthy Jews

steal innocent animals to torture and slaughter to look for means to make more filthy money? It's a shame Hitler did not exterminate each one of you. You're not even human."[14]

The more politically sophisticated leaders in the movement denounce or try to temper these attitudes, insisting that protestors participate for the right reason—to help animals—and not to work out their own xenophobia, and organizers have largely succeeded in channeling moral shrillness so as to broaden the movement's popular appeal. In one example, animal groups promoted a California bill to ban the private killing of dogs and cats—designed to discourage any human consumption of these animals. When Asian-American groups denounced the bill as racist, animal groups had it withdrawn.

In its early stages especially, the movement attracted extremists, prophets in the Old Testament style who took pride in standing outside the moral mainstream. Says one activist, "Ten years ago, it was hard to find any normal people in the movement. Before 1983 or so, most of the people in it were social misfits—that's the reason a lot of them went into animal rights."[15] Its recruits have changed during the 1980s, though the movement has retained a strong, sometimes disturbing, streak of the arrogance that comes from moral rectitude. The temptation to adopt fundamentalist rhetoric remains strong.

———

Moral outrage and missionary zeal encourage diverse and sometimes extreme political actions, and animal rights groups have tried a great number of them. At the annual "Great American Meat-outs," held throughout the country since 1985, activists distribute vegetarian recipes and samples, and have steakouts, takeouts, speakouts, and write-ins. Protestors are given toll-free numbers of animal-abusing companies like slaughterhouses and poultry farms, and soon tie up their phone lines. Animal rights groups held a "Rock for the Animals" evening at the Palladium, a New York disco. To demonstrate that "What L'Oréal does to animals is enough to make us sick," PETA staged a Barf-In in front of the company's New York headquarters, and protestors pretended to vomit into an oversized papier-maché toilet. This event was followed by the distribution of "barf bags" that could be mailed to the cosmetics company. On Saint Valentine's Day 1990, L'Oréal received thousands of black hearts from PETA supporters. These are memorable and effective activities because the news media enjoy covering them, attracted by amusing slogans, elaborate costumes and props, and Hollywood celebrities.

Some animal rights tactics, however, test and even break accep-

ted limits of political action. Activists engage in "direct action" to
achieve immediate results instead of going through the indirect mechanisms of law and regulation. They frequently break into laboratories to free experimental animals. They carry out civil disobedience
to pressure the state into remedial action and to impress the public
with their moral fervor. Often, protestors occupy offices or sit down
in the street and allow police officers to carry them off. While making a public statement, they satisfy their own consciences through
this form of moral testimony. Direct action and civil disobedience,
both illegal, are mainly adopted when protestors believe that "normal channels" of protest are too slow or have been exhausted.

Animal rights groups were quick to adopt extreme tactics. The
ALF broke into its first American laboratory in 1979; Pacheco infil-
trated Taub's lab in 1981. The ALF imported tactics from its British
counterparts, and Pacheco was inspired by the dramatic actions of
Greenpeace and by his stint on the *Sea Shepherd*. But activists have
also been driven to militancy directly by their moral sentiments. If
animal experiments are evil, the equivalent of another Holocaust,
then almost any measure can—and should—be taken to stop them.
As crusaders with passionate convictions, animal rightists would feel
remiss if they did not do everything in their power to stop abuses.
They reject reformist tactics as inadequate, and use radical actions
to distance themselves from welfare groups. Some activists had
worked in welfare groups and became frustrated with the slow pace
of change. Most favored radical tactics from the time they joined
the animals' crusade, inspired by the rhetoric and imagery of animal
cruelty and by their own sense of outrage.

Radical tactics are threatening to split the animal rights movement. Most recent movements, from civil rights to anti-abortion,
have indulged in some illegal actions; our society condones a certain
level of direct action and civil disobedience. There are, however, distinctions between illegal methods that are destructive and those that
are not. Destroying a neurology lab goes far beyond blocking en-
trances to a building, which merely inconveniences occupants. Here
we see cleavages between fundamentalists and pragmatists in the
movement, for not everyone supports sabotage as a political tactic.
Indeed, the leaders of pragmatist organizations want to curb the extremes of moral militancy, including break-ins and physical damage,
that could damage the credibility of the movement. And even fundamentalists distinguish violence against property, which they support,
from that against humans. In Britain, the Animal Liberation Front

has claimed responsibility for car bomb attacks on veterinary researchers. But to date, no American animal rights group, including the ALF, officially condones personal violence, partly because it would sour public opinion.[16] At the 1989 Summit for the Animals, representatives from more than sixty animal rights groups unanimously condemned violence against any animals, including humans.

Nonetheless, individual activists have occasionally expressed a tolerance for personal violence. Chris DeRose, President of Last Chance for Animals in Los Angeles and suspected member of the ALF, predicted in an interview that at some point an animal exploiter would be killed. Why? "Frustrations. The system is not moving fast enough to make these changes, so people feel they have to take the law into their own hands." The interviewer asked, "Would someone who is considered more radical than you be able to justify the murder of a pharmaceutical chief?" DeRose: "They might be able to justify it. That's up to the individual."[17]

Only one American is known to have taken steps to act on her murderous rage. In November 1988, Fran Stephanie Trutt was arrested for placing a radio-controlled pipe bomb near the parking place of Leon Hirsch, president of the U.S. Surgical Corporation. Had it exploded, the bomb could have killed those people within thirty feet. Dubbed the "Bow-Wow Bomber" (*Newsday*) in a case of "Puppy Love" (*Daily News*), Trutt was an unstable loner who passionately loved her four dogs—for which she demanded visitation rights when in prison. U.S. Surgical's use of live dogs in demonstrating its surgical staples aroused her fury more than any other animal issue. She had moved in and out of New York animal rights groups for several years, making group leaders uneasy with her eccentric and demanding tone in pursuing her special concern about dogs. She progressed quickly from trampling azaleas at a 1986 demonstration against U.S. Surgical to planting a bomb. Fortunately for Hirsch, Trutt was arrested as she was putting it in place.

Trutt was caught because she was helped by two "accomplices" who were, in fact, in communication with the police. They were employees of Perceptions International, a surveillance organization that monitors and infiltrates animal rights groups, and which had been hired by U.S. Surgical. They had befriended Trutt and, according to press reports, had suggested killing Hirsch, paid for the bomb, talked her out of doubts she had (even on the night she placed the bomb), and drove her to the parking lot to plant it. In April 1990, Trutt, hoping to be reunited with her dogs sooner, accepted a plea bargain and, in July, was sentenced to a ten-year jail term, suspended after thirty-two months.[18]

Animal rights groups were divided in their reactions to this messy case. Friends of Animals, its national headquarters in the same Connecticut city as U.S. Surgical, provided both legal and moral support for Trutt, especially following the accusations about Perceptions International. Friends of Animals had been organizing protests against U.S. Surgical for eight years, and found a bug planted in its own office soon after Trutt's arrest. But most in the movement seem to feel that the fewer cases like Trutt's, the better. One prominent activist said, privately, "I hope she fries." Others sympathize with Trutt's anger, and one said, speaking of Hirsch, "I could really see him dead. A nice bullet hole through the head. He's simply awful." Murderous thoughts, however, are far from murderous actions.

Whatever extreme tactics activists are willing to use—and some can stomach shocking ones—animal rights fundamentalists share a reluctance to moderate their demands or actions. Convinced they are morally correct, it appears immoral to accept partial solutions. "We don't want larger cages. We want empty cages," says Tom Regan.[19] This unwillingness to compromise distinguishes the fundamentalist fringe of animal rightists from the rest of the animal protection community, for whom improved conditions represent a clear victory.

In addition to dilemmas over tactics, the rights movement faces moral choices over which species to save. The overwhelming majority of attention and funding still goes toward helping a few species of easily anthropomorphized mammals. But virtually every species has its protectors, as the language of rights can be applied to any creature. The World Society for the Protection of Animals recently condemned rattlesnake round-ups in Texas, partly for environmental reasons but more because of the reptiles' suffering. The caption for the photo accompanying the article read: "This decapitated snake is fully conscious whilst it is tormented." Some readers might find the photo of the snake head simply creepy, but the Society worries about its pain.[20] PETA complains of the poor treatment of crustaceans: "A moose is a goose is a chimp is a child, but is a lobster still a thing?"[21] The editor of the *ARIES Newsletter* is concerned for bees used in scientific experiments and crickets threatened by pest control efforts.[22] The banana slug of Northern California, slimy and yellow and up to ten inches long, also has its defenders, who picketed the Guerneville Banana Slug Festival in 1989 on the grounds that "A whale or a slug or a tiger—it doesn't make any difference."[23]

It does make a difference, however, to the potential financial supporters courted by all animal protection groups. Animals with large eyes, furry bodies, and communicative cries arouse sympathy; bees and banana slugs are not likely to gain as much support. Fundamentalist groups must balance the selective sympathies of supporters with the inclusive sympathies of activists—a tension common to all organizations that depend on direct mail contributions to support a few moral virtuosi who carry out the actions.

The ownership of pets is also a source of tension in the movement. Some activists believe that having pets is in itself a form of "fascism." George Cave writes "I remember feeling early on that what is now termed the 'companion animal bond' was commonly a distasteful relation of domination and servility, and that the irritating, yapping miniature dogs of suburbia were a sorry replica of their noble wolf ancestors."[24] Jim Mason, coauthor of *Animal Factories,* expresses a similar view: "We have brought the animal into our domain and in doing so we have disturbed her/his life absolutely. Many say that this is better for the animal's own welfare, but they speak, of course, from a grievously self-serving, homocentric culture. Who are we to determine the welfare of others' lives? . . . We play out our power trips, our ego problems on our pets."[25] Indeed, the *Animals' Agenda* found in a 1985 survey that only half of the staff and leaders of animal rights groups approved of pet-owning.[26]

Animal welfarists favor pet-owning, for they are less concerned with the supposedly independent purposes of an animal's life than with preventing pain and cruelty. They are not inclined to ask what is wrong with placing an animal in a loving human environment, for that is their ideal—to humanize animals as the objects of care and affection. After all, thousands of years of breeding have shaped the responses, pleasures, and desires of domestic species to meet human tastes and expectations.

The issue of pet-owning presents a strategic dilemma for rights groups, however, since leaders and members often disagree. Philosopher Peter Singer is quick to point out that he has no pets; yet groups which depend on public contributions could not survive if they openly debunked the ownership of pets, for this is what underlies sentimental anthropomorphism. The movement partly masks disagreement on this issue by calling pets companion animals. When Trans-Species changed its name to the Animal Rights Mobilization in 1990, enhancing its direct mail efforts, it modified George Cave's opposition to pet-owning, warning simply that "dogs and cats are different from humans. If you choose to live with companion animals, don't expect them to behave like humans, and don't mutilate them to conform to your aesthetic tastes."[27]

———

The single-mindedness of many animal rights groups has obstructed efforts to form strategic relationships with other protest movements. The *Animals' Agenda* has consistently promoted such links and chided animal protectionists for their narrowness.[28] Donna Spring, head of the Disabled and Incurably Ill for Alternatives to Animal Research, feels that "the strength of the animal rights movement will rest on how well we are able to coalition and coalesce with other social movement groups—peace groups, social justice groups, feminists, as well as some of the new spiritual movements that are coming out."[29] Such links could prove crucial to the future of animal rights.

The ecology movement is ideologically compatible in many ways. Environmental writers like J. Baird Callicott and Roderick Nash see kindred concerns in animal rights, and try to make theoretical links.[30] But environmentalists also have some misgivings about animal rights in both its philosophical and political dimensions. The Greens, a network of 200 grassroots groups, have been reluctant to accept animal rights positions. Its "lifeforms" working group developed proposals for vegetarianism, and against animal experiments, cosmetics testing, hunting, trapping, and fishing for sport, but the Greens' consensus machinery (by which all members must come to an agreement before decisions can be made) blocked their adoption.

Some feminists have actively embraced animal rights in their writings and political activities, finding parallels between the domination of women and of animals. Carol Adams' *The Sexual Politics of Meat* documents historical and rhetorical links between the two; meat eating has long been associated with virility, and vegetarianism with femininity. In Berkeley, Feminists for Animal Rights lists the names of animals that men in patriarchal societies have applied to women: "chicks, bitches, pussies, foxes, dogs, cows, beavers, birds, bunnies, sows, kittens, lambs, hens, shrews, geese, fillies, bats, crows, heifers, vixens." The same brochure pairs a photo of a woman bound and gagged with that of a cat trussed and constrained. It claims that men often discern the same characteristics in both animals and women—irrationality, childishness, instinctive behavior, emotionality, and inferiority—and hence have treated them similarly: as objects for enslavement, entertainment, rape, or experiments.[31]

Sympathetic articles in recent issues of the *Progressive,* the *Village Voice, Zeta,* and *Signs* seem to indicate a revaluation of animal rights by writers on the Left. John Sanbonmatsu asks, "Animal Liberation: Should the Left Care?" His answer is yes, "for both ethical and pragmatic-strategic reasons." He argues that the animal rights movement fits every traditional criterion of a radical social justice movement except that it focuses on animals rather than humans. Yet, he observes, "To the vast majority of the Left, the animal rights issue seems appallingly trivial." He criticizes this attitude as mirroring "the prevailing societal view which places 'Man' at the center of the universe."[32] In *The Progressive,* Jean Bethke Elshtain similarly concludes that "We humans do not deserve peace of mind on this issue. . . . Animals are not simply a means to our ends."[33]

Animal rights activists are awkward in their handling of these occasional gestures from other social movements: "Animal rights groups don't go out and make a point of taking part in building coalitions. That's why environmental coalitions don't pursue animal issues."[34] Fundamentalist urges make many animal activists believe their own issue is of such overriding importance that solidarity with others is not urgent. Awkwardness is also sometimes based on political naïveté. The Animal Rights Coalition of Minneapolis advertised a 1986 speech on "feminine [rather than feminist], gay and animal rights." Ingrid Newkirk even chides feminists: "Women are suggesting that men give up power, yet women can't understand why it is taking them so long! How long will it take women to relinquish their power *over others?* How long will some feminists go on munching on the greasy bones of little murdered birds? Dressing in the skins of slaughtered cows and wild creatures?" Anti-fur protestors carried a sign at a demonstration denouncing "Corporate woman: Ms. Macho wears her cruel status trophy to the office. Never underestimate her haughty inhumanity." And despite PETA's Barf-In against L'Oréal, PETA never mentions that L'Oréal is a Nestlé subsidiary, missing the chance to link its own boycott with one of the most popular left-liberal boycotts of recent years—against the marketing of baby formula in developing nations. Not exactly the way to build coalitions.

The links between animal rights and other protest movements remain at the theoretical level, developed by the philosophers, journalists, and politically sophisticated in the various movements, but not adopted by many rank-and-file. Their sentiments are different, and concentrate overwhelmingly on animals. As one observer at the June 1990 demonstration in Washington noted: "Not one single banner acknowledged racism, classism, capitalism, homophobia, and other dominant supremacist mentalities."[35]

How did animal rightists so quickly gain the upper hand in the animal protection movement, repainting the public image of the movement and raising ideological questions that even traditional groups had to address? And why, in the 1980s, were fundamentalists more successful than pragmatists in attracting members and formulating issues? In order to compete with welfare organizations for direct mail support, the new animal rights groups presented themselves as more active and energetic; their flamboyant protest and moralist tactics were their proof. Their rhetoric of good and evil, their images of pain and exploitation, played better than arguments about the costs and benefits of animal use. The traditional style of compromise and negotiation, without the glare of the media, was less effective in raising funds than the dramatic footage of memorable media events. Animal rightists knew how to turn the special emotional charge conveyed by animals into a moral issue.

The fundamentalists were also able to solve the challenge of all voluntary groups: how to get people to work for your cause when you cannot pay them. They discovered that demonizing opponents and exaggerating evils are effective ways to energize supporters and hold their commitment. To mobilize time and money, protest movements must rely on those who feel most strongly about an issue—precisely those most likely to be moral extremists. For them, denunciation of their opponents becomes more satisfying than efforts to communicate. The result is that "the very structure of a voluntary political organization tends to produce an inability to hear or understand what others are saying."[36]

The radical rhetoric and moralist tactics of the fundamentalists surely help explain their success. But to fully understand the emergence and rapid growth of the new groups and the appeal of their ideological position, it is useful to explore their roots in the hundred-year-old history of animal protection, and their relationship to the anti-instrumentalism that developed in the environmental movement of the 1960s and 1970s.

FIVE

The Compassionate Tradition

In 1888, Leonard Eaton, President of the American Humane Association, described the group's purpose at its twelfth annual meeting: "Animals are now regarded by the more reasonable and intelligent portion of the community as having rights that humans are bound to respect. . . . A cruel community will, of necessity, be an ignorant and vicious community."[1] Convinced that kindness to animals was essential for human moral development, nineteenth-century humane societies reflected the charitable impulses of privileged elites, whose members formed organizations to develop humane education and to enforce anticruelty laws protecting both children and helpless animals—"dumb brutes." This tradition provided the roots for a welfare movement that arose after World War II and engaged a broader constituency less condescending in its attitudes toward its beneficiaries. Yet the associations retained a reformist agenda, avoiding extreme positions that might undermine their mainstream appeal, their financial and political support, or their policy influence.

The compassion driving the humane and welfare movements became an essential dimension of animal rights. Welfarists preached lessons about the protection of animals that the emerging animal rights groups absorbed quite fully—so fully, indeed, that they could criticize welfarists for not living up to their own ideals.

American humane societies are descended directly from British organizations. Britain's first animal protection bill, introduced in

Parliament in 1800, was to ban bull baiting—the dubious practice of letting packs of dogs torment a bull for human entertainment. The bill failed. But following a series of aborted proposals, a bill finally passed both houses in 1822, protecting draft and farm animals from unnecessary cruelty. Two years later, a group of wealthy men formed the Society for the Prevention of Cruelty to Animals (SPCA) to lobby for further legislation as well as to demand enforcement of the 1822 Act. Enforcement grew increasingly vigorous; the society hired its own private constables, and, by the end of the nineteenth century, there were over one hundred of these officers. After 1900, enforcement activities dwindled, as horses—the main beneficiaries of SPCA actions—were replaced by motor vehicles, but by this time the RSPCA (in 1840, its most prominent patron, Queen Victoria, allowed the society to be called "Royal") was a favorite charity of the upper classes.

The British humane movement focused on lower class cruelty; its attitudes toward vivisection were more ambivalent. The RSPCA began to oppose experiments on live animals in the 1860s. However, its membership seemed split on vivisection. For this reason, when an 1876 Act instituted a mild licensing system for experimenters, the society gladly dropped the issue. However, anti-vivisection demonstrations continued into the 1900s, often composed of poor and working class people who suspected that scientific experiments were taking place in certain orphanages and charity hospitals. Medical groups organized to protect research interests and, in 1906, a Research Defense Society was established to promote confidence in medical science and convince the public of the importance of animal experiments for human health. Scientists claimed to be on the side of progress, and they discredited the anti-vivisectionists by drawing on elite fears of the "uneducated," "hostile," and "hysterical" masses. Anti-vivisection societies declined as a public force; science was too popular in Victorian Britain, especially among the upper classes who supported the protectionist movement.[2]

Subject to a slight time lag, a similar pattern evolved in the United States. Efforts to form an animal protection association in America began in the 1830s, but failed to coalesce in an organization until, in 1866, Henry Bergh, the son of a rich New York shipbuilder, used his social connections to form the American Society for the Prevention of Cruelty to Animals. While living in St. Petersburg as Secretary of the American Delegation to Russia, Bergh had observed with horror the cruel treatment of carriage horses. On the way back to America, he attended a meeting of the RSPCA in London. Deciding to devote himself to the "defense of the friendless dumb beast," he proceeded to raise money to form a "humane and civilizing charity" in New York.

Other groups proliferated, organized by people who, like Bergh, belonged to wealthy urban elites.[3] George T. Angell, law partner of abolitionist Samuel Sewell, founded the Massachusetts SPCA, although he was best known for organizing the American Humane Education Society in 1889 to protect children and teach them compassion. The two organizations shared a single board of directors, reflecting the fact that early societies linked the protection of animals and children as part of a single humanitarian goal. By the end of the century, there were 700 humane organizations throughout the country. Conservative and highly respectable, they were among the most influential voluntary associations in America.

Protection of animals became the rallying cry of this new humane movement, and sentimental anthropomorphism its vision. The societies saw two groups as especially needing moral education—children and the lower classes—and animals provided living lessons for them. Children's books preached kindness to animals, and pets were seen as a tool for developing their moral awareness. Thus a Bostonian, Sarah Josepha Hale, wrote the nursery rhyme "Mary Had a Little Lamb," which closed,

> "What makes the lamb love Mary so?"
> The eager children cry—
> "O, Mary loves the lamb, you know,"
> The Teacher did reply.[4]

Controlling the abuse of animals was also a way to impose a bourgeois moral sensibility on the lower classes, which were perceived as lacking moral discipline and respect for social order. For the humane movement, as the name implies, protection of animals from undue cruelty went hand in hand with the moral improvement of humanity.

Women played prominent roles in many of the new groups. The increasing differentiation, in the nineteenth century, between public and private spheres, workplace and home, separated male and female roles. Middle class women were confined to the sentimental realm of "feelings." The burgeoning humane movement provided possibilities in a field devoted to caring and compassion and, therefore, socially accepted as appropriate to female skills. Explaining the involvement of women in the animal welfare movement, a 1924 American Humane Association publication expressed the sentiments of the time: "The heart of American womanhood has always been sympathetic for the lot of the unfortunate. Her deep seated instinct for right and justice has been seen in all of the great social reforms."[5] Nonetheless, in a pattern that has persisted to the present, women were overrepresented among rank-and-file members, yet underrepresented in leadership positions.

Throughout the nineteenth century, the humane societies focused on the pain inflicted on animals used for work and entertainment. The treatment of carriage horses was a visible problem in the growing cities. But toward the end of the century, America was also becoming a center for medical experimentation and animals were increasingly necessary for research. A number of animal lovers turned their attention to the perceived cruelties of vivisection and formed their own group within the SPCA. Encouraged by 1884 legislation in Massachusetts banning vivisection in elementary and secondary schools, they began to press for anti-vivisection laws. Their actions embarrassed most traditional SPCA leaders and their wealthy patrons, who saw anti-vivisectionists as eccentric extremists.

In subsequent debates, some claimed that science—evolutionary biology—had demonstrated the affinity between animals and man and should be defended as paving the way for increased compassion, while others felt betrayed by modern science—biomedicine—and viewed animal research as an affront to the spiritual values that should guide compassionate behavior. Still others used the issue of animal experimentation to express their skepticism about doctors and scientists as an arrogant, secretive, and even cruel elite. Yet most were dazzled by the advances in immunology and public health during the decades following Pasteur's and Koch's 1876 discoveries linking specific diseases to specific microorganisms. Public ambivalence toward modern science—awe and dread, confidence and skepticism—have persisted to this day, providing a rich vocabulary for animal activists.

The promises of medical science weakened support for those who wished to eliminate animal research. Forced to address the issue, the powerful humane societies called for restrictions to reduce unnecessary pain for animal subjects, but not for the abolition of research. In 1892, the American Humane Association, for example, called for laws "prohibiting the repetition of painful experiments on animals for the purpose of teaching or demonstrating well-known accepted facts."[6] However, the Association considered vivisection acceptable with the use of anaesthetic, if it would contribute to the discovery of new knowledge. Gradually the American anti-vivisectionists were marginalized, persisting only as a fringe group. The humane and anti-vivisection forces went separate ways, rejoining only with the development of the animal rights movement in the 1980s.[7]

The humane societies, however, maintained considerable continuity in the twentieth century. Their agendas continued to be shaped by their location in major cities. Their boards of directors and members were urban people, and their target was the most visible example of animal cruelty in cities, the wretched horses pulling trams and carriages. When motor vehicles replaced horse-drawn carriages in the early years of the century, the humane societies turned their attention to other urban issues. They built animal hospitals, shelters and clinics, rescue leagues, rest homes for work animals, and animal cemeteries. They fought for leash laws, sound pet care, and humane education in the schools. Such activities made the organizations less visible to the public.

Frustrated by this limited activity, several groups split off from the humane societies in the early twentieth century. Some tried to tackle issues such as the horrors of slaughterhouses and cruelties of trapping wild animals, forming their own specialized societies such as the Anti-Steel Trap League. However, its cause was not adopted by the major animal welfare organizations, and the league foundered from lack of support. Similarly, the societies paid little attention to the issue of cruelty in slaughterhouses, although the industry used archaic methods of slaughter long after the invention of humane killing devices. An animal welfare advocate of the 1960s explained the "deterioration" of the movement during this early period: "A sophisticated, materialistic, amusement-seeking public" regarded the issue of animal cruelty as "a hobby for the supersensitive, stupid people who worry about things which do not exist."[8]

After half a century of relative quiescence, animal protection began to make the news again in the 1950s. If we are right in linking animal protection with bourgeois domesticity, its reemergence at this time is understandable. The 1950s saw strong social and political efforts to reinforce domestic family life after the strains of the war years, to spread the image of detached suburban houses with picture-perfect nuclear families cared for by full-time mothers and emotionally enriched by pet dogs.

Several new groups formed in the 1950s, often in response to the fear that the growing market for research animals threatened personal pets. The Animal Welfare Institute was founded in Washington, D.C., in 1951. In 1954, some members of the American Humane Association broke away to form the Humane Society of the United States (HSUS), because, "A great many people throughout the United States were aware of the tremendous need for a strong humane group that would actively endorse and work towards eliminating . . . the more obvious cruelties and injustices imposed on animals."[9] HSUS activities, initially driven by concerns about research, soon extended to a wider range of issues, including trapping, the conditions of animal shelters, the protection of wildlife, slaughterhouses practices, the overbreeding of animals, and the use of animals for entertainment. A third group, Friends of Animals, began operation in New York in 1957. Together, these groups represent the emergence of a new kind of animal welfare movement. While the early humane tradition tried to change individual behavior and attitudes toward animals, these new groups also occasionally sought to change institutional practices.

They also introduced more aggressive tactics. In 1966, HSUS joined the Maryland State Police in a raid on the facilities of a dog dealer who had been collecting strays to supply medical research laboratories. The chief investigator of the state police, a member of HSUS since 1961, had been monitoring the dog auctions supplying animals to labs. He organized the raid and HSUS arranged to have *Life* magazine reporters on the scene. A picture of the facility appeared on the front cover of *Life,* captioned: "Concentration Camp for Dogs." The event brought public attention to the "animal slave trade" in which lost or stolen pets were picked up and sold to dealers who trucked them off to universities or pharmaceutical laboratories. HSUS offered awards for information leading to the arrest and conviction of abusive animal dealers, and hired its own investigators to expose illegal suppliers. Some even posed as dealers themselves to discover abuses first hand.

The new activities had legislative results. The federal Humane Slaughter Act of 1958 required packers to provide anesthesia and to stun animals prior to slaughter. Nineteen Congressional bills were introduced in the early 1960s to control the laboratory use of animals, culminating in the Laboratory Animal Welfare Act of 1966. This, the first federal law dealing with the care and treatment of laboratory animals, required licensing of dealers and registration of laboratories, and set minimum standards (for certain species) for food, water, and sanitary conditions, although it said nothing about research procedures themselves. A 1970 amendment added requirements for the use of appropriate anesthetics and tranquilizers, and extended protection to all warm blooded animals.

In the public hearings prior to the 1966 act, Congress heard testimony from people who had lost pets to laboratories, and from HSUS and other organizations concerned about the growing business of dog dealing.[10] These groups did not propose to abolish the use of animals in research, but wanted research labs to purchase animals only from licensed dealers. They were disturbed by the cruel irony, perhaps the ultimate betrayal of proverbial canine loyalty, that former pets made good research subjects since they were obedient and would not bite humans. These organizations were not, though, opposed to vivisection in general.

Nor did the welfare groups take action against pound seizure laws that required animal shelters to release unclaimed dogs and cats to research institutions.[11] Only in the 1970s, under pressure from the radical flank of the animal protection movement, did more and more welfare societies promote legislation to prohibit the use of pound animals in research. By then, the societies began to take more seriously their goal of assuring domestic animals a humane life and, barring that, a humane death.

———

Tension within the movement grew with the increasing animal welfare activism of the 1960s. A handful of groups—usually driven by a single forceful personality—went far beyond traditional welfare concerns. These prophets heralding the animal rights crusade were isolated voices decrying not just the unusual cruelty of cockfights, dog dealers, or sadistic pet owners, but many practices—the wearing of furs, the eating of meat—that were an accepted part of American life. They were people like Cleveland Amory of the Fund for Animals, Alice Herrington of Friends of Animals, Helen Jones of the International Society for Animal Rights, and Ellen Thurston of the American Fund for Alternatives to Animal Research. Too radical for existing welfare societies, they founded their own groups. They were animal rightists before the term, or even the ideology, had been created.[12]

The Fund for Animals, founded by Cleveland Amory in 1967, epitomizes this step in the evolution of the animal welfare movement. Amory, a large and gruff Harvard graduate with patrician roots, wanted to "put some cleats on the little old ladies in tennis shoes" with a group that was more oriented toward political action than humane education.[13] Like many of the new generation of welfare groups, the Fund was driven by the dynamism of its founder, who at the time wrote a column for *TV Guide* and appeared regularly on television talk shows. New members/contributors typically learned of the Fund through Amory's interviews on television and radio.

The Fund was best known for its efforts to save groups of burros, mustangs, and wild goats, and it started the Black Beauty Ranch in Texas as a preserve for these species. Wolves caught the Fund's fancy in the early 1970s, and the Endangered Species Acts of 1969 and 1973 provided ammunition for saving them. In order to change public perceptions of the animals, Amory appeared on talk shows with two domesticated wolves—themselves later poisoned by a deranged cat lover. The Fund's Washington office, opened in 1972, worked to protect timber wolves in Minnesota from hunting, and to stop fashion shows that included coats made from wolf furs. Committed to environmental rhetoric, the Fund failed to condemn furs made from ranch animals, despite the preferences of more radical staffers.[14]

In 1977, Ellen Thurston founded the American Fund for Alternatives to Animal Research in New York to raise and disseminate money for research into alternatives to live animal testing and research. It began to give out small grants totaling over half a million dollars. More than half went to one of its own science advisors, Joseph Leighton, a pathologist at the Medical College of Pennsylvania. Although almost all its funds went into developing alternative tests, $700 was used to purchase a dog dummy to loan to veterinary colleges, and $18,000 per year has been devoted to courses for students and teachers of biology. Thurston and her science advisor John Petricciani claim that "Most of the animal defenders who support alternatives research are abolitionists who are also realists, who work within a framework of what is possible . . . in the long run, the replacement approach should eliminate very many more [animals than a regulatory approach would]."[15]

Thurston's and Amory's activities reflected a growing radicalism among animal welfarists in the 1970s due partly to frustration with the conservatism of the humane tradition and partly to awareness of broader issues like environmental threats or the callous pursuit of profit by private companies. The effort to protect animals in new contexts and the accompanying proliferation of tactics would accelerate over the next decade.

———

The animal welfare organizations that had grown steadily through the postwar period became an important inspiration and source of information for the animal rights movement at the end of the 1970s. They gathered and published useful information on laboratory research, trapping, hunting, and other uses of animals. Even more, they inspired a new generation of activists. Compassion for animals, based on romanticized and anthropomorphic sentiments, became an essential ingredient of the emerging rhetoric of animal rights.

The large animal welfare organizations still dominate the animal protection movement in money and members. Indeed, they have gained from the recent interest in animal rights, expanding their membership and increasing their services while continuing their traditional activities: the education of children, the care of stray pets, and the prevention of outright cruelty. They are often defensive about their role. As one activist put it, "I'm tired of other activists assuming that I'm politically unsophisticated, too moderate, or afraid of confrontation, simply because my main emphasis is humane education."[16] HSUS established a legal department and began giving more attention to public relations in the 1970s. To extend its outreach, it held annual conferences and increased the size of its staff. Its membership has grown exponentially to top 1,000,000 in 1991. The Massachusetts SPCA, largest of the many SPCAs, has a professional staff of 350 and assets of over $60 million. The New York-based ASPCA, the direct descendent of Bergh's organization, has 300,000 members and assets of $40 million. No fewer than six animal protection groups have assets over $10 million.[17]

Their wealth has in fact made these large societies vulnerable to attacks from a new generation of animal rights activists, who claim that large salaries are being paid without large results for animals. The heads of the large societies earn over $100,000 annually. In 1989, according to *Animals' Agenda,* nine staff members of the Massachusetts SPCA received salaries over $70,000.[18] Yet, critics ask, how many animals have been saved? Because they compete with animal welfare groups for direct mail contributions from the same population, animal rightists insist that they are far more effective. PETA, for instance, points out the high percentage of its contributions that goes "directly" to helping animals rather than to overhead, and boasts of its low staff salaries. In fact, however, its overhead rate is higher than that of HSUS or the Massachusetts SPCA.

Animal welfare organizations have been rocked by such attacks. Tied to the assumptions and values of their forebears, they accept the instrumental use of animals when essential for human well-being. While they borrow radical language by engaging in "rights talk" and arguing that all life has intrinsic value, the welfare groups are willing to make cost benefit calculations that weigh animal rights against human needs. HSUS asks: "What does it mean to recognize the rights of animals? It means that before we make use of any animal . . . we should weigh our desires and needs against those of the animal—giving equal consideration to each—to see which is of overriding value."[19] And in the spirit of the nineteenth-century compassionate tradition, HSUS remains concerned about the effect of cruelty to animals on the morality of human beings. In 1979, HSUS President John Hoyt called for "sensitivity, commitment, and sacrifice" for the cause of animal welfare reform; "The greatest task facing the humane movement today is the task of assisting man in the recovery of his own humanity. For unless he is able to affirm himself as one with the world he is intent upon destroying, it will matter little that we have acted to protect a few million animals."[20] Tied to their ongoing programs, especially involving strays, welfare groups have retained as their primary goal reforms that will stop unnecessary cruelty.

Animal welfarists still perceive their supporters primarily as pet lovers. Their mailings have a special character designed to appeal to pet owners. They are personalized, addressing people by their first names, praising volunteers for their work, and publishing the names and sometimes the pictures of community volunteers. They provide advice—even special recipes—for the care of pets. They print memorials to pets: "Chablis—in memory of my beautiful friend who always kept my lap warm" and "honorarials" to people: "Thank you Dave and Debby for contributing your services." A group called Volunteer Service for Animals circulates stories about the heroic activities of their volunteers and "special people lists." And they run a "Golden Bone Club" for those who "remember VSA every week of the year."

But membership does not imply participation in decisions, which remain the prerogative of the staff and leadership. Aside from infrequent rallies or marches, members' participation in animal welfare organizations is restricted to letter writing and financial contributions. The limited involvement of members has left these organizations vulnerable, and some of their active constituents found that the new rights groups provided more opportunities for direct grassroots engagement in the struggle for animal protection.

The growing animal rights crusade has affected the rest of the animal protection movement in diverse ways. The radicals have especially influenced the ideologies and attitudes of many staff members, whose devotion to animals made them sympathetic to arguments drawing on sentimental anthropomorphism. Rights arguments merely carry to an extreme many of the sentiments about animals that already motivate welfare society staffers, who often join rights groups too. The older organizations themselves have adopted increasingly strident objections to many uses of animals. They criticize the unnecessary repetition of research involving the use of animals, seek to restrict dissection of animals in science classes, endorse alternatives to animals in substance testing, and campaign for additional inspectors to enforce the Animal Welfare Act. But despite the hyperbole about the horrors of animal research, they do not propose abolishing all use of animals. The literature of the large national groups does not suggest that animals have moral status equivalent to that of humans. Nor have these groups usually encouraged direct political activism by members. Thus rights groups portray the welfare community as stodgy and rigid, and manage to steal away many active and devoted members. The differences between moderate welfarists and radical rightists are highlighted by the persistent problem of what to do with stray animals.

Most humane societies operate shelters where unclaimed animals are killed. The organizations shield donors from this fact by emphasizing their adoption programs, and some shelters claim to be "no-kill" (they send animals elsewhere for the dirty work, or accept only clearly adoptable animals). Yet groups founded on compassion for animals kill (or as they say, "put down") from twelve to twenty million animals a year—roughly the number of animals killed annually by trappers. Animals are treated with compassion before being killed, but the stark contrast between loving care and death makes shelters especially poignant for those who work in them. Says one such worker: "Very often what they get is the best five days of their lives. They are entitled to a stress-free environment, a disease-free environment. They're entitled to be kept warm and dry and played with and to get attention, and they're entitled to a humane and digni-fied death."[21]

Despite one hundred years of humane education efforts, many people still do not take proper care of their pets, and shelters see the results. The manager of a California shelter complains, "It's very difficult to work at an animal shelter and continue to love people. You have to remind yourself that we're all the same, that people are our brothers too. It's very difficult when you see the kinds of things they do."[22] Pets are part of the family, but many families are destruc-tive: "Man's best friend has become man's biggest victim," says one writer.[23]

The animal protection movement tries to place abandoned ani-mals in good homes, but only one in five is ever claimed or adopted. Members of the animal welfare and animal rights movements them-selves adopt large numbers of pets; many activists have five or ten or more animals of their own. Even in densely populated New York City, not only did 72 percent of the animal rights demonstrators in-terviewed in 1988 have more than one animal, but 31 percent had animals from more than one species. But such efforts are not on a sufficient scale to deal with millions of animals a year. Hence the shelters.

Animal rights groups have tried to resolve the dilemma by build-ing, not animal shelters, but "sanctuaries," as protective refuges. In-stead of painless death, they provide the means for animals to live out their "natural" lives. Some of the animal sanctuaries are for stray animals, others for retired work or laboratory animals. They are costly and often elegant. The Defenders of Animal Rights, for exam-ple, sent out mailings to raise the $500,000 needed to complete a pet sanctuary. For a contribution of $1,000, a donor's name is on a plaque. For $2,000, one's name is on a kennel. Another sanctuary is promoted as "a unique housing development for underprivileged felines." It contains "kitty condos" where cats can nap, with large windows for our "sun worshippers" and for "an entertaining birds-eye view of the great outdoors." This sanctuary, in the middle of a thirty-five-acre wildlife area, costs about $600,000 a year to run. One California group named DELTA (Dedication and Everlasting Love to Animals) houses 400 abandoned dogs and 200 rescued cats, which live in their own three-bedroom home and outdoor recreation area.[24] Homeless humans should be so lucky.

Sanctuaries are not without their critics. There are simply too many dogs and cats, so that most specialize in certain species they know they can care for. But a no-kill shelter in Elmsford, New York, accepts all animals; it has over 400 dogs and cats. Unfortunately, it lacks room for so many, and dogs are kept on short leashes and, according to critics, not given adequate care: "I understand what she's trying to do, but unfortunately you can't save everything. There's a point where your head has to take over your heart, and that's very hard."[25] Both HSUS and the ASPCA oppose no-kill shelters as cruel to many of the animals.

Pat Derby, who operates the Performing Animal Welfare Society, a sanctuary near Sacramento, California, expresses the sentimental anthropomorphism that encourages sanctuaries. Some of her animals have whimsical names, such as Lucretia and Lucifer Leopard or Seymour and Gwendolyn Grizzly. She insists that animals' intentions are always innocent—"An animal will never pursue an altercation except for a really valid reason." "There's no real neurosis in animals," and "An animal just knows everything; they know—this is a corny phrase—all the secrets of the universe." Derby is convinced that they do not abuse this knowledge: "A human can say one thing and mean another. Animals don't do that. Animals say what they mean." Derby's concept of compassion not only blurs the boundaries between species, but reverses roles. When asked if she "owns" her companions, she replied:

> Not at all. I think they own me. I mean I'm not kidding. Look at my domestic cats. [Her outstretched hand motions around the room—a cat is perched on every comfortable surface from floor to eye level.] I mean if I owned them, they wouldn't be clawing up the furniture and peeing all over everything. . . . I don't interfere with what they do in their lives. I really think, in a sense, I'm just sort of the servant—I do whatever is necessary for them to be comfortable. And that's a choice that I've made. Right now, look, Valerie is lying on the clean clothes. I'm not going to stop her and she knows I'm not going to. So that's the difference between owning something and not."[26]

After thousands of years in which animals served humans, some humans are now serving animals, in the name of compassion and animal rights.

———

The formation of radical groups alongside existing ones is characteristic of many protest movements, attributed by most observers to frustration with the plodding pace of social change. Disillusionment with reformist strategies is expressed in both ideological and tactical innovations. In the civil rights movement, for example, the legal strategies of the NAACP gave way in the 1950s to the nonviolent boycotts and protests of the Southern Christian Leadership Conference. Then the lunch counter sit-ins of students led to the formation of the Student Nonviolent Coordinating Committee, and to its increasingly violent tactics in the 1960s, which themselves were eclipsed by more confrontational groups in the ghettos of large Northern and Western cities.[27] In each case, new recruits helped to break the inertia of old tactics. In like manner, the antinuclear movement turned to direct action in 1976 and 1977, as the failure of reformist strategies frustrated many activists, especially younger, more left-leaning recruits.[28]

Compelled by similar moral sentiments, radical and reformist wings of social movements are often capable of sustained cooperation. Yet heightened competition for resources creates conflict, and allied groups may come to trade accusations of "sellout" on the one hand, and "political naïveté" on the other. Moderate organizations in a movement usually control greater resources, because they attract broader support from the rest of society. If unable to tap into these resources, movement radicals develop low-cost tactics (street protests rather than lobbying Congress). Or they heighten their radical rhetoric in hope of obtaining some resources even while they claim to spurn such support as a sign of cooptation. In some cases, radicals gain resources through strategic alliances or by direct takeovers of existing moderate organizations. The animal welfare community has provided these kinds of opportunities to the emerging animal rights movement.

Adding to the frustration of existing participants in the welfare movement were the beliefs of the new recruits—both encouraged radicalization. Animal protection was transformed mainly by evolving ideas about animals. The traditional language of "humane" compassion implied a powerful group helping powerless beneficiaries, a form of charity that does as much to satisfy the givers as it does to aid the recipients. But when activists defined animals as beings with emotions and interests rather than simply objects of pity capable of pain, they began to adopt the rhetoric of "welfare." The main form of American welfare is Aid to Families with Dependent Children: its beneficiaries are presumably innocent and deserving of systematic aid. The notion of welfare lies partway between private charity and a full concept of individual rights. The gradual radicalization of the animal protection movement thus followed changing images of animals; from pitiful objects of charity, to innocent beings with interests of their own, and—finally—to autonomous individuals with a right to their own lives.

Humane and welfare groups were necessary precursors to the animal rights movement, yet also a convenient whipping boy when rights advocates needed to prove their radical bent. Driven by compassion, for decades the animal welfare movement mobilized large numbers of animal lovers to protest cruel and painful treatment of animals. The reformist agenda created a system of shelters and led to legislative reforms. But institutional uses of animals—for substance testing and medical research, for food and fur, for education and entertainment—continued. By the late 1970s, many animal lovers were disaffected with the slow pace of reform, and new recruits questioned the efficacy of the moderate strategies of the humane societies. Like Cleveland Amory and other harbingers of changing attitudes, many humane society supporters and staff were ready to assimilate the activist values and ideological critiques generated in the late 1960s and 1970s by the environmental movement.

SIX

Animals
in the Wild

Rooted in the indignant compassion of the animal welfare
movement, the contemporary animal rights movement also incorporated the critique of exploitive attitudes toward nature developed by
the environmental movement. Beyond their concern about pollution
and limits to growth, environmentalists called attention to the threat
of species extinction, blaming large industries devoted to whaling,
trapping, and the trading of commodities such as ivory. Environmentalists developed a set of related critiques—of uncontrolled economic
growth, massive development projects, and the elevation of profit
above human values—that proved useful to animal rightists. No issue dramatized the new sensibilities more powerfully than the Canadian seal hunt.

In the Gulf of St. Lawrence, the ice was said to have a red tinge
after the seal hunt every March, when 100,000 seals were killed for
their pelts. Most prized of all were the babies, which, for the first
three weeks of life, have furry white coats. With their large eyes, they
could bring out sentimental anthropomorphism in almost anyone. A
Canadian film crew—expecting only to film seals in their natural
habitat—caught part of the 1964 hunt, and the sight of baby seals
being clubbed and spiked in the head caused outrage throughout the
industrialized world and generated a major controversy, attracting
the attention of both environmentalists and animal welfarists.

Brian Davies, then executive-secretary of the New Brunswick
SPCA, merged his welfare perspective with the political arguments
of environmentalists: "I discovered that an over-capitalized sealing

industry was intent on killing the last seal pup in order to get a return on its equipment, and that those who profited from the seals gave not one thought to their suffering."[1] Davies buttressed this critique of instrumentalism with an explicit anthropomorphic description: "Their hind flippers were like two hands crossed in prayer, and again, the five fingernails. I can well imagine why many biologists consider sea mammals the most advanced form of nonhuman life."[2] Whether for anthropomorphic or other reasons, whales, dolphins, seals, and other sea mammals have aroused tremendous sympathies.

Davies later described the first baby seal he saw killed. "He was a little ball of white fur with big dark eyes and a plaintive cry . . . *he was only ten days old.* He went to meet, in a curious, friendly and playful way, the first human he had ever seen and was . . . by that same human . . . clubbed on the head and butchered on the spot. He was skinned alive. I saw the heart in a body without a skin pumping frantically. From that very moment . . . ending the commercial whitecoat hunt was a cause that consumed me." As in a religious conversion, he knew his life would henceforth be devoted to what he called a "crusade against cruelty."[3] Cruelty, not species preservation, was the issue for animal protectionists who joined the environmental cause.

Animal rights activists readily adopted the environmental critique of instrumentalism, even though they often differed from environmentalists in their attitudes toward individual animals. Ecologists, convinced that sustainable environments require a balance among various species, focus on the maintenance of ecological communities in which plants and animals are interdependent. What happens to individual animals is not important. They accept that, in nature, animals compete with one another for the necessities of life. From the biological point of view, survival of the species, rather than of particular individuals, is the issue. In contrast, animal rightists feel for the pain of particular animals, sometimes even rejecting a species orientation as "environmental fascism" that violates the rights of individual animals for some greater collective good.

Yet the environmental movement left several essential legacies to animal rights activists. The critique of instrumentalism provided a powerful ideology that the animal rights movement could adopt even when its goals diverged from those of environmentalists. And the environmentalists also refined a range of strategies, embodied in the Greenpeace model of high-risk activism supported by direct mail fundraising. Many environmental groups of the early 1970s provided examples of radicalism that encouraged animal activists to transcend the limits of the welfarist tradition of animal protection. If the humane societies appealed to the hearts of animal lovers, environmental arguments appealed to their minds, to their desire for an ideological rationale.

———

Concentrating on the protection of wildlife and land from urban and industrial development, conservation societies have existed in the United States at least since the Sierra Club was founded in 1892. A new kind of environmental group began to appear in the 1960s, inspired partly by Rachel Carson's 1962 book *Silent Spring,* an attack on the use of DDT. Carson developed a view of nature as a complex and highly integrated set of relationships between living things, relationships that humans ignored at their peril. Her image of a fragile ecological balance brought together concerns about wildlife and pollution, supporting the belief that human actions were threatening environmental integrity.[4]

The 1960s saw increased political activity by existing organizations, notably the Sierra Club, as well as the formation of new organizations. Scientists collaborated with lawyers to form groups like the Environmental Defense Fund and the Natural Resources Defense Council. In 1969, Congress passed the National Environmental Policy Act requiring federal agencies to prepare environmental impact reports before undertaking large construction projects, and giving legal standing to citizens who wished to sue for enforcement.

This "right of standing," an important strategic legacy, has allowed animal rights activists to sue on behalf of wildlife even if they were not themselves affected.[5] According to Joyce Tischler of the Animal Legal Defense Fund (ALDF), her organization is more likely to win lawsuits to protect wild animals than those to help domestic animals, because it usually does not have to fight for standing in the courts.[6] In the 1980s, animal activists used environmental laws to delay the construction of new animal laboratories in San Francisco, Berkeley, and Stanford because of improper environmental impact statements. The Animal League Defense Fund stopped California's annual mountain lion hunt for several seasons, on the grounds that environmental assessments had not considered factors like the loss of lion habitats, wildfires, and future hunting seasons.

The American environmental movement of the 1970s left another strategic legacy in its style of protest. Groups like Greenpeace, founded in Canada in 1971, used direct action tactics to bring attention to environmental threats. "Exemplary actions"—pouring blood on the headquarters of polluting corporations, occupying towers to unfurl banners—serve to publicize an issue: they are adopted more for their symbolic value than for their practical effects. They suggest the sense of moral urgency that motivates both environmental and animal activism, the belief that breaking the normal rules is justifiable because the cause is so important.[7] In a society dominated by television, memorable symbolic action is also vital for recruiting new members to a protest movement. And tabloid newspapers, with their lurid headlines and large photographs, may be a more useful forum than the traditional press.

Environmental actions were financed through the technique of "direct mail." Hundreds of thousands joined and contributed to environmental groups in the early 1970s, drawn by direct mail solicitations.[8] This important innovation has since transformed the operations of most social movement organizations, including those for animal protection. By sending fundraising letters to people around the country most likely to contribute—typically, those who have contributed to similar groups—an organization can raise funds relatively cheaply. An industry of several hundred "list brokers" has formed to maintain, trade, rent, or sell lists of people thought to have certain political sympathies. Direct mail consultants are available to procure the right lists—the price of a list varies according to how current it is and whether it is a proven winner—and to develop a package of letters and brochures specifically targeted to particular groups. (Hence the stream of solicitations one receives after contributing to one organization or subscribing to a particular magazine.) Greenpeace is a model for direct mail fundraising—it now boasts several million supporters around the world—and many animal rights groups successfully use its list, suggesting the overlap between environmental and animal rights contributors.

Many animal rights groups adopted the Greenpeace model of protest, using direct mail campaigns to finance highly visible and often highly risky activities by a small cadre of committed individuals.[9] The organizations use their feats and exploits to solicit money, so that the audience for direct action consists of supporters as well as the general public. This style of elite activism contrasts with the approach of most civil rights and antinuclear groups, which were more concerned with either mass participation or legislative lobbying. The Greenpeace model aims more to create a public image than to encourage mass participation. It would prove especially useful to animal rights organizers.

The rhetoric and ideology of the environmental movement provided further ammunition for the animal rights movement. Traditional environmental groups had wanted to preserve nature for the use of future generations. But 1970s activists felt that the natural world had "inherent worth," no matter what its value for human use. Ecosystems should be preserved for their own sake, and land, animals, and plants should not be considered mere resources to be used up in economic production. Environmentalists linked exploitation of nature to capitalism, Western science, and Judaeo-Christian religious traditions. Eco-feminists linked exploitation to male attitudes of domination. The critique of instrumentalism flowered in the environmental and feminist movements of the 1970s.[10]

The new generation of animal activists of the late 1970s drew on the rich vocabulary of environmentalism. They learned the tactics of the environmental movement, using direct mail to recruit members, exemplary actions like hanging banners from cranes and bridges to gain publicity, and the rights of standing to launch legal battles. Many, like Joyce Tischler, who participated on the fringes of the environmental movement without feeling this was her real interest, later applied these tactics to animal rights.[11]

Among the issues preoccupying environmental groups was the protection of endangered species, and they quickly allied with animal welfare groups in the early 1970s. The two movements often pursued the same goals for different reasons. While animal protectionists concerned themselves with those animals that humans exploit, environmentalists concentrated on animals in the wild, including elephants, whales and, of course, the Canadian seals.

———

The battle over the Canadian seal hunt has continued since the exposé of 1964. During the late 1960s, critics used photographs and films to publicize the hunt around the world. These were not easy to obtain, for a hunt lasts only a few days, often in bad weather, on ice floes scattered over many miles. Coverage in Europe was especially important, for most sealskins were sold there. A tactical victory came in 1968 when Britain's largest newspaper, the *Daily Mirror,* featured extensive coverage of the seal hunt, including a lurid front page photo of a baby seal being clubbed and the headline "The Price of a Sealskin Coat." The following year *Paris-Match* ran articles on Davies and the seal hunt. The Canadian government gradually restricted methods of killing and set quotas on the number of seals to be taken each year.

Davies founded the International Fund for Animal Welfare in 1969, as environmental groups such as Greenpeace and animal welfare groups like the Fund for Animals joined in his seal campaign. The environmental actions of the early 1970s encouraged diversified tactics—perhaps the most memorable being the Fund's spray-painting of baby seals to render them useless to hunters. (Although good for media attention, this tactic was short-lived, as the paints proved water soluble.) Yet the first significant success came only in 1983, when the European Economic Community banned products made from Harp and Hooded seals. The campaign against seal hunts continues in many parts of the world—Norway, the Bering Sea, the coasts of South America and South Africa. In dramatic tabloid style, the *Daily Mirror* ran another article in 1989 entitled "And STILL the Slaughter Goes On," drawing parallels between Norway in 1989 and Canada in 1968.[12] Even in Canada, the hunt continues, now using small boats to go after Harp seals several weeks old rather than large ships to hunt newborns. By the end of the 1980s, over fifty thousand seals were being captured annually. In 1988, the Canadian government allocated $5 million to revitalize the small-boat hunt. As an added insult—in the eyes of activists—the seals' meat was sold to fox and mink ranchers, who fed it to their animals to promote thicker pelts.

Efforts to save dolphins, also dating from the 1960s, show similar convergence of animal protection and environmental themes. If seals trigger a "cute animal" response, a compassion in line with the humane tradition, then dolphins demand attention by virtue of their perceived intelligence. Since 1961, scientist and psychoanalyst John Lilly has been popularizing dolphin capacities.[13] Through his Human/Dolphin Foundation he has also tried to develop a language for communication between the two species, although out of respect for dolphins he recommends never keeping them in captivity for more than one year. He warns that dolphins are so easily bored that to see their intelligence "you have to think in terms of complex puzzles or you'll never get a dolphin to do anything."[14] Despite his inability to uncover conclusive evidence of great intelligence or the existence of a dolphin language, Lilly has tantalized the public's imagination. Whether because of Lilly or the television show *Flipper,* Americans sympathize readily with dolphins.

This sympathy spurred another protection campaign. Dolphins speed around the oceans in herds numbering in the hundreds, and several species in the eastern Pacific travel with schools of yellowfin tuna. Tuna boats in the 1960s began using purse-seining techniques: huge nets, hanging from floats, which can be brought up and closed shut, catching whatever has swum into them. Fisherman herded the dolphins with speedboats and explosives, knowing the tuna would follow them into the nets. Along with the tuna, the nets caught large numbers of dolphins—hundreds of thousands each year. When environmentalists began a boycott of tuna, they were joined by the Humane Society of the United States and other animal welfare groups. This coalition gained a victory when the Marine Mammal Protection Act was passed in 1972 to reduce the kill of marine mammals in the course of commercial fishing "to insignificant levels approaching a zero mortality and serious injury rate."

Despite the legislation, dolphins were not fully protected. Even though annual quotas were reduced each year, from 78,000 in 1976 to 20,500 in 1984, there was little monitoring, and many observers on the fleets claimed that kill levels were much higher. Then, under Ronald Reagan, amendments to the Act froze the quota at 20,500, while funds to develop alternative fishing methods were reduced. Common estimates are that six million dolphins have been killed in purse seines in the eastern tropical Pacific (80 percent of that region's total). In addition, squid and salmon fishers from Japan, Korea, and Taiwan recently introduced plastic driftnets in the north Pacific. Up to thirty miles long, they catch all living creatures: dolphins, seals, even seabirds. In response, the Earth Island Institute and other groups pushed for a label on tuna cans reading "The Contents of This Product Have Been Captured with Technologies That Are Known to Kill Dolphins." The United Nations passed a resolution calling for a worldwide ban on driftnets by 1992, and it appears the three countries will comply.[15]

In April 1990, the three largest sellers of canned tuna in the United States announced they would only buy tuna caught in dolphin-safe nets. StarKist, Chicken of the Sea, and Bumble Bee—which together represent 70 percent of the American tuna market—were mainly responding to pressure from children, who are often enamored of dolphins as they learn about them in school. They had organized letter-writing campaigns to companies and legislators, and succeeded in having tuna removed from menus in several school districts around the country. It was pressure from his eight-year-old daughter that helped convince Senator Joseph Biden to introduce the bill concerning tuna can labels.[16]

Once converted, the tuna companies were quick to exploit the same anthropomorphic sentiments that had previously given them trouble. StarKist ran a television commercial picturing dolphins at play. It said that they talk to each other—and talk faster and with a higher pitch when they are nervous; have friends of the same age; give birth one at a time; nurse their babies until they are ready for solid food; and even babysit for each other. StarKist bragged that its fishing methods killed no dolphins. At the same time, controversy continued over whether Bumble Bee was indeed following dolphin-safe guidelines.

Another controversy over dolphins in the late 1980s pitted animal activists against the United States Navy. The details of how the Navy has been using dolphins, in a program begun in 1960, are officially secret, but in addition to research on underwater propulsion, they have apparently been used for surveillance around ships and for recovery of items lost in water. The controversy juxtaposed the symbolism of peaceful, playful dolphins with the brutal instrumentalism of the military, for critics charged that the animals were being trained to guard nuclear submarines and kill enemy divers. When fifteen environmental and animal rights groups sued in 1989, on the grounds that the program lacked an environmental impact report, the Navy agreed not to use dolphins to guard submarines at its Bangor Depot in Washington state.[17]

Campaigns against whaling have had even more influence than efforts to protect seals or dolphins. The Fund for Animals, Greenpeace, and later the Sea Shepherd Society have pursued the whaling industry since the early 1970s. Mainstream tactics include lobbying the International Whaling Conference. This organization, founded in 1946 so that whaling nations could coordinate the size of their catches, turned critical of whaling in the early 1970s. Greenpeace testified against illegal whaling at the conference in 1981, and a moratorium on commercial whaling was declared in 1982. But these groups are better known for their dramatic direct actions interfering with whaling operations. In 1979, the Fund's *Sea Shepherd* rammed the *Sierra*, a Portuguese whaler operating illegally, and was seized by the Portuguese police who stripped and damaged the *Sea Shepherd*. Its crew scuttled it on New Year's Day 1980. One month later, a bomb mysteriously sank the *Sierra*. Greenpeace's *Rainbow Warrior*, operating out of Amsterdam, has been involved in similar incidents.

Environmental and animal protection groups find the large sea mammals appealing symbols of peaceful existence. An article in the *Greenpeace Examiner* states, "Like man (*Homo sapiens*) on land, whales and dolphins (*Cetacea*) at sea stand at the pinnacle of evolution . . . [humans'] dominance has been manifested in an unceasing drive to conquer, exploit, and control that has profoundly conditioned our present individual, social, institutional, and environmental existence. . . . Cetaceans stand in poetic contrast to human history. . . . Despite their dominance, these creatures are gentle and passive."[18] Just as a critique of instrumentalism permeates the condemnation of humans, so anthropomorphism animates the admiration for cetaceans. Dolphins are "the people of the sea." And individual humpback whales can be "adopted" through the Whale Adoption Project of North Falmouth, Massachusetts.[19]

Concern for baby seals harks back to the humane tradition's concern for "the dumb brute," but cetaceans—fish-like mammals that live in the sea—are attractive because they symbolize autonomy. They live on their own, beyond prying human eyes, in social relationships we only dimly perceive. And their intelligence defines them as deserving of rights. They are therefore favorite fundraising tools, even though today some populations—of certain whales, at least—are probably increasing.[20] When three whales were trapped in a hole in the ice in October 1988, Americans were willing to spend $6 million to save them.[21]

Environmental and animal welfare groups became frequent allies in the 1970s, as campaigns to save sea mammals drew on themes from both traditions. Intelligence and cuteness appealed to sentimental anthropomorphism, while commercial interests could be attacked as the systemic basis of animal exploitation. The conjunction of these issues in these early campaigns helped to shape the animal rights position.

While a handful of such well-funded groups as Greenpeace brought world attention to the mammals in the sea, a larger number of environmental and animal protection groups focused their attention on endangered land animals, especially those easy to glamorize or anthropomorphize, such as lions, cougars, and apes. Contributors to the World Society for the Protection of Animals allocated their money to specific animals and habitats: African elephant, black rhino, mountain gorilla, beluga whale, tropical rainforest, or coral reef. Campaigns over particular species were able to link conditions

of the animals in the wild with the worldwide trade in the animals
or products made from them.

Elephants have aroused wide public sympathy, for, like whales,
their size and longevity often make them symbols of primordial wisdom and tenacity. Protecting individual elephants is also a matter of
species preservation, for they are disappearing fast. Perhaps ten million inhabited Africa in the early part of the century; around 1.3
million still existed in 1979. By 1989, there were as few as 600,000
left, with poachers killing 70,000 each year for ivory, often circum-
venting, through local corruption, the voluntary quotas set by individual African nations. In the late 1980s, Wildlife Conservation International claimed that 80 to 90 percent of ivory in world markets
was illegal. With the price of ivory skyrocketing in fifteen years from
twelve dollars to over five hundred dollars a kilo, many poor African
countries could hardly afford the measures to stop poachers
equipped with assault rifles. The problem was especially acute for
Kenya, where large game parks were important sources of tourist
revenue but also easy targets for poachers.

Campaigns for elephants concentrated on the consumers who
purchase ivory products, for bans on killing elephants would fail as
long as there was consumer demand for ivory. The African Wildlife
Foundation ran full-page ads in major American papers with a bold
headline to bring the issue home: "Today, in America, Someone Will
Slaughter an Elephant for a Bracelet," featuring a photograph of a
carcass with its face hacked off. As with the tuna boycott, one tactic
of animal protectionists was to make consumers think about the implications of their individual purchases. But the tuna boycott was
effective because it aimed at several large, image-conscious corporations; ivory consumers were more anonymous and diffuse.

In a moving letter, the Friends of Animals appealed to consumers: "By the time you finish reading this letter, an elephant will
have died." It added an animal rights perspective to environmental
concerns: "Besides threatening an entire species, today's elephant
holocaust involves tremendous individual suffering. After all, 'species' is only a human-coined abstraction; when death pours out of a
rifle, it's always specific animals that do the suffering."

The elephant campaign won a major victory in October 1989,
when the Convention on International Trade in Endangered Species
of Wild Fauna and Flora (CITES, formed in 1973 to monitor, restrict, and sometimes eliminate international trade in endangered
species) voted to ban all trade in elephant products. During its first

year the ban did seem to reduce ivory trading and prices, and hence African poaching.[22]

The focus on a limited number of species has allowed organizations like the International Primate Protection League (IPPL) to maintain a global perspective.[23] The IPPL publishes a newsletter that juxtaposes articles on abuses in roadside zoos, safari parks, and scientific experiments with information on protective efforts and the native conditions of animals still in the wild. Such organizations spend much time fighting uses of their favored species in captivity— an issue of little interest to environmentalists. The contrast between the (often romanticized) life of animals in nature with their abuses under human captivity makes for powerful moral rhetoric. With 2,500 members around the world, the IPPL focuses on the international trade in primates and monkeys, publishing articles on smuggling, poaching, import prices, and the conditions and deaths of animals in transit. It has field representatives in two dozen countries, both those—in Asia, Africa, and South America—where primates and monkeys originate, and those to which they are shipped. Englishwoman Shirley McGreal founded the IPPL in 1973 while living in Thailand, a point of origin for many animals; she now lives in South Carolina, where—among many other activities—she operates a sanctuary for several hundred gibbons.

Most organizations for primates protest the flow of animals from the wild to captivity, and attempt to move some back, or at least into sanctuaries, but the Gorilla Foundation concentrates on portraying gorillas as part of the human family. It is a fundraising tool for Penny Patterson, who since 1972 has taught sign language to Koko, a gorilla born in the San Francisco zoo. A funding appeal touts "an astonishing breakthrough in our understanding of the world. The news is that a very remarkable gorilla named Koko has changed myth into fact . . . by speaking to humans." She is said to use "the very same language used by the Deaf," a bit of anthropomorphic fancy rather demeaning to deaf humans, given the simplicity of Koko's communication. The reader is invited to "become part of Koko's extended family."

Almost any endangered species can become the object of some group's attention. CITES has been petitioned and has agreed to protect species of bats and certain species of reef-building coral. Major construction projects in the United States have been blocked or delayed by unique species: the spotted owl stopped a large logging operation in Oregon, and the notorious snail darter helped stop construction of a large Tennessee dam. Wolves, coyotes, and other predators have their fervent supporters.[24] Shrimp nets in the Gulf of Mexico must have trap doors through which sea turtles can escape.[25] Worldwide communications links have allowed activists to mobilize to save single animals anywhere in the world. For example, when Colombian peasants captured an injured Andean condor in the remote Northern part of the country, the World Society for the Protection of Animals arranged to have the bird brought to a zoo near Bogota. The students of the Clifton College Preparatory School in Bristol, England, paid for its expensive X-rays and treatment.[26]

While environmental and animal protection groups have worked together to protect endangered species around the world, the issue of domestic hunting and trapping of wild animals has attracted only the protectionists. The number of animals killed is large: over 100 million birds each year, over 50 million mammals. Most of these are rabbits and squirrels, but in the 1988–89 season, almost 5 million deer were killed, 22,000 bear, even—the list goes on and on—90 musk ox.[27] Animal rightists oppose all hunting as cruel, and they criticize environmental groups that favor or tolerate hunting in order to preserve natural balances. Animal groups criticize the Izaak Walton League, the National Wildlife Federation, and others for actively supporting hunting, and the Defenders of Wildlife, the Nature Conservancy, and the Sierra Club for tolerating it.[28]

American hunting, fishing, and trapping are regulated by state-level fish and game commissions, which set hunting seasons, place limits on fish and game catches, sell licenses, and monitor and manage animal populations. Animal rightists—who have attacked hunting more aggressively than animal welfare groups—charge these commissions with managing populations, not to maintain natural equilibria, but to maximize the numbers of animals that can be hunted or fished. Financed heavily by fees from licenses—which total half a billion dollars a year nationally—they artificially inflate populations until they need to be culled through hunting. Activists claim the commissions are composed primarily of hunters, fishers, and trappers, with no representation by people concerned with protecting animals. They also claim that many states even have laws *requiring* commissioners to have sporting licenses (our own calls to ten states found only one where licenses were required). In 1989, the Animal Legal Defense Fund sued the Massachusetts Fisheries and

Wildlife Board to change its composition, in what it hopes will be a series of such challenges.[29]

Activists blame state governments for encouraging hunting in other ways too. Several groups, led by the Fund for Animals, have attacked Florida's government for sponsoring a deer hunt for children eight to fifteen years old, designed to introduce them to the sport.[30] In New York and New Jersey, the Committee to Abolish Sport Hunting has, for fifteen years, been fighting efforts to open additional state parks to hunting. It closed only one park, at a cost of $35,000 and two years of work, but thirty-two new parks were opened to hunting. In an exceptional national action, HSUS has spearheaded a drive to close National Wildlife Refuges to hunting and trapping. The powerful National Rifle Association and hunting groups strongly oppose such efforts, and animal protectionists have so far gained only a handful of victories.

Hunting taps into a cluster of America's oldest myths and images.[31] From Daniel Boone, who became the country's first national folk hero in 1784, through the novels of James Fenimore Cooper, to stories like Ernest Hemingway's "The Short Happy Life of Francis Macomber," the hunting of wild animals has symbolized an escape from the constraints of home, family, and civilization—a way to test or prove one's manhood, to learn the wisdom of nature, to live off the land, and to extend human control over other species. Mostly shorn—in the New World—of its aristocratic context, hunting has been a rugged, populist struggle between Man and Nature, set in mythic places like the Wilderness, the Frontier, and the Wild West. Hunting and gun ownership are woven together into a libertarian individualism. Yet, for more and more urbanites (today only 7 percent of Americans hunt) and for many women (90 percent of hunters are men), these images have grown stale, sometimes even laughable. A cartoon character from the comic strip *Bloom County* bemusedly questions the tradition: "This morning, I was watching one of those manly hunting shows on TV. . . . Some big cracker wearing fatigues was holding up a fat duck whose fanny he'd just shot clean off. Then he said this: 'Healthy-lookin' sucker, ain't he?'"[32]

Hunters defend their sport by claiming that they are conservationists whose license fees help preserve wildlife. They have lobbied legislators, and thirty-seven states have passed laws making it illegal to harass hunters when they are in pursuit of game on state-owned land. Several of these laws have been challenged in the courts and found unconstitutional. More importantly, they have rarely been enforced to stop the increasing numbers of animal advocates who follow hunters into the woods.

Fishing, like hunting, is managed by state commissions, but receives far less attention. Trout lack the heart-wrenching appeal of large-eyed deer or the wild glamour of bears and mountain lions. With scales rather than hair or fur, with no way to whimper or cry, with neither cuteness nor humanoid features, fish are difficult to personify. Tuna were a problem only when catching them killed dolphins. An *Animals' Agenda* article on the *Exxon Valdez* oil spill described the impact on otters, seals, eagles, seabirds, even deer (which died after eating oil-coated kelp), but not fish.[33] Yet some animal rightists, following the inexorable logic of their moral position, have come to the defense of fish. Their position is necessarily spare and abstract, without the emotional resonance and fund-raising appeal of puppies and fawns, but several writers have articulated it nonetheless. In 1988 and 1989, two such articles appeared in the *Animals' Agenda*; one in the *Animals' Voice*.[34]

Trapping animals for their furs has long been a target for animal protectionists, though fewer animals are killed in trapping (roughly fifteen million each year) than in hunting (fifty to seventy million, excluding birds). Until the late 1980s, the fur issue was synonymous with trapping, and the trapping issue was dominated by debate over the steel leg-hold trap. In this classic animal trap, two steel jaws spring together when an animal steps into it. It provided critics with extensive ammunition. The pain of the animals was paramount: all were hurt; many were badly mangled; a large portion broke teeth trying to free themselves; some gnawed off their own limbs. The traps often caught unintended animals, sometimes pets and hunting dogs, sometimes what trappers called "trash animals" like rats, birds, and opossums. In a relatively urban state like New Jersey, 1,000 pets were caught in traps from 1976 to 1979.[35] The suffering of lost pets became the staple of fundraising appeals in the welfarist tradition. HSUS reported a gruesome case from Florida of a Labrador retriever that caught its tongue in a trap. The tongue was ripped off, and the animal had to be killed.[36] In addition, critics argued that virtually all the advanced industrial countries have banned the trap, replacing it with more humane designs.

The critique of specific traps broadened into an attack on the entire trapping industry. Critics said that few trappers were professionals, citing the figure of 1 percent.[37] Most made no more than a few hundred dollars annually. Animal protectionists portrayed amateurs as less careful about where they placed traps and how often they checked them, leaving animals to suffer longer. Citing a Yale study which found that 86 percent of trappers were under twenty years old, activists stereotyped the typical trapper as a teenager out for fun.[38]

In one prominent battle over trapping, in the mid-1980s, Susan Russell, vice-president of Friends of Animals of New Jersey, attacked the fur industry directly. She argued before Congress that 80 percent of the furs trapped in the United States were sent abroad for processing, supporting few domestic jobs. While the fur industry claimed that hundreds of thousands of New Jerseyans would be put out of work by a proposed state ban, Russell calculated the number as one hundred eighty-three. She juxtaposed the moral issue against the instrumental goal: "Because an activity is income producing doesn't make it right. The New York drug trade is estimated at $54 billion, making the fur trade look like peanuts, and 'employs' 300,000 people in the New York area alone. Because of these revenues, should we legalize heroin?"[39]

In response to persistent lobbying, a handful of states have passed moderate legislation. New Jersey banned steel-jawed leg-hold traps; Florida, traps made of steel; Massachusetts, leg-hold traps set on dry land. Other states require trappers to check their traps every twenty-four hours so that animals do not suffer long. Similar congressional bills are introduced each session. For example, in 1983, a bill to prohibit trade in furs from animals captured in steel leg-hold traps had 125 cosponsors but—like many others—failed.

Various national lobbying organizations have tried to block restrictive legislation. The National Trappers Association, the American Fur Resources Institute, and other industry groups are natural opponents. Yet a representative from the National Wildlife Federation also testified against the 1983 bill. She used the language of environmental management: "Wildlife research, control of wildlife damage, and harvest of renewable wildlife resources are all frequently accomplished most efficiently and effectively by trapping." She also referred to the pitiful natural life of wild animals: "Animals taken in leg-hold traps die in ways that are no more or less severe than when they die naturally. Proper use of leg-hold traps can cause less painful and protracted deaths than those which wild animals might otherwise experience."[40] Those concerned with animals, she concluded, should fight the destruction of habitats, not traps.

The hunting question has frequently divided environmentalists and animal rights advocates. In an exchange in the *Green Letter,* an ecologist extolled the pleasures he found in hunting: a spiritual experience, a way of reconnecting with nature, of attaining intimacy with one's environment, of momentarily escaping the artificiality of urban life. He criticized the word "cruel" when applied to hunting as "an awfully human word," implying that animal activists are naïve about the natural fate of wild animals. Another Green responded that it is cruel for humans to hunt when they have a choice, but contemporary hunting is rarely for subsistence. Yet even this writer admitted that "hunting is not *inherently* inappropriate, unecological, or cruel," it is just that, in advanced industrial societies, it is all three.[41] In contrast, most animal rights activists find hunting inherently objectionable.

_____

Despite frequent cooperation, environmentalists and animal protectionists remain opposed on a critical principle. Erik Mills of Action for Animals expresses the divergence: "I have some troubles with the environmental movement that says, well, it's only one animal, and we're concerned with species. At the same time, at an animal rights conference a couple years ago, two young folks told me they'd rather see coyotes extinct than to suffer the way they do, with poisoning programs and trapping. I said, well, why not have black folks extinct so they didn't have to go through slavery?"[42] Increasingly, however, animal protectionists have reached out to the environmental movement to find common ground. *Animals' Agenda* changed its subtitle from *The Animal Rights Magazine* to *The International Magazine of Animal Rights and Ecology,* on the grounds that "Most of us already consider ourselves environmentalists," and the name change would "allow us to reach out to people who may have a great deal of sensitivity to animals, yet do not consider themselves animal rights activists."[43] Patrice Greanville, one of the magazine's regular columnists, often writes about the need to link with environmental groups. Nonetheless, one animal rightist lamented that, "Those of us who have entered the Greens have done so with the hopes that perhaps this movement will have a better record [on animal protection] than the environmental movement as a whole. And I think I've come out with mixed feelings about whether that's the case."[44] Clearly, tensions persist.

Contrasting images of nature may underlie these divergent concerns. A spokesman for the environmental "land ethic," philosopher J. Baird Callicott, insists that, "The most fundamental fact of life in

the biotic community is eating . . . *and being eaten.* Each species is
adapted to a trophic niche; each is a link in a food chain, and a knot
in a food web. Whatever moral entitlements a being may have as a
member of the biotic community, *not* among them is the right to
life."[45] Life is hard in the wild, ecologists insist, and the double meaning of the word "wild" encourages a rough enthusiasm. Dave Fore-
man, founder of Earth First!, enjoys his place in the food chain as
he hunts and eats the meat of the game he kills, and he claims to
anticipate the day when his corpse is food for carrion. For him, this
comes close to an ecologically sound, natural existence. For Earth
First!, domesticated herds that overgraze are a larger problem than
the hunting of wild animals.

The tensions between animal protectionists and environmentalists suggest the ironies of anthropomorphism. To the extent that animal activists project human intentions and behaviors onto animals,
they risk losing the ability to understand "natural" behaviors. Domesticated animals have been changed by thousands of years of
breeding; humans have bred dogs to behave the way we expect: to
be loyal, eager, cute. But experience with domesticated species may
not pertain to nature. A journalist described an unfortunate incident
in which well-intended observers saved a newly hatched sea turtle
from a mockingbird. When the predator was scared off, and the
baby made its way toward the water, hundreds of the turtle's fellows
appeared and rushed for the ocean, too. But they had received a false
signal, and a flock of birds attacked and devoured them. Protectionist interference had upset nature's mechanisms.[46]

The issue of wild-animal sanctuaries highlights the tensions between environmentalists and animal protectionists. Sanctuaries are
not ecosystems, but bland artificial environments created to take care
of a handful of individual animals. Some groups nonetheless try to
combine environmental and animal protection approaches. In Lin-
coln, Nebraska, the Wildlife Rescue Team nurses injured animals to
health in order to return them to the wild. Carol Odell, who founded
the organization in 1979, is trying to redress some of the imbalances
humans have created in nature, arguing that "most of the animals
come in to us because of man's interference." She refuses to give
names to the animals under her care, disavowing personal affection
for them. "For their sakes, they need to be wild."[47]

The practices of indigenous peoples further underline the differences in perspectives. Many environmentalists have looked to Native
American traditions for sound attitudes and practices, assuming that

they lived in exemplary balance with their habitats.[48] Around the globe, 500 million indigenous people still live as hunters and gatherers, in 15,000 separate groups. These peoples use and kill animals, and few environmentalists are willing to criticize a lifestyle they view as preserving the balance of nature. Whether or not they still live in harmony with nature, these groups themselves resist animal rights demands. Indigenous Survival International, formed in 1984 by native peoples from Alaska, Canada, and Greenland, issued a statement positing environmental balance as a counter to animal rights: "It is ironic to see animal rights activists, who are primarily urban dwellers who have lost their relationship to nature, attacking the way of life of Native people, who still live in harmony with the natural habitat." Along with other organizations of indigenous peoples, such as the Inuit Tapirisat of Canada and the Inuit Circum-Polar Conference, the ISI fought antitrapping proposals by animal rights groups, using the language of environmentalism: renewable resources, conservation, even "spiritual bonds with other species, including those [we] harvest."[49] At the same time, native groups are advertising and labeling their fur products to distinguish them from more commercial ones.[50]

These indigenous groups contacted Greenpeace, which suspended its anti-fur campaign in the mid-1980s. Greenpeace remained opposed to cruel trapping methods and the killing of wildlife to satisfy luxury markets, but was concerned with the effects of its campaign on Canada's indigenous peoples. Accused of espousing cultural genocide, Greenpeace established a committee to examine the question of "living resources with particular reference to aboriginal and subsistence uses." After years of fighting the seal hunt in the Pribilof Islands of Alaska, Greenpeace dropped its protest in 1984, as the native Aleuts moved to a subsistence-only hunt with traditional methods of killing and skinning. But for animal rights sympathizers, indigenous hunts are, as one of them told us, "just another excuse to kill animals."[51] Left-leaning groups are sensitive to charges of cultural imperialism, but most animal activists feel that animal lives are more important than cultural traditions.

Despite tensions, the animal rights movement has itself begun to influence environmental groups, which have extended their range of concerns. Brian Davies' International Fund for Animal Welfare, for example, has expanded into the protection of dogs in Korea, kangaroos in Australia, bees in Costa Rica, endangered species of birds in Thailand, elephants in Africa, monkeys in the Philippines, and whales. In its fund-raising brochures, the Fund has even picked up the stock animal rights target, the Draize Test for cosmetics, in which substances are put into the eyes of white rabbits. The logic of animal rights has taken Davies from the ice floes of Canada to Madison Avenue, from seals to bunnies, as the movement embraced new issues.

———

Protest movements learn from each other, sometimes because knowledgeable people move from one to another, sometimes through simple observations and precedents. Despite philosophical differences, the environmental movement provided organizational, strategic, and ideological inspiration for animal rights. As animal rights groups formed, they gained members from welfare groups, and strategic models from environmentalists. Animal rightists could build on increased public awareness of the plight of animals in the wild. They could draw on a rhetoric critical of large business, bureaucracy, and instrumental uses of animals, as well as on the middle-class sentiments behind this rhetoric. And the Greenpeace model of activism would prove fruitful in fostering radicalism on the fringe of the animal protection movement. Still missing was an ideology consciously linking the systemic critiques of environmentalism with the compassionate sentiments of the early animal welfare tradition. Beginning in the late 1970s, several philosophers would provide this ideology, sparking an explicit animal rights crusade.

SEVEN

Philosophers
as Midwives

As "professionals" of moral discourse, philosophers who deal with ethical questions have a natural—and central—role to play in moral crusades, and they were crucial to the birth of the animal rights movement. Just as philosophers, poets, and priests had questioned the treatment of animals in the eighteenth century, so do many philosophers criticize the uses of animals today. But beyond their role as social critics, moral philosophers are attracted to this issue as a way to explore such fundamental philosophical questions as "What does it mean to be human?" and "What are the bases of moral rights?" Some debate these issues in the professional arena, but many philosophers have taken activist roles, developing moral arguments to generate political advocacy.

Philosophers served as midwives of the animal rights movement in the late 1970s. Through their prolific writing, they combined the emotional appeal of the humane and welfare traditions with the institutional critique of environmentalists. Through their ideas, the animal rights movement developed an agenda that won the hearts and the minds of people seeking ways to articulate their growing concern for animals. The moral sentiments were there; so were models of engaged activism; what was needed was an explicit ideology that could link feelings to actions on behalf of animals.

Almost every animal rights activist either owns or has read Peter Singer's *Animal Liberation,* which since its publication in 1975 has become a bible for the movement. Singer is an Australian philosopher committed to the analysis of moral disputes, and in the preface to his 1971 Oxford thesis, published as *Democracy and Disobedience,* Singer urged philosophers to leave their abstract word games and take stances on moral issues:

> If philosophers are to say anything of importance about major issues, they must go beyond the neutral analysis of words and concepts which was, until recently, characteristic of contemporary philosophy in Britain and America. Moral and political philosophers must be prepared to give their opinions, with supporting arguments, on the rights and wrongs of complex disputes.[1]

This argument was a call to arms for his profession, heavily dominated at that time by an analytic tradition more concerned with clever language analyses than moral issues.[2]

Singer grounded his argument about the treatment of animals in a utilitarian perspective. For utilitarians, ethical decisions should be made by adding up all pleasures and pains that would result from different choices, and choosing the option yielding the greatest aggregate pleasure (or happiness). Jeremy Bentham, founder of utilitarianism, had specifically applied his philosophy to animals in 1789: "The day *may* come when the rest of the animal creation may acquire those rights which never could have been withholden from them but by the hand of tyranny . . ."[3] Following Bentham, Singer believes that all pleasures and pains, even of nonhumans, must be tallied for a proper moral calculus. He developed his position in several writings, including a widely read 1973 essay in the *New York Review of Books.*[4]

In *Animal Liberation: A New Ethics for Our Treatment of Animals,* Singer argued that humans must take into account the fact that animals are capable of suffering and enjoyment.[5] It is just as arbitrary to disregard the suffering of animals as that of women or people with dark skin. To assume that humans are inevitably superior to other species is "speciesism"—an injustice parallel to racism and sexism.[6] Animals, in other words, are worthy of moral consideration: "What we must do is bring nonhuman animals within our sphere of moral concern and cease to treat their lives as expendable for whatever trivial purposes we may have." Articulating the intuitive feelings of those inclined toward sentimental anthropomorphism, Singer's plea for equal consideration has since become the principle of the movement, and "speciesism" has become a key catch word.

Singer did not, however, claim that all lives were of equal worth or that all beings should be treated in identical ways. It would make no sense to give a dog the right to vote, since dogs cannot understand what it means to vote. But dogs can feel pleasure and pain. It is this characteristic, Singer argued, that brings them into our moral calculus: "The basic principle of equality does not require equal or identical *treatment;* it requires equal *consideration.*" Beyond this right to equal consideration, however, Singer's utilitarian framework discourages discussion of absolute individual rights; it examines only aggregates, and views individuals less as autonomous actors than as sites for pleasures and pains. His critique of speciesism recognizes "that there are morally relevant differences between species—such as differences in mental capacities—and that they entitle us to give more weight to the interests of members of species with superior mental capacities." He denies, however, "that species membership *in itself* is a reason for giving more weight to the interests of one being than to those of another."[7] Each individual being must be judged for its own particular capacities for pleasure.

Singer's utilitarian approach allows animal experimentation if suffering is minimized and the research has a high probability of yielding aggregate benefits that outweigh the individual pain. Nor does Singer unequivocally reject all animal products. It is permissible to eat free-range eggs, for these hens can "live comfortably. They do not appear to mind the removal of their eggs."[8] He allows for differences between species in their sense of pain; it is probably permissible to eat an oyster but not a shrimp, but because we cannot know with certainty if mollusks feel pain, those who wish to be certain should avoid them as well. For Singer, then, suffering is the problem; the use of animals for human ends, if considerate and painless, is not in itself to be condemned.[9]

Animal Liberation contains far more than philosophical discussion. Half the book documents, in gruesome detail, what happens to animals used in agriculture and research. The book also provides practical advice: vegetarian foods and cookbooks, names of animal organizations, and further reading. In effect a 300 page how-to guide, *Animal Liberation* played a crucial role in helping to form the animal rights agenda. For those already active and concerned with animals, it provided philosophical arguments and justification for what they wanted to do. It gave the incipient movement an ideology and a vocabulary. Joyce Tischler, then a law student and later founder of the Animal Legal Defense Fund, says: "Singer's book influenced us all. It gave us a philosophy on which to hang our emotions, feelings, sentimentality—all the things we had thought were bad; it gave us an intellectual hat to put on our heads."[10] Activism for animals was no longer just compassion; it had recourse to systematic philosophical arguments. For people like Tischler, who had been active in other social movements—for women's rights, for environmental protection—a coherent ideology was an important part of political action.

Singer also opened up a new vista for animal protectionists. He pushed beyond the welfarist concentration on pets and the environmentalist concern with wild animals to pursue institutional abuses he thought would be hardest to stop. Singer felt animal abuse was an inevitable part of big business and science. He adapted the political attack on instrumentalism, an attack honed by environmentalists, to practices they had not considered.

Avon Books published an inexpensive paperback edition of *Animal Liberation* in 1977, and almost all animal rightists own a copy. When describing their conversion to animal rights, rank-and-file activists inevitably talk about Singer's book. They mention his critique of speciesism, and they reiterate his descriptions of cruel practices in factory farming and research laboratories. These descriptions have been more influential than his philosophical arguments. While many pragmatists in the movement accept Singer's philosophy, most fundamentalists reject his utilitarian position allowing the use of animals if anticipated benefits exceed the costs of suffering. While fundamentalists use his book in recruiting members, they find it too moderate. Singer is not an "animal person," many say. He has no particular fascination, interest, or love for animals, and no companion animals. One activist, herself living with eight cats, complained, "He's very highly evolved intellectually, but there's no emotion, no feeling. . . . He's cerebral, not an animal lover. . . . You'd think he could at least take an animal or two from the pound."[11] The growing crusade for animals soon outpaced Singer's position, as protestors developed an uncompromising stand against any use of animals for human ends. Tom Regan emerged as the philosopher articulating the rights perspective of these fundamentalists.

———

The same year Singer published *Animal Liberation,* Tom Regan, professor of philosophy at North Carolina State University, published an essay entitled "The Moral Basis of Vegetarianism." Regan had been trained in analytic philosophy, and his M.A. and Ph.D.

theses, on beauty and goodness respectively, dealt with the meanings of the words rather than what was actually beautiful or good. The Vietnam war changed his academic approach, leading him to study pacifism and to explore Mohandas Gandhi's writings on animals and vegetarianism. Like Singer, Regan wanted to bring the insights of moral philosophy to politics and policy questions.

Gandhi and vegetarianism shaped Regan's intellectual trajectory; the death of his dog during the same summer was an emotional jolt. He writes, "My head had begun to grasp a moral truth that required a change in my behavior. Reason demanded that I become vegetarian. But it was the death of our dog that awakened my heart. It was that sense of irrecoverable loss that added the power of feeling to the requirements of logic."[12] In a published interview Regan put it more tritely: "Philosophy can lead the mind to water but only emotion can make it drink."[13] Regan's intellectual and political activities have focused ever since on animals; he has written and edited a stream of articles and books, and founded the Culture and Animals Foundation.[14]

In a position more extreme than Singer's, Regan argued that animals have inherent worth as living creatures, and should never be used as resources. Regan came to this view gradually; in a 1982 essay he admitted animals could be used in some experimental research.[15] However, only a year later, he published his central treatise, *The Case for Animal Rights*,[16] developing a more absolutist position that broke from utilitarianism. This view reflected the emerging sentiments of an increasing number of animal activists, as the philosophies of fundamentalists and pragmatists in the animal rights crusade began to diverge.

Regan built his case by arguing for the similarities between humans and other mammals, developing in effect the theoretical basis for a strongly sentimental anthropomorphism.[17] From common sense, from the way animals behave, and from their evolutionary proximity to humans, we have every reason—according to Regan—to conclude that normal mammals have many complex aspects of consciousness, including perception, memory, beliefs, desires, preferences, intentions, and a sense of the future. They have needs and desires and organize their lives with the intention of satisfying them. Animals, argues Regan, are "subjects of a life," which they can perceive as going well or badly. Thus, like humans, they "have a value of their own," independent of their utility for humans. Inherent worth does not come in degrees; a creature either has it or does not.

Having inherent worth gives an animal the absolute right to live its life with respect and autonomy. Regan explicitly attacks the utilitarian perspective: "On the rights view, we cannot justify harming a single rat merely by aggregating 'the many human and humane benefits' that flow from doing it." For Regan, the rat has worth beyond the benefits it can provide to humans.[18]

Just as Singer argued that some animals may lack the capacity to feel pain, so Regan admitted that some animals may lack many attributes of consciousness. But since we do not know how aware they are, we must treat them all as conscious beings:

> We simply do not know enough to justify dismissing, *out of hand,* the idea that a frog, say, may be the subject-of-a-life, replete with desires, goals, beliefs, intentions, and the like. When our ignorance is so great, and the possible moral price so large, it is not unreasonable to give these animals the benefit of the doubt, treating them *as if* they are subjects, due our respectful treatment, especially when doing so causes no harm to us."[19]

It is this willingness to attribute human qualities to frogs—to believe they may be conscious subjects and worthy of respect—that distinguishes animal rightists from the general public.

Regan also elaborated a moral critique of instrumentalism, insisting that instrumental considerations can never excuse immoral practices. No benefits to humans (or even to other animals) from scientific research and substance testing can change the moral case against animal experiments. Nor is the validity of research a relevant justification; whether or not tests are valid or necessary for scientific understanding, they are wrong simply "because they violate the rights of laboratory animals."[20] Regan also rejects the premises behind animal tests: that companies must earn profits, that they must continuously introduce new cosmetics or hair sprays.

Uncompromising in his attack on instrumental attitudes, Regan dismisses any willingness to sacrifice individual animals for the sake of species survival as "environmental fascism." That a species is endangered confers no additional rights; to Regan, rights are already absolute. He denies the potential conflict between individual rights and species survival: "Were we to show proper respect for the rights of the individuals who make up the biotic community, would not the *community* be preserved?"[21] To environmental philosophers such as Mark Sagoff, the response is clear: "This is an empirical question, the answer to which is 'no.'" Nature, Sagoff argues, is not fair, and ecological balance often requires the sacrifice of individual organisms.[22]

Philosopher J. Baird Callicott also pursues the weakness of Regan's rights argument when applied to the wild. If individual animals have some right to be protected, doesn't it follow that humans should try to exterminate predators? The doe cares little if she is killed by a wolf or a human hunter; both are trying to violate her rights.[23] Callicott believes that humans could treat domestic animals as Regan wishes, for they are already part of our community, but that wild animals call for an environmental perspective.

Regan believes that an uncompromising moral position is a better way to protect animals than Singer's utilitarianism: "Those who accept the rights view, and who sign for animals, will not be satisfied with anything less than the total abolition of the harmful use of animals in science—in education, in toxicity testing, in basic research."[24] This was an appealing ideology for a moral crusade. It articulated the beliefs that already motivated many activists, it justified their goals in philosophical terms, and it reassured them as they tried to abolish animal exploitation.

A densely reasoned, 400-page philosophical text, *The Case for Animal Rights* did not win the readership of Singer's *Animal Liberation*. Most activists and many casual participants have read Singer's book; few Regan's. Even Regan admits that his book, "is a work of serious, methodical scholarship, written in the language of philosophy, 'direct duties,' 'acquired rights,' 'utilitarianism,' the whole lexicon of academic philosophy. It can be rough going for someone unfamiliar with the field, but I make no apologies for its difficulty. Physics is hard. In my view, moral philosophy is harder."[25] Many people within the movement confuse the arguments of the two philosophers, adopting Regan's ideas but attributing them to Singer. Regan says "I cannot begin to count the number of times I have sat through discussions or read essays in which my views regarding the rights of animals were attributed, not to me, but to Singer."[26] But despite the confusion, it is Regan's rights argument—not Singer's utilitarianism—that has come to dominate the rhetoric of the animal rights agenda, often pushing it beyond reformism and pragmatism.

Mary Midgley is a British philosopher who, like Singer, was promoting the value of moral philosophy before this became trendy.[27] Less well known in the United States than Regan or Singer, she argues in *Animals and Why They Matter* that "rights" and "speciesism" are useful political slogans, but muddled philosophical concepts.[28] Midgley refers to rights as "the really desperate word," used as a last resort to bolster weak arguments. Implying equality, the concept is more useful for progressive reforms within a group that is already clearly defined than for expanding the boundaries of a group to include new categories of members. Defining those deserving of rights is ultimately arbitrary, based not on philosophical arguments but on intuitions.

Similarly, while she admits the political utility of the label "speciesism," Midgley believes it is limited as an analytic category. It is not precisely parallel to "racism," for "Race in humans is not a significant grouping at all, but species in animals certainly is. It is never true that, in order to know how to treat a human being, you must first find out what race he belongs to. . . . But with an animal, to know the species is absolutely essential."[29] Furthermore, species boundaries shape our sympathies, for humans—like most other animals—bond more fully with those of their own species. Midgley insists, "There is good reason for such a preference. We are bond-forming creatures, not abstract intellects."[30] Close contact with members of its own species is vital for any complex creature to develop its full range of potential faculties.

Attachment to one's own species, however, never excludes sympathy and bonding with others. In fact, all known human societies have incorporated animals, forming what Midgley calls "mixed communities." Successful domestication and exploitation of animals actually requires close knowledge and empathy with their moods, reactions, and other mental states. Pet-owning is merely the strongest form of this bonding, although Midgley points out that it is an extension of human bonds, not a competitor: "One sort of love does not need to block another, because love, like compassion, is not a rare fluid to be economized, but a capacity which grows by use."[31]

Midgley's argument from compassion seems to support an animal welfarist or pragmatic position, for she sees no philosophical reason for treating all species the same. She also favors arguments from compassion for practical reasons, because the abstractions and absolutes of the rights position are remote from popular belief. Her position draws on Singer's strongest point—that avoidance of suffering is key to the moral treatment of animals—without his more controversial insistence on aggregating across individual beings. She also avoids the weakness of Regan's anthropomorphic projections concerning the mental states of other species. Compassion suggests sympathy for other species without requiring anthropomorphic identification with them—a strong basis for animal protection arguments.

Singer, Regan, and Midgley helped generate a lively debate among professional philosophers, yielding both a popular and a professional literature in the late 1970s and 1980s that disseminated animal rights ideas. The Society for the Study of Ethics and Animals, founded in 1979, began holding annual meetings and established a journal, *Ethics and Animals,* for philosophical debates on animals and their treatment. In 1984, *Between the Species* began publishing a mixture of essays, interviews, and fiction dealing with the relationships between humans and other species. Several mainstream philosophy journals have had special issues on animal rights, including *Etyka* in Poland, *Inquiry* (Norway), *The Monist* and *Philosophy* (United Kingdom), and *Ethics* (United States).[32]

While most philosophers have entered the animal rights debate purely as academics, others are activists as well, and it is often hard to distinguish between their intellectual and political activism. Steve Sapontzis, who teaches at California State University at Hayward, is an example. A vegetarian since his teens, he read Singer's book and Regan's article on vegetarianism around 1977, and his "personal and professional lives came together."[33] He began teaching special courses on the ethics of animal use and, by 1981, was publishing articles and making speeches on the topic. A book followed in 1987,[34] and he became co-editor of *Between the Species.* But in 1981, he was also involved in political action. After helping Elliot Katz found Californians for Responsible Research in 1983, Sapontzis soon left because he disagreed with Katz's ambitions to create a national organization (it became In Defense of Animals). He also helped Brad Miller start the Humane Farming Association; served on the Animal Welfare and Research Committee at the Lawrence Berkeley Laboratory; sits on the boards of the San Francisco Vegetarian Society, PAW PAC, and the International Network for Religion and Animals; and is president of the Hayward Friends of Animals—a group devoted to improving conditions at the local shelter. Sapontzis' professional philosophy and his political activism reinforce each other.[35]

George Cave, the philosopher who founded Trans-Species Unlimited, has misgivings about the activities of professional philosophers. He attacks those academic philosophers writing about animal rights for their lack of moral outrage:

> There is something morally abominable about the "objective" debates on moral issues which often take place in a university context, when a propelling sense of moral outrage is altogether lacking. A controlled sense of moral outrage is the absolutely indispensable prerequisite for keeping one's true moral goals in view; it is *not* equivalent to naïve or dogmatic emotional fervor or fanaticism.[36]

Other philosophers, however, defend their profession for bringing to the movement "intellectual breadth and respectability."[37] Sapontzis, for example, suggests that philosophy helps show that the movement is not anti-intellectual, as many scientists claim; it provides important tools for debating the other side in sophisticated ways; and it educates college teachers about animal protection so that they pass that knowledge on to their students.[38] According to Tom Regan, as many as 100,000 college students discuss animal rights in philosophy courses each year.[39] Nonetheless, as Cave argues, the abstractions of philosophical thought often seem to conflict with the imperatives of political action.

———

Philosophical arguments are limited. They cannot prove that animals do or do not have rights, since rights claims, based partly on intuitions, cannot be clinched by logical debate or empirical proof. To people with strong pro-animal convictions formed by compassion for pets, the arguments of the animal rights philosophers are plausible. To others, they fall flat. Disputes over moral values can be explained sociologically, but not settled by philosophical debate. Logical arguments can uncover inconsistencies, clarify positions, and reconcile intuitions and positions, but they cannot "disprove" most intuitions.

For example, Singer cannot prove conclusively that a human's pleasure in eating a pork chop is trivial compared to the suffering of the pig; this is an intuitive judgment about the relative meaning of pleasure and pain in different species. Philosopher Mary Anne Warren points out similar limits in Regan's arguments. Like Midgley, she claims that there is no distinct trait that proves inherent worth, no visible characteristic to demonstrate the case: "It is probably impossible to either prove or disprove the thesis that animals have moral rights by producing an analysis of the concept of a moral right and checking to see if some or all animals satisfy the conditions for having rights. The concept of a moral right is complex, and it is not clear which of its strands are essential."[40] Instead, she claims, there are degrees of inherent worth based on the ability to communicate, to have a self-image, to plan a life. Regan denies this, for it implies that humans could have more inherent worth than other species.

The limits of philosophical discourse are captured by a dilemma frequently posed by animal rights philosophers. They argue that there is no more justification for experimenting on intelligent, healthy animals than on severely mentally disabled humans. Their point is that neither sentience nor intelligence nor capacity to lead a full life is a sufficient criterion to separate all humans from all nonhumans (and, hence, to allow experiments on the latter but never on the former).

For most people, membership in the human species is itself a morally relevant boundary, and they find the idea of experimenting on retarded humans repugnant and outrageous. Animal activists, however, extend their loyalty to all species. Men and women do not define their loyalties because of philosophical argument. Loyalty is a moral intuition based on values and experience. While philosophy can help articulate existing intuitions, it can rarely change them.

Frustrated over the limits of philosophical arguments about rights, several writers join Midgley in resurrecting compassion as the basis for animal protection. Feminist Josephine Donovan criticizes both Regan and Singer as overly rationalistic, individualistic, and abstract, and she claims that, in their quest for criteria, they in fact maintain boundaries between different forms of life. In the work of women artists, she claims, "the boundaries between the human world and the vegetable and animal realm are blurred. Hybrid forms appear: women transform into natural entities, such as plants, or merge with animal life." She discerns a feminist voice that "respects the aliveness and spirit . . . of other creatures and understands that they and we exist in the same unified field continuum. It appreciates that what we share—life—is more important than our differences. Such a relationship sometimes involves affection, sometimes awe, but always respect."[41] Debunking arguments over what constitutes rights, many feminists, like ecologists, emphasize the importance of community. They believe we owe loyalty and compassion to animals, not because of their qualities, but because we are connected with them in a single community.

Some feminists have drawn on the work of Carol Gilligan to return the concept of caring to animal protection philosophy. Morality demands not just that we recognize the abstract rights of strangers, but that we do good for those around us out of sympathy and love. The stray dog put to sleep at the pound suffers from lack of care, not lack of freedom.[42] If, as Gilligan suggests, women are more likely to have a caring perspective than men, this would help explain their greater participation in the animal protection movement. But again they hardly require elaborate, abstract philosophies to support their activity.

Some critics have attacked Singer's claims, more have debunked Regan's. Others—especially ecologists and feminists—argue that philosophical conceptions of individual rights and interests must be replaced by recognition of the direct connections between humans and animals. Still others, like George Cave, are tired of philosophical debates altogether, and want to focus on protest rather than talk. The prominent philosophies of animal protection in fact allow distinctions to be made in the treatment of individual animals–whether on the grounds of sentience, ability to live a full life, or place in the mixed community. Yet many activists apply their arguments to break down all distinctions. Ultimately the intellectual debates have been less persuasive as philosophy than as political ideology.

———

Explicit ideologies are vital to protest movements, giving form to shapeless feelings and reassuring participants about their grounds for acting. Sheer anger or frustration do not by themselves bring protestors into the streets. People need to link their feelings to an explanation, a cause, perhaps to a villain. And they need some vision of alternatives. Ideologies provide the rationale for social action.

That a handful of moral philosophers could help spark a powerful social movement suggests that they appealed to moral sentiments already widely spread. In their lives and their writings, the animal rights philosophers combined the emotional compassion driving the humane tradition with the critique of instrumentalism developed by the environmental movement. They appeared at a time when environmental and biomedical ethics were emerging as professional fields, bent on influencing public policy and social practice. This was heady stuff for philosophers disaffected with the analytic tradition. Singer, Regan and others were exhilarated to find that their profession could say something to nonprofessionals about how to live, and they wanted their writings to spawn social action. Though their ideas have not in fact coalesced into a single widely accepted ideology, they provided philosophies that could be used in recruiting new members, educating those already in the movement, and persuading policy-makers and the public to change their values and practices. Activists were ready to apply these ideas to a series of specific arenas where they felt animals were being abused.

EIGHT

From Rabbits
to Petri Dishes

After the successful 1977 campaign against the Museum of Natural History, Henry Spira needed a new target. He knew that another glaring abuse, like the cat sex experiments, would be a decisive way to engage public sensibilities and attract media attention. Ideally, however, it should involve more animals than the sixty cats saved at the museum, since a string of trivial victories might weaken his campaign. In 1979, he decided to attack the Draize test, which was a way of establishing the safety of cosmetics by observing their effect on rabbits' eyes. If the sexual preferences of mutilated cats seemed a frivolous justification for experiments, how much more so would a new shade of lipstick seem. Cosmetics testing—an issue bound to mobilize action—brought Spira to Revlon's Fifth Avenue headquarters in May 1980.

Since 1944, product testers have put cosmetics and other household products—anything that might get into people's eyes—into the eyes of rabbits in order to check for irritation. Rabbits are used in this Draize test precisely because their eyes are large and sensitive and because they produce fewer tears to wash substances out. The rabbits are constrained to keep them from wiping the materials out of their eyes, and at regular intervals testers examine the eyes for redness, swelling, opacity, and other ill effects. Test rabbits are albinos so that eye pigment will not confuse the observations.

The Draize test might well have been designed as a recruiting device for the animal rights movement. The color photographs used by the cosmetics industry to train technicians in recognizing eye changes could, when employed by the animal rights organizers, arouse public anger and compassion. The grotesque red swelling around the eye against the pure white fur is shocking. Rabbits— gentle, cute, huggable animals—were sure to arouse sympathy.

The Draize test used several hundred thousand rabbits each year, while other tests for toxic substances employed an estimated 14 million animals annually. Because of the limited use, few vested interests were likely to defend the Draize. Yet, because it involved rabbits, the test was more likely to attract public sympathy than those using mice and rats. Ultimately, Spira anticipated, a victory against the Draize test would be a starting point for campaigns against other substance tests.

In pragmatic fashion, Spira first attempted to talk to managers at Revlon, a cosmetics industry leader. After a polite reception but few concrete results, he began to construct a coalition of animal groups, eventually numbering over 400, called the "Coalition to Stop the Draize Rabbit Blinding Test." Funded by the Millennium Guild, a philanthropic organization involved with animal welfare, in April 1980 the coalition announced its plans to attack Revlon. Through negotiation backed by large demonstrations, the campaign succeeded in gaining extensive financing of research into alternatives to live animal tests.[1]

How had victory been achieved so swiftly? For one thing, it was a partial victory. The tests were reduced but not stopped. Funds began to flow for alternatives research, as large corporations, sensitive about their image, sought to avoid bad publicity. On this score, cosmetic companies were vulnerable, for they provide almost indistinguishable products to individual members of the public, who might remember that a company tortures rabbits more easily than they would recall the quality of the product. Also, the cosmetics companies saw potential benefits to themselves in the whole affair. Alternatives research seemed a promising investment, since the live animals used for testing were expensive. And if a company's rivals were also shamed into contributing, no competitive advantage would be lost. Manufacturers could actually benefit from the animal rights movement if it helped them find cheaper ways to meet government testing regulations.

Protest against substance testing helped the animal rights movement develop its critique of instrumentalism. The profit motive of the industry had little to do with moral values or critical consumer needs. To activists, cosmetics companies were creating artificial markets ("one more shade of mascara") to make money. Arguments about freedom of consumer choice appeared absurd in the case of hundreds of shades of lipstick. And with 1,300 brands of shampoo already available, consumers were hardly clamoring for one more. Why was it necessary to have more and more new products and ingredients that required testing? Animal defenders were angry that commodities had become more important than rabbits and did not necessarily reflect real consumer needs. For Spira, cosmetics testing was an opportunity for a broader critique of consumerism.

———

The Draize was only one of many substance tests. Another, the LD_{50} (Lethal Dose fifty percent) test consumed far more animals, several million each year worldwide. This test is used to ascertain the toxicity of substances such as household products or pesticides.[2] Again, Spira established a coalition against the LD_{50}, but he changed his strategy. This time, he targeted Procter & Gamble, an industry giant with a good record on social issues, and a producer of a range of household products other than cosmetics. Instead of money for alternatives research, he asked Procter & Gamble to change its own internal procedures. The changes could then be publicized as an industry standard. The company began taking steps to cooperate, largely because, like the Draize, the LD_{50} was a vulnerable target.

The LD_{50} test has been used since 1927, but its applicability to humans is still scientifically controversial, and Spira tapped the technical disputes to support his rhetoric. If rats die from eating a daily breakfast of a cleanser, how will a woman be affected if she gets it on her skin? There is a long history of scientific disagreement over the LD_{50} test; scientists had first questioned it in 1957. In 1973, toxicologist Gerhard Zbinden called the test "a ritual mass execution of animals." In 1982, the National Society for Medical Research said the test "is no longer scientifically justified," and the Pharmaceutical Manufacturers Association published a position paper questioning it. Even the director of the National Institute of Environmental Health Sciences and the National Toxicology Program called the test "an anachronism." In 1983, a writer for *Science* concluded that "animal rights groups and scientists in general agree that the test is now outdated and has limited value." But the test continued to be used until the attacks from animal rights groups.[3]

The cosmetics industry was quick to shift the blame for the Draize and LD_{50} tests onto federal regulators. The Cosmetic, Toiletry and Fragrance Association published a statement in the early 1980s titled "Cosmetic Manufacturers Have a Legal Duty to Test Their Products." It said the "FDA [Food and Drug Administration] has by regulation affirmatively required that industry undertake safety testing utilizing live animals." Some FDA officials denied that their regulations specifically required the LD_{50}.[4] However, other statements strongly suggested use of the Draize test. Responding to a query from a Maryland state legislator, the Commissioner of Food and Drugs said, "The Draize eye irritancy test is currently the most valuable and reliable method for evaluating the hazard or safety of a substance introduced into or around the eye. . . . Since certain tests should never be carried out in human beings and since at the present time there are no adequate alternatives, whole animal testing remains unavoidable."[5] It has continued, while the FDA has continued its ambivalent stance.

The FDA does not, in fact, require any tests for substances marketed as cosmetics, unless they contain color additives or certain restricted ingredients (such as mercury or chloroform). But if a product is marketed without tests, its producer can be held liable for mislabeling if the product turns out to be hazardous. Even this liability is removed if the product has the label, "Warning—The safety of this product has not been determined." Many cosmetics companies have abandoned animal testing, and all have distanced themselves from it. Elizabeth Thomas, a spokesperson from Maybelline, is characteristic: "I want to state emphatically at the outset that we at Maybelline are philosophically and operationally opposed to the indiscriminate or cruel use of animals in research. As a matter of policy, animals are used to provide safety and efficiency data only when alternative, government-approved methods are not available."[6] Many of these companies, however, have merely pushed the responsibility for testing onto their primary suppliers and independent laboratories.

It is apparently not difficult to avoid testing new cosmetics on animals, for dozens of companies are doing so. An animal rights group called Beauty Without Cruelty provides information and encourages purchase of "cruelty-free" products. Its newsletter, "The Compassionate Shopper," a guide for the politically engaged, lists many companies that do not use animals in testing or production. Instead, these companies use substances that have already been tested, or "natural" products such as beeswax, honey, and oatmeal.

Human volunteers, including, it is claimed, company presidents, wear the cosmetics to test for irritation. The Body Shop, created in Britain in 1976, began opening stores in the United States in 1988, and has four hundred shops worldwide. This company, linking animal and environmental concerns, uses recycled paper and biodegradable plastic, keeps packaging to a minimum, and offers refills if the customer brings in the old bottle. It also asks suppliers for a statement that no animal testing on materials has occurred in the last five years. A company representative claims, "There is a vocabulary of caring that is emerging, and consumers want products that don't harm anything."[7]

Cruelty-free companies tap into two ideological themes in the animal rights movement. One is the holistic, sometimes "New Age" idea that life should be simpler, with fewer refined, processed ingredients. We are told to trust fruits and vegetables. The Body Shop seems almost a greengrocer, with Kiwi Fruit Lip Balm, Honey and Oatmeal Scrub Mask, Sage and Comfrey Open Pore Cream, Cucumber Cleansing Milk, Seaweed and Birch Shampoo, Rice Bran Body Scrub, and Peppermint Foot Lotion. The other theme is the critique of instrumentalism: managers who have the potential to profit from a new product should be the ones to run the risk if the product irritates human skin. Animals should not be tools. Whether or not company presidents test substances on their own skin, the idea provides a powerful image.

There are few if any ingredients which have not, at some point, been tested on animals. Competitors are quick to point out that "cruelty-free" companies are simply using ingredients already tested on animals by other companies (like the no-kill animal shelters that simply send animals elsewhere to be put down). The FDA does require that all color additives be tested on animals. Thus, when Affirmative Alternatives claims to "offer a comprehensive line of cosmetic, personal care, and household products that have not been tested on animals," it stretches the truth. Cruelty-free companies often rely on substances already given expensive testing by large companies, or on raw ingredients sold (and tested) by others. However, because their products require no *new* animals, they are seen as an improvement over the development of ever new and frivolous cosmetics.

———

Carrying greater risks, new prescription drugs are subject to more stringent regulations than cosmetics. And because the testing of new drugs is linked to health advances rather than personal appearance, it has greater public support. The views of the syndicated columnist "Abby" may be typical. In response to a letter signed "For Human Rights," Abby defends her position on animal rights: "I am opposed to the use of live animals for testing household products and cosmetics. I am not opposed to using live animals for medical or biomedical purposes where there is no alternative method of testing."[8]

Both pragmatists and fundamentalists in the movement deploy arguments about the limited applicability of animal tests to humans. Says one flyer, "Thalidomide causes serious birth defects in the off-spring of pregnant women who take it, but does not produce defective offspring in most species of animal." Other brochures describe the tragic episodes of thalidomide, DES, Oroflex, Zomax, and other drugs—all developed and tested on animals but causing serious side effects in humans—to show that animals are inadequate models for human disease.[9]

Activists also question the necessity of constant innovation, although, sensing public attitudes, they are less likely to apply this argument to drugs than to cosmetics. Drug companies, concerned about the effect of the movement on their public image and profits, have been dissociating themselves from cosmetics companies. In the 1960s, they bought up cosmetics firms, but in the 1980s they began selling them. Faced with declining profits and the financial strains of retail stores, Squibb sold Charles-of-the-Ritz in 1986; Lilly sold Elizabeth Arden in 1987; and Schering Plough sold Maybelline in 1990. "Drugs you need," says the director of a trade group, "One could live without cosmetics."[10]

The testing of chemical products raises other issues. Corporations normally use animal tests for cosmetics and pharmaceuticals to provide evidence that a *new* substance is safe and can be marketed. But tests on chemicals are often used by regulators, scientists, citizens' groups, and public health officials to show that *existing* substances may cause cancer and should be taken off the market. Chemical companies introduce more than 500 new chemicals each year, but about 63,000 chemicals are already in common use, and barely one-tenth have been fully tested for carcinogenic properties.[11] Requiring animal tests can thus be an onerous constraint on the chemical industry.

Even without pressure from animal activists, the chemical industry has long been critical of animal tests. For example, an industry lawsuit delayed for two years the publication of a Department of Health and Human Services annual report listing carcinogens—on the grounds that chemicals should not be listed on the basis of animal tests alone.[12] For chemical companies, as well as drug and cosmetics firms, cost is the motivation shaping their perspective on animal testing. "There's nothing like a little financial incentive to get people to consider alternatives," says Christine Stevens, president of the Animal Welfare Institute.[13]

According to animal rights fundamentalists, animals should not be used to test either mascara or miracle drugs. The benefits to humans cannot, for Tom Regan and others, outweigh the suffering of the animals. Feminists for Animal Rights looks to holistic medicine not just for shampoos, but even for "alternatives to prescription drugs that have existed for thousands of years and have withstood the test of time and experience."[14] But a pragmatist position would allow some animal testing for drugs that might save human lives.

The campaigns against animal testing have not abolished animal tests, but fewer animals are used. A modified form of the LD_{50} uses five or ten animals rather than fifty or one hundred. Draize tests use diluted versions of the formulas, and fewer rabbits, which are now commonly anesthetized. As *The Economist* wryly reports, "now that regulators insist that animals should be treated better, fewer are needed to spot biological effects."[15] In 1986, Spira, who merged his coalitions into Animal Rights International, claimed a 75 percent reduction in acute toxicity tests. He quoted an article from *Science:* "The classic LD_{50} test has now been virtually eliminated in favor of tests using judiciously selected dosages on fewer animals."[16] The total numbers of animals has dropped. Most companies managed to cut their use of animals by one-third or more in the early 1980s, although some went even further. Colgate reduced animal use by 80 percent in six years.[17] Avon claimed to reduce its use of animals by 33 percent in 1982 and 31 percent in 1983, testing only substances that differed from those previously tested, and stopping the tests at the first signs of toxicity.[18] The movement had, by any standard, been very effective.

Animal rights groups more fundamentalist than Spira, especially PETA, presently want an immediate ban on all animal testing. In 1988, PETA's resolution to this effect won more than 10 of Avon shareholder votes. Instead of negotiating and communicating with Avon, PETA exploited the testing issue for its own purposes. In April, 1989 Avon's chairman privately told a PETA representative that the company would soon announce it was ending live animal tests. Nonetheless, a week later, PETA announced an international boycott of Avon products and gave the chairman a "Pinocchio Award" for lying, prompting many activists to mail false noses to the company. In June, Avon announced a permanent end to animal tests, as planned. PETA claimed all the credit, although Avon representatives say it was Spira's close cooperation and pressure over several years that had helped the company develop alternative practices.[19] Revlon also ended its testing. Like Avon, it had already reduced its use of animals by 90 percent.[20] Other companies have followed along. In 1990, Mary Kay Cosmetics, perhaps tired of ridicule in *Bloom County,* also announced a moratorium on live-animal testing.

Ironically, many animal protection organizations will miss the Draize and LD_{50} tests if they are abolished. For if the most shocking uses of animals are ended, their own recruitment may suffer. Not only PETA, but the ASPCA, the International Fund for Animal Welfare, and many other groups use the issue of substance testing as a means to raise funds. Because they must balance their urgent calls for action with reassurance that they can deliver results, they find substance testing a perfect cause. Many of the brochures sent out by the large, direct mail organizations describe the tests prominently, and the photographs of Draize rabbits are gruesome. Sometimes, organizations take credit for the reductions in these tests; more often, they neglect to mention the changes in corporate policies. A brochure still being sent by the ASPCA in 1990 listed "The Ten Most Unwanted" abuses of animals. The LD_{50} was at the top of the list, even though its use had by then been drastically cut. The accompanying photo is typical. The substance is being given to a rodent with a syringe, and it looks as though the animal is receiving a large hypodermic shot right in the face. A grisly and compelling moral shock, but one based on a dwindling practice, as the search for alternatives to animal testing continues.

Because the animal rights movement has accelerated the development of alternatives to live animal testing, diverse methods are being developed. *In vitro* cell cultures are a favorite method. Some cultures are groups of single cells; others form tissues; others replicate the functioning of particular organs. One test measures the clotting ability of blood extracted from horseshoe crabs, which are then released back into the ocean. Others use egg membranes, which have blood vessels—unlike cell cultures—but no nerves. An "agarose diffusion" test uses mouse cells mixed with agar, a seaweed derivative. Its results are the same as those of the Draize test 81 percent of the time, with the discrepancy resulting from the even greater sensitivity of the agarose method. Even better, the agarose test costs $50 to $100 per product rather than $500 to $700 for the Draize test, and it takes twenty-four hours rather than several days or several weeks. Noxell, producer of Noxzema and Cover Girl, has substituted the agarose for the Draize test, arguing that the two tests yielded similar results ninety percent of the time.[21]

Several private companies are already marketing alternatives using cell cultures. There are "living skin equivalents" in chambers arranged so that nutrients can be put in and waste removed, and substances tested on the skin. One company, Organogenesis, is also preparing bone and pancreas equivalents. The National Testing Corporation has an *in vitro* alternative to the Draize test called Eytex, using a mixture of fifty-three proteins that resemble the makeup of the human cornea. The mixture turns cloudy if an irritant is introduced. Many cosmetics companies claim to be satisfied with the results they obtain from Eytex.[22]

Computer models are also used as alternatives to *in vivo* testing. One program can recognize chemical structures that are similar to known toxic ones. Kurt Enslein of Health Designs has entered data on 6,000 chemicals known to be toxic, so that the computer can generate similar compounds without further testing. He claims his predictions match those of other tests 80 percent of the time.[23] Complex computer models of organisms are sometimes used to eliminate substances at early stages, avoiding even cell testing. A regular sequence of ever more expensive tests allows many dangerous substances to be weeded out quickly and cheaply. Whole animal tests come only at the final stage to evaluate substances expected to be safe.

Other techniques replace higher organisms with lower ones such as earthworms, sea urchin eggs, protozoa, plants, and invertebrates. Toxicologist Jerald Silverman of Ohio State uses protozoa, measuring the dosage that makes 10 percent of them lose their normal swimming ability. Advanced technologies such as gas chromatography, mass spectrometry, and radio immunoassay are also useful. Data banks have been extended so that existing tests need not be replicated. To further the spread of these developments, several English-language journals specifically focused on toxicology and testing were founded in the 1980s. Some of these journals are oriented toward the academic community, others to industry.[24]

The Center for Alternatives to Animal Testing at Johns Hopkins has emerged as a world center of research on alternatives. Established in 1981, the center, by 1983, was funding sixteen research projects around the country. It has continued to give twelve to twenty small grants each year, in amounts up to $20,000. Funding has come from most of the largest chemical and cosmetics companies, including Johnson & Johnson, Mary Kay, Benetton, Chanel, Walgreens, Exxon, Du Pont, Mobil, Procter & Gamble, and Avon. Through its newsletter and conferences, the center has helped gather and spread information about new techniques. By 1984, articles in the newsletter were reporting tremendous progress in promising alternatives but warning that proper validation of these techniques would take years. Test results must be compared for a wide range of substances in many laboratories, to show that they are as good or better than older animal tests. The Ames test for mutagens, which uses bacteria instead of mice, took about fifteen years to go from an experimental stage to widespread use. The Hopkins Center hopes to reduce this period through improved communication among scientific laboratories. In 1986, Bausch and Lomb provided $130,000 for the first step, a complete review of the research on alternatives, both published and in progress. The Soap and Detergent Association also began a validation program in 1988, examining fourteen proposed alternatives to the Draize test to find the five that seemed most promising.

———

Because it involves the internal operations of large companies, substance testing has been especially well suited to the pragmatists' negotiating style. But while Spira is satisfied with the steady progress in alternatives research, fundamentalists in the animal rights movement are less happy. They point out that after the large initial grants, the amount of money contributed by most corporate supporters of the Johns Hopkins Center is very small, in the range of $25,000–$35,000 per company per year. They criticize the slow adoption of new techniques. Ten years after the first announcements of funding for alternatives, validation of these techniques has barely started. Some critics assert that researchers working on alternatives are more concerned with funding and their own careers than with the animals that might be saved. Anxious to find evil enemies, fundamentalists look to the motivation behind actions. For Spira, in contrast, "if a large corporation reduces the number of animals it uses, it isn't important whether it does this because it cares about animals or because it is seeking to avoid unfavorable publicity. The animals who are spared suffering will be better off either way."[25]

Substance testing is an area where animal rights organizations can, if they wish, portray themselves as aligned with progress and technical efficiency. Spira manages to make the *testers* sound like Luddites opposed to technological change. He claims his goal is "to review archaic, repetitive animal tests and to substitute cell cultures, computer and mathematical models." These will "give the research community more elegant, less expensive, and more accurate science."[26] But this stance is not palatable to the fundamentalists, many of whom attack Spira for helping the testers. The director of PETA's "Compassion Campaign," Susan Rich, says simply that animal tests are "scientifically invalid, ethically indefensible, and are not required by law."[27] PETA wants total, immediate abolition, not Spira's gradualist strategy of "reduction, refinement, and replacement." For example, as Spira was working with Procter & Gamble to reduce animal use, PETA was introducing shareholder resolutions to force the company to stop animal testing altogether. Spira responded, "It seems to me that when a corporation is responsive to our concerns, it makes no sense to clobber them over the head. . . . It would be unfortunate to give industry the impression that it is useless to deal with and respond to animal rights concerns."[28] But to an uncompromising fundamentalist, "clobbering" the corporation makes perfect sense.

The risk of fundamentalist rhetoric is that companies harden their positions in response. Even while companies were publicly changing their testing practices, behind the scenes the Cosmetic, Toiletry and Fragrance Association—the cosmetics industry's trade group—began collecting funds for a public relations offensive against animal protection, with its president insisting, "We are not dealing with rational opponents. We are dealing with zealots who cannot comprehend that a child's life is more important than a dog's."[29] Faced with some animal groups that privately negotiate and others that publicly denounce, this industry combines concession and smear.

In some cases, criticism from a protest movement can force corporate and government bureaucracies to overcome inertia and reexamine existing procedures. In the area of substance testing, the animal rights movement has encouraged changes that sometimes benefit the companies as well as animals. Spira says, "Such major corporations as Avon, Bristol-Myers, Colgate, Hoffman La Roche, Mobil and

Procter & Gamble have drastically reduced their use of animals by about two-thirds through asking such basic questions as: Is this test really necessary? Can this information be obtained without using animals? With fewer animals? With less painful methods?"[30] Both the fundamentalists and the pragmatists in the animal rights movement have attacked substance testing, and both have doubtless had an impact. But, backed by public protests, pragmatic negotiation for cost reduction and alternatives research has resulted in greater changes in the use of animals than the urgent demands by fundamentalists for immediate abolition.

NINE

Test Tubes with Legs

The use of animals in scientific research is at once the most emotional and the most controversial, the most broadly publicized and the most widely criticized of all the issues raised by the animal rights movement. Admitting no moral boundaries between human and animal life, the fundamentalists in the movement want to abolish all animal research regardless of its merits or potential benefits. The pragmatists, urging cost-benefit calculations, insist that, at the very least, such research be more fully scrutinized. Opposition to animal experimentation highlights in starkest form the implications of the extreme animal rights position, for there are human lives to be saved through such research.

Animal rights brochures and magazines are filled with shocking images of maimed and tortured research animals. Posters at demonstrations portray experiments as painful and cruel. But beyond the appeal to compassion, the protests against animal experiments reflect the larger ambivalence in public attitudes toward science: respect for the free pursuit of knowledge is tempered by moral concerns about how that knowledge is obtained; a sense of awe about our technical capacities is countered by a fear that they have outrun our ability to control them. Concerns about the instrumentalism of science have fueled the animal rights movement. But research using animals has been widely valued for its contribution to medical care, and in the battle for public opinion, scientists have actively pursued this point. Thus, science is the most controversial target of the movement.

After World War II and the establishment of the National Institutes of Health (NIH), biomedical research burgeoned, increasing the demand for laboratory animals. This was the period when medical laboratories used pounds and shelters as sources of research animals, sparking the public concern that resulted in the 1966 Animal Welfare Act. Intended primarily to prevent former pets from ending their days in research labs, neither the Act nor its amended version in 1970 dealt with the care and treatment of research animals. Animal welfare groups remained dissatisfied, but biomedical research, associated with improved medical care and the control of major diseases, seemed immune to criticism. Just as the prestige of modern science had banished anti-vivisectionists to the fringes of society in the early twentieth century, so science and its significant medical gains retained immense authority in the years following World War II.[1]

Uncritical support of science, however, began to wane in the 1970s with growing public awareness of the social and moral implications of many scientific advances, especially in medicine. The emerging field of bioethics developed a professional discourse around the moral issues generated, for example, by the increased technical ability to prolong life.[2] While philosophers debated the ethical implications of science, sociologists analyzed science as a social construct, and critiques of science proliferated. Jürgen Habermas and Paul Feyerabend, for example, argued that modern science has taken on the unquestioned status once reserved for religion.[3] Along with professional scrutiny came demands for "social assessment of science," implying public accountability and regulation. Debates on "the limits of scientific inquiry" examined the proposition that some kinds of research should not be done at all.[4] These discussions focused on both the social impacts of science and the ethics of research methods, including both human and animal experimentation.

The disputes over science and technology during the 1970s aired several themes that would later enrich the rhetoric of animal protection, especially its attack on instrumentalism. The controversies raised questions of equity. Can potential benefits to some people justify the costs to others? The cost to the environment, as in the development of nuclear power? The risks to vulnerable research subjects such as children? The disputes raised questions about research priorities, in particular the balance between high-technology medicine and simpler measures of disease prevention. Should resources be directed to technologically sophisticated clinics to save very premature infants, or to prenatal care that would prevent many premature births? The accountability of science was challenged. Who should participate in decisions about research priorities and practices? And critics of biomedical research aired moral and religious arguments over the sanctity of life and the moral responsibility of scientists—all questions later pursued by animal rights activists.[5]

Revelations at the Nuremburg trials about Nazi medical research had established the need for careful regulation of experimentation with human subjects. The Nuremburg codes, followed in 1964 by the Declaration of Helsinki, had elaborated rules for biomedical research based on voluntary, informed consent. However, cases such as the Tuskegee syphilis experiments, in which black males were unwittingly the subjects of a study of the natural history of untreated syphilis, came to public attention in the 1970s and brought congressional attention to the persistence of questionable ethical procedures.[6] Congressional hearings and the press paid special attention to the need to protect "most vulnerable subjects," that is, children, fetuses, prisoners, the retarded, and others vulnerable to coercion and incapable for one reason or another of voluntary, informed consent. The notion that research subjects could be "innocent victims" was adopted by animal rights advocates such as Hans Ruesch, who, extending the concept from humans to animals, wrote about "the slaughter of the innocent."[7]

During the 1980s, activists from several social movements were articulating alternatives to contemporary scientific and medical practices. Ritual medicine and New Age devotees engaged in "holistic" practices that relied less on scientific procedures than on mental attitude.[8] Environmentalists called for healthy lifestyles and preventive dietary regimes. Feminists such as Evelyn Fox Keller outlined a "feminine" scientific practice, less intrusive and manipulative, and retaining empathic sensitivity to the voice of nature.[9] The feminist movement celebrated women such as Jane Goodall and Dian Fossey for embodying this ideal, living among the apes they studied rather than capturing them for observation in research labs.[10]

This climate—in which large segments of the educated middle class grew skeptical of scientific expertise and practices—encouraged animal activists to shift from the protection of research animals to their liberation, from the idea of welfare to the rhetoric of rights. Younger animal advocates were more likely than their elders to blame the accepted practices of science rather than to condemn individual scientists as deviant. After 1981, they began to demand not just better regulation of animal research, but its abolition, and they escalated their tactics to match the imperatives of their moral stand.

Early on the morning of February 21, 1989, six animal rights activists climbed atop a 160-foot construction crane at the site of a new animal research facility at the University of California at Berkeley. Calling themselves the Coalition against Militarism, Animal Abuse, and Environmental Hazards, they denounced the new facility as "a major research center of the U.S. military, developing biological warfare and employing abusive animal testing and dangerous toxic agents." The protesters unfurled banners demanding "No Toxic Animal Lab" and "Stop Germ Warfare Lab." In seeking a moratorium on the construction of the facility and an end to all animal research on campus, they expressed their moral outrage in dramatic terms: experimentation was from a "dark age," it was an "ethical disaster." And when university administrators called them terrorists, one of the protestors responded, "I don't see terror in climbing a crane. People who carry out research on animals are terrorists." Protestors occupied this moral high ground for a week, even though police chased them from the snug operator's cabin to the top of the crane. They came down when the university agreed to press only trespassing charges, a misdemeanor, and to drop a civil suit for several hundred thousand dollars to cover the cost of construction delays.

A memorable media event, the occupation followed several years of protest against animal research at Berkeley. Animal rights groups had demonstrated, lobbied state legislators, caused minor damage, and filed several lawsuits against the university. One woman had parked herself on campus in a restraining chair like those used to harness research monkeys, fasting in hopes of provoking moral outrage among passersby. Elliot Katz, a veterinarian who had organized much of the animal rights protest at Berkeley, exploited the image of "Berkeley-Gate" to attract tens of thousands of recruits to his organization, In Defense of Animals.

Ironically, the new building was itself a response to animal protectionists, an effort to improve animal conditions by consolidating the campus's twenty-two separate animal labs. But the activists' moral stance allowed little room for compromise—they wanted to stop research, not improve conditions—and, as a result, the building had been the focus of contention since the first plans were developed in 1985.

Those who believe that animals have absolute rights demand the elimination of all animal research. Condemning the instrumental rationality of science, they find it morally unacceptable to reduce animals to the status of raw materials, in pursuit of human benefit: "We don't consider animals to be a tool, the test tube with legs."[11] Improving conditions is not enough, for as one poster puts it, "Lab animals never have a nice day."

Anti-vivisectionists insist that immoral methods can never be used to support even the most worthy goals. They support their impassioned argument by comparing laboratories to Nazi death camps: "For animal researchers, the ends justify the means. This argument has a familiar ring: Hitler used it when he allowed experiments to be done on Jews."[12] Harking back to the humane tradition, activists further argue that exploitation of animals in laboratories teaches and condones cruelty and crime. SUPRESS (Students United Protesting Research Experiments on Sentient Subjects) asserts that:

> The social dangers of encouraging and even forcing students to kill and torment defenseless creatures are too obvious to belabor. Violence begets violence. It only follows that such a traumatic and emotionally desensitizing experience at such an early age has to be the springboard that eventually leads to vandalism, rape, child abuse, torture and murder.[13]

Similarly the American Anti-vivisection Society argues that the practice of having medical students practice surgery on healthy dogs teaches "future physicians to be callous and devoid of compassion."[14]

Animal rights groups accuse scientists of sadism, arrogance, and deviance, of acting like "lobotomized robots." Activists pick up on language. Speaking at a conference Steve Rauh, a former Sierra Club editor, was appalled by the words of a Berkeley researcher that: "The remains of animals from U.C. [University of California] are now disposed of by a commercial company at a location outside Berkeley." Said Rauh: "The word *disposed* bothered me a lot—'disposed of.' I have an attitude about life as being sacred, so I got a little annoyed." Again he quoted the researcher: "Incineration is the main means of disposing of animals that have been killed in pounds, and many humans are similarly processed." Rauh commented, "The word *processed* sent a chill up my spine. Because if this man is doing the research that's supposed to save my life, I thought, what's he thinking and what does he feel, and where is that research going?"[15]

The scientist had chosen precise and emotionally neutral terms; the activist felt such neutrality inhuman, cruel, and threatening to his own self. Gruesome stories are rife in the movement. Such stories attest to the cruelty of scientists; images of evil, dehumanized, sadistic scientists pervade animal rights publications.

A brochure from United Action for Animals, called "Science or Savagery?" exploits a thesaurus of shocking images to call its members to action:

> The truth is that millions of dogs, cats, monkeys, rabbits, horses, zoo animals, farm animals, reptiles, dolphins and other animals are * SCALDED * BAKED ALIVE * CRUSHED * SUFFOCATED * POISONED * IRRADIATED * DRIVEN INSANE * ELECTRIC SHOCKED * BLASTED BY EXPLOSIVES and more—all in the name of "scientific" research but in truth having nothing to do with human or animal health.[16]

The International Primate Protection League circulates a description of a grim device for severing animal heads and keeping them alive (patented in May 1987). Grotesque and pathetic photographs of primates in restraining chairs, dogs with missing limbs, cats with open wounds: these are printed in fundraising brochures and enlarged in provocative posters. They provide support for the urgent calls to action on behalf of animals.

———

Appealing to sympathy for animals, the movement has ready access to media attention and the hearts of millions. While some news coverage is critical—especially when violence is involved—many articles reflect the sentimentalism so important to the movement. A reporter describes one research animal: "No. 875 is a furry little cat with black and white markings like those on a pinto pony. Her head seems halved by colors, with one eye rimmed in black, the other in white. She has no name because nobody wants her. When someone visits her, she mews and rubs her head on the cage's bars, scratching herself with her visitor's fingers. She's going to be killed for medical experimentation."[17] The *San Francisco Chronicle* describes in empathic detail the life of rat #1913 from his birth and the moment he first opened his eyes, through his weaning and maturation, to his death. "The furry stump of 1913's head lay motionless on a paper towel at the base of the blade, its black, bulbous eyes staring . . ."[18]

Just as the sentiments of animal protectionists support their belief that all animals—not only pets—deserve moral consideration, so the perceptions of scientists support the belief that certain animals must be used as tools. Focusing on the benefits of their research—to scientific progress, to medical care—they simply fail to see a moral dilemma. Like surgeons, they find ways to maintain emotional distance from the animals they use. Through elaborate mechanisms, researchers "construct" their animals to be something alien and hence manipulable; they usually refuse, for example, to name the research animals and refer to them interchangeably as "he," "she," and "it." Scientists are professionally socialized to objectify their research animals in this way, and the routines of their daily practice reinforce their training. Yet they also prefer the term "sacrifice" to killing, perhaps admitting some sentimental attachment that must be covered by a euphemism.[19]

Scientists strongly defend their use of animals. For some, the protection of science has become a counter-crusade. Just as animal rightists use a language of urgency to save animals, so scientists describe the value of animal research as "vital," "life-saving," the solution to "devastating" and "life-threatening" disease. Certain of the social worth of their calling, they argue that science is expanding the frontiers of knowledge, and is essential to medical and social progress. Professional autonomy, they feel, is necessary for such progress. Threats of regulation frequently evoke references to Lysenkoism or the persecution of Galileo. Feeling besieged by the increasing regulations imposed on their research, many scientists defensively dismiss criticism as antiscience, a return to the Dark Ages. When attacked as immoral, cruel, careerist, or greedy, scientists respond with disbelief, confusion, and outrage. Their attackers must be insane, misanthropic, or simply uninformed. Thus, scientists frequently suggest that animal activists—"fruitcakes," "weirdos," "nuts"—give up their right to therapeutic interventions that were developed through animal research.

————

Ignoring this response, animal rights activists pursue their moral critique of science. The entire world, according to many activists, is becoming simply a resource to be used and manipulated for the sole purpose of creating ever more powerful tools. One critic finds the origins of AIDS in this attitude: "Self-interest combined with the world view that everything is an object is what motivated the doctor who is said to have invented the AIDS virus—either on purpose or by medical accident."[20] The widely publicized Baby Fae case in 1984 became a case in point. Scientists at the Loma Linda University Medical Center in California implanted a heart from a seven-month-old baboon in a newborn human infant. Describing the experiment as "ghoulish tinkering," an experiment with no possible utility beyond the advancement of scientific careers, fundamentalists envisioned a scenario where animals were systematically captured, bred, and killed for purposes of organ transplantation.

Animal research is most likely to be targeted if it has no immediate applications to human health, for animal activists can portray such research as useless, self-serving, and self-evident. Behavioral psychology has been a target of protests since the beginning of the century, when anti-vivisectionists attacked John Watson's studies of the effect of deprivation on animal behavior.[21] To the Humane Society of the United States, behavioral research seems to discover the obvious. In 1984, John McArdle, then research director of HSUS, described psychologist Harry Harlow, who studied the effects of isolation on infant primates, as "devising a seemingly endless series of new methods and devices to torment and torture" them. What did he discover? asks McArdle. Neither a grand new theory nor a breakthrough in treatment of troubled human beings:

> Strip away all of the jargon, the self-serving platitudes, and pseudo-science, and you can summarize Dr. Harlow's conclusions in two sentences: mother love is important to young primates; and if you raise an individual of a naturally social species in isolation, it will have problems adjusting when reintroduced to that society.[22]

When reduced to such seemingly obvious findings, research projects appear to be superfluous.

Anti-instrumental arguments also revolve around money. Animal rightists believe that science is "draped in a cloak of concern for humanity" but that—in fact—it is a money-making enterprise pursued for personal gain. A woman at a demonstration wears a hat which is a tiny cage containing a toy monkey surrounded by greenbacks. Animal experimentation, writes a CEASE member, "serves the economic—not scientific—interests of thousands of research institutions."[23] In attacks reminiscent of William Proxmire's Golden Fleece Awards, activists deplore the taxes wasted on "useless" research that produces few results. Money spent on drug research could be used for educating young people; dollars spent on AIDS research could be used to care for AIDS patients. A PETA leaflet lists the "abuses our taxes support": "$500,000 to discover why monkeys clench their jaws in anger; $102,000 to study the effects of gin as compared to the effects of tequila in Atlantic fish; $30,000 to turn rats—natural teetotallers—into alcoholics; $1,000,0000 to study the mating call of the mosquito; $148,0000 to determine why chickens grow feathers; $525,000 to study the differences in vomiting mechanisms between cats and dogs."[24] Taking a cue from Pentagon watchdogs who bemoaned $500 wrenches, the Animal Protection Institute of America attacks "the age of the $30,000 chimpanzee and the $50 mouse." Seizing upon some of the seemingly specious projects selected for funding, the Institute implicates all as unworthy.

Activists seize upon disagreement within the scientific community in order to challenge the scientific grounds for animal experiments. In particular, they exploit debates over the relevance of animal models.[25] Are rats the appropriate test subjects for evaluating the safety of cyclamates? Are chimps relevant subjects for research on AIDS?[26] Were animal tests adequate to predict the strokes experienced by recipients of the artificial heart?[27] Animal protectionists also tap the endless debate among scientists over the relative role of prevention and cure in the improvement of human health. Picking up on tensions between science and society, they turn them to their own ends. They criticize a "slash and burn" approach to cancer (surgery and radiation) based on animal experiments, claiming that such research diverts attention away from the importance of diet, improved sanitation, and uncontaminated food in improving health and preventing disease: "Animals, like ordinary people," claims Michael W. Fox of HSUS, "are the victims of a medical mind-set on disease and disease treatment instead of preventive medicine."[28]

Activists argue that animal research is outmoded because of alternatives, proposing, for example, that the new techniques for substance testing be used in biomedical research as well. The Medical Research Modernization Committee, a group of 650 health care professionals, wants to decrease the use of primates to study AIDS because people with AIDS are willing to volunteer. And the *Animals' Agenda* has proposed "neomort" studies—an increased use of cadavers and brain-dead humans in medical education and research.[29] Mobilization for Animals has circulated a list of such alternatives to the use of animals in experimentation; only the self-interest of the "vivisection industry," they claim, stands in the way.

Scientists, however, insist that live animal models are essential, that alternatives are simply not feasible in many areas of research.

The deans of the thirteen medical schools that make up the Association of Medical Schools of New York issued a statement acknowledging the need for stewardship on behalf of animals, but they reaffirmed the use of animals as "indispensable" and condemned the "tactics of intimidation and violence which undermine our democratic traditions and threaten the principle of free scientific inquiry."[30]

But pleas for freedom of inquiry elicit accusations of arrogance. A psychologist in the animal rights movement calls it "science-ism, the blind dogma that science is right regardless"—a dogma that allows scientists to say, "'Just trust us.'"[31] Questioning the accountability of science, a writer for the movement claims that the practices of science are "protected by the weapon of secrecy . . . which has fostered an increasingly uninformed public." She quotes Thomas Kuhn's observation that scientists have enjoyed "unparalleled insulation . . . from the demands of laity and of every day life. . . . There are no other professional communities in which individual creative work is so exclusively addressed to and evaluated by other members of the profession."[32] Capitalizing on exposés of scientific fraud, animal advocates insist that, "Animal experimentation is one of the biggest frauds perpetuated by the scientific community, which is allowed to go on unscrutinized. We hope that more fraud-busters will begin to reveal its damage."[33] Frustrated by traditionally closed access to the work and findings of scientific researchers, the movement has decided to undermine society's confidence and trust in the profession. The social role of science—including the cost of medicine and its relevance to human needs—were already the subject of press coverage and congressional inquiry by the 1980s, and in this context the arguments of the animal rights movement appeared credible to many people. Science provided a potent set of issues for recruiting activists, for eliciting public support, and for justifying attacks on laboratories.

To gain credibility, the animal rights movement mobilized its own professional experts—among scientists, physicians, and veterinarians sympathetic to the cause. Movements opposed to modern science and medicine—Creationists, Laetrile groups, opponents of genetic engineering—all object to science on moral grounds, yet employ scientific arguments to strengthen their causes.[34] Animal rights groups are no exception.

Organizations such as the Association of Veterinarians for Animal Rights, the Scientists' Group for Reform of Animal Experimentation, the Medical Research Modernization Committee, Psychologists for the Ethical Treatment of Animals, and the Physicians' Committee for Responsible Science began to form in the early 1980s to challenge the attitudes and practices within their professions. Research psychologist Donald J. Barnes explains his conversion to animal protection:

> Five years ago today, I held the position of research psychologist and principal investigator at the School of Aerospace Medicine, Brook Air Force Base, Texas. I resigned on March 1, 1981. . . . Not only did I face the ignominious truth of the meaninglessness of 16 years of personal and professional investment; I had to hear the echo of more than 1,000 rhesus monkeys screaming with indignation and pain.[35]

At an investigation by the National Academy of Sciences, scientists sympathetic to the movement talked about their former "blind faith" in science. They claimed to have been duped by the "wall of propaganda" that keeps the public from the truth. And they argued that scientists seek "twenty-first century solutions for problems with nineteenth century methodology."[36] These professionals lend legitimacy to demands for legislative and policy change. They serve as advisors to the animal rights organizations, write articles for their mailings, and speak at demonstrations. By arguing that animal research is often useless and unnecessary, and that alternative research procedures are available, they convey an image of mainstream science as barbaric and immoral. Veterinarians Andrew Rowan and Nedim Buyukmihci, physiologist Barbara Orlans, and physician Neal Barnard are prominent animal advocates. An organization called the Scientists' Center for Animal Welfare (SCAW) was founded in 1979, dedicated to the principle that "a humane concern for animals should be incorporated into our conduct of science." It runs workshops and educational programs to promote "responsible inquiry." Such groups, supporting the pragmatist agenda, seek reforms through communication, negotiation, and compromise.

The technical debates were accompanied by direct action. PETA set up "research investigation teams," using NIH grant applications accessible to the public to identify vulnerable targets. Because NIH provided the support for most of the biomedical research projects under attack, and because its offices are located not far from PETA's national office, it became PETA's major target. In July 1985, eighty members of PETA occupied the offices of the director of the National Institute of Neurological and Communicative Disorders and Strokes at NIH, demanding that the agency stop funding the University of Pennsylvania head injury research, institute a policy to include an outside observer approved by the animal rights community in NIH investigations, and appoint a mutually agreeable party to the national council of each of the NIH's member Institutes. The agency eventually suspended the Pennsylvania primate project.

The fate of the seventeen monkeys rescued from Taub's laboratory in 1981 became a major issue. PETA, supported by other animal rights organizations, demanded that the monkeys be sent to an animal rights sanctuary called Primarily Primates. They held regular demonstrations at NIH, culminating in a vigil, called a "conscience camp," that lasted 125 days. They also sued the agency for custody of the animals. In September 1986, the U.S. Fourth Circuit Court rejected their suit, ruling that animal protection groups have no right to speak for animals. NIH sent five of the monkeys to the San Diego Zoo and the rest to a primate center in Louisiana where they were to be retired. Veterinarians recommended euthanasia for three of the seven remaining monkeys but were blocked by PETA's legal actions. PETA demanded guardianship rights over the monkeys, arguing that they were leading "very boring, very bleak, and very desperate lives," and that they should be treated like minors, available for custody. PETA's hysteria over these monkeys—terming the case a *"must win"* situation in fundraising appeals—shows a fundamentalist concern with the symbolic value of a case rather than with the number of animals involved. In July 1990, after nine years of protest, PETA lost its suit.

NIH remains a target of the animal rights movement. Its Office of Protection of Research Risks receives over 300 letters a month demanding that the "torture" of animals in research laboratories be controlled. It receives three to four letters a week from Congress requesting site visits. In 1980, only 5 percent of the work in this office related to animal research. This number increased to 50 percent by 1988 as NIH responded to movement complaints and increased its laboratory inspections.[37]

While PETA supplies emotional rhetoric and encourages civil disobedience, the ALF believes that more radical direct action is essential: "We believe we are in the same position as the black people who decided they would no longer sit in the back of the bus," said an ALF demonstrator.[38] Another explained her involvement: "They [scientists] have the money, the media, but they don't have the TRUTH. We have the Truth." She told a reporter that she expected to be caught during a raid and to go to jail, but that this was necessary: "It's almost like living in Germany in the '30s."[39] This attitude placed ALF on the virtuous side of a moral crusade, as part of a resistance movement battling against the powerful but morally bankrupt forces of science. As such, all manner of rhetoric and strategy could be condoned.

The success of the raid against the University of Pennsylvania encouraged other incidents, including bomb scares, threatening phone calls, and destructive actions such as the firebombing of labs, trashing of facilities, theft of animals (sometimes leaving a copy of Singer's *Animal Liberation* in their place), vandalism of equipment and research records, and burning of buildings. These incidents have delayed and, in some cases, stopped research.

The number of illegal actions has increased. According to NIH, there were no reported break-ins at NIH-supported labs between 1978 and 1983, but in 1984 there were ten. In 1987, the ALF claimed responsibility for striking fourteen research labs in California, as compared to one in 1986. From 1983 through 1987, in California alone, animal rights protestors caused an estimated $4.5 million in damages.[40] A handful of actions were especially costly. In February 1986, ALF activists raided a lab at the Riverside campus of the University of California and stole 467 animals. They set off a $2.5 million fire at the University of California at Davis in April 1987 and vandalized eighteen automobiles. Such actions have resulted in the prosecution and conviction of only three people, a fact that has prompted several congressional bills that would make lab break-ins a federal offense and engage federal investigatory capabilities.

Most animal rights groups claim to discourage their members from harassing individual researchers, but they cannot stop such activities. One Berkeley researcher was contacted by FBI agents who believed that a bomb—which accidentally killed the man who made it—could have been designed for him. Photocopied lists of research scientists circulate at many demonstrations. One, distributed by individuals at a New York demonstration, provided home addresses and telephone numbers of researchers, indicating which apartment buildings had doormen. It read: "Some have termed this list 'Dial a Ghoul,' however it is hoped that your inquiries will be of a civil nature." To some animal rights activists, intimidation, harassment, and even violence are justified by the end goal of abolishing animal experiments.

———

As the actions proliferated, scientists responded. Several major protests suggest the interplay between the actions of protestors and scientists' responses. In April 1987, when Trans-Species Unlimited began a series of demonstrations at the Cornell Medical School in Manhattan,[41] the target was a study of barbiturate addiction, funded by the National Institute on Drug Abuse (NIDA), using cats as experimental subjects. The principal investigator, Michiko Okamoto, had been working on the project for thirteen years with the ultimate goal of helping doctors prescribe drugs without addicting patients. Trans-Species selected this experiment for its potential emotional punch, since it used cats and studied drug addiction. Its demands focused not on laboratory conditions, but on the efficacy of the research, arguing that drug abuse was a complex social issue that could not be solved simply by understanding physiological mechanisms. With so many humans suffering from drug addiction, why spend tax dollars to hook cats too?

Trans-Species organized demonstrations and letter-writing campaigns. NIDA received 10,000 letters and inquiries from about eighty congressional representatives. Okamoto received threatening phone calls at home and at work. A committee of the American Society of Experimental Therapeutics reviewed Okamoto's work and found it "impeccable." But in response to the pressure, in August 1987, Cornell officials met with Trans-Species leaders and told them the experiments would end. In a public letter they ambiguously stated that "The research . . . that required the use of the cat model has essentially been completed." Trans-Species claimed victory. In October, however, Okamoto submitted a renewal proposal to NIDA to continue her addiction research for the year beginning June 1988, including further experiments on cats to be followed up by rat research. The project was strongly supported by the peer review system and NIDA granted her $600,000. When Trans-Species leaders learned this, they renewed their protest, accusing the university of "betraying the public trust."

Late in 1988, Okamoto returned her grant money to NIDA, writing, "As much as I want to continue my long interest in the study of the mechanisms of drug dependency using the feline model, recent developments both inside and outside the University have made it difficult for me to proceed with the experiments as proposed in my renewal grant."[42] Cornell claimed that this was the investigator's own decision, but there was also a need to preserve institutional credibility. Poorly prepared to deal strategically with the pressure from animal rights groups, Cornell's response was fragmented and indecisive, providing little institutional support to the researcher.

This was the first time a researcher had voluntarily returned funds because of pressure from the animal rights movement. As one reporter put it, it "sent tremors through the biomedical research community."[43] The director of NIDA blasted Cornell: terminating the research would "set a disastrous precedent in our battle against those who would eliminate the use of animals in research." He believed that "the productivity of public funds that we have invested in this project has been compromised."[44] Scientists from around the country deluged both the medical school and the university with letters condemning the action.[45] The university had "bowed to the demands of Yahoos." "Shame on Cornell and all American universities who are unwilling to stand up for their faculty." Professional society statements announced that the decision "strikes at the heart of academic freedom." It was "a major victory for special interest agitators who would impose their philosophical and religious views on the whole of American society."

In 1988 and 1989, another protest, against experiments at the New York University medical school, was less successful. NYU maintains a monkey colony at Sterling Forest, north of New York City, and a researcher there was conducting experiments on addiction to toluene, a solvent used in many paints and glues. The monkeys addicted themselves by administering their own doses of the drug. As in the Cornell campaign, Trans-Species insisted there were many human drug addicts who could be clinically studied and helped, sparing the need for addicting new subjects (the monkeys). Though the same group launched both campaigns, against similar experiments, the NYU effort had little impact.

NYU's response was consistently aggressive. Each year, it preempted demonstrations by holding earlier news conferences to explain the work in its animal research laboratories. The day before the April 1988 demonstration, for example, the public communications department of the medical school called a press conference in which scientists described the medical value of their research. It featured a child who would have died had he not been treated with a procedure developed from research using cats. He and his mother, with down-home Kentucky accents, were appealing witnesses. The next day, when television news programs reported the protest, they featured the child, providing NYU a victory in the battle of moral images. This type of response, more pro-active than re-active, is increasing, as research institutions learn from each others' mistakes.

In addition to its public relations, NYU consistently defended the researcher and his work and admitted no abuses or poor laboratory conditions. It simply tightened security, letting the protestors march, chant, and get arrested. The university won another symbolic battle when the protests took place in front of NYU administrative offices located in the main library building. Shouts and chants were directed at a place symbolic of learning, while the experiments occurred forty miles away. Fewer protestors showed up in 1989, and there was no protest in April 1990. A tough response worked for NYU.

On the West Coast, Stanford University and the University of California at Berkeley both drew protests in the late 1980s when they announced plans for new and improved animal research facilities. At both universities, activists attacked environmental impact reports as inadequate, appealed to town–gown frictions, and engaged in disruptive actions. Many of the protestors at the two universities were the same, notably those organized by Elliot Katz and In Defense of Animals. But the two universities responded differently.

Stanford organized an aggressive response to animal protectionists. President Donald Kennedy, himself a biologist and former head of the U.S. Food and Drug Administration, is an articulate spokesman for many areas of science policy. He actively defends the need for animal research in public speeches and articles. He even traveled to Sacramento to defend construction of Berkeley's new animal facility. Stanford's vice-president in charge of relations with government, Larry Horton, has also written about the animal rights movement and prodded others to fight it. "People on the defensive never win anything," he said, as he criticized several other universities for taking a low profile in hopes that the issue would fade away. For several years in the late 1980s, he spent roughly one-quarter of his time on animal care issues.[46]

In contrast to Stanford, a wealthy private university relatively protected from pressure by elected officials, Berkeley is directly accountable to the state legislature for its funding and must win approval for the planning, design, and construction of new facilities. The Berkeley crane occupation cost the university (and ultimately California taxpayers) an immediate $300,000, and even more in heightened security for the remainder of construction—five guards at all times, and even a bomb-sniffing dog. The building was rede-signed to include bulletproof windows. Moreover, Berkeley officials feared that the letter-writing campaigns of activists could cause de-lays, investigations, and—although this has not yet happened—rejec-tions of new projects. However, both students and faculty at Berke-ley value the university's tradition of political dissent, and animal activists can reserve Sproul Plaza in the center of campus for their demonstrations. The university even provided rooms for nonviolence training before one of the direct actions against it. Although followed by police, protestors are allowed to wander through the campus and buildings as long as they do not disrupt regular activities.

Stanford has a public relations advantage because of its prestig-ious medical school and its research associated with medical applica-tions. Stanford is one of the world's leading centers of research on heart transplants, relying heavily on dogs obtained from pounds. When the California legislature was debating a bill to prohibit sales from pounds, Stanford organized a group of transplant recipients to lobby, sporting buttons saying "I got my heart at Stanford," an emotional appeal to match that of animal activists. In contrast, Berkeley has no medical school. While several Berkeley researchers doing basic research have pointed out the potential medical implica-tions of their work, their case appears weaker. Anti-vivisectionists can play on widespread public skepticism about research that lacks immediate practical applications.

Out of these and other cases, a counter-movement is forming to defend scientific research. In parallel to the animal rights movement, its tone is generally strident and dismissive. It is also learning that strong responses, like those of Stanford and NYU, work better than ambiguous ones. Drawing on these lessons, the scientific community has tried, in some cases, to negotiate; in others, to undermine the animal rights movement; and in general, to fight the battle of public opinion.

―――――

In a conciliatory effort intended to facilitate negotiation with ani-mal protectionists, the American Association for the Advancement of Science (AAAS) voted at its 1989 annual meeting to approve the affiliation of the Scientists' Center for Animal Welfare. The decision was controversial, as many AAAS scientists were concerned it would legitimate the antiscience message of the broader animal rights move-ment. But others perceived the group as a "moderate voice on a very shrill issue," and believed that affiliation might limit the influence of the more extreme voices in the animal rights movement.

While some scientific societies are conciliatory, the American Medical Association has tried to undermine animal protection groups. In 1989, it announced an "Animal Research Action Plan" to contest their tax-exempt status, build its own database for monitoring animal rights activities, and push the federal government to establish a special unit to investigate animal rightists. The idea was to isolate hard-core activists, on the theory that "the general public is up for grabs. These people can be scared away if they come to see the violent tactics of the movement as dangerous and counterproductive."[47] At a 1989 news conference, an AMA representative claimed that, "As we speak, [animal activists] are infiltrating the schools and influencing our children so they will oppose biomedical research and denigrate those who conduct it."[48]

Engaged in a battle for public opinion, scientists are increasingly trying to match the moral strategies of their adversaries. But for reasons of confidentiality and good taste, most researchers are reluctant to show pictures of sick patients that might counter the emotional images of research animals displayed by animal activists. Emotional confrontation is not part of the scientific style. Publicists for the scientific community tend to favor point-by-point rebuttals of anti-vivisectionist positions. Some radio talk shows allow detailed arguments, but the format of television news is the "sound bite." Even the print media prefer short quotations that will contrast one position quickly with another.[49]

The research establishment has nonetheless improved its public relations, using catchy phrases, visual images, and emotional appeals to counter those of the animal activists. Some scientists are bringing reporters directly into their laboratories hoping to show the value of their work and to demonstrate their efforts to minimize pain. But it is difficult to allay people's fears about the suffering of animals by opening up the labs. As one campus veterinarian told us: "You can't win that way. People see animals in cages, and assume they're suffering. It could be the happiest animal in the world, but it will look bad on television if it's behind bars."[50]

Few scientists are inclined toward grassroots organizing, and few have the political skills to deal with public controversy. Nonetheless, some scientists have organized on university campuses to dampen the animal rights influence. A Stanford group called Citizens for Life, Education, and Research (CLEAR) tries to counter anti-vivisectionist arguments by publishing and circulating educational material. At Berkeley, students and faculty formed the Association for Animals and Animal Research (AFAAR) in March 1988. It quickly changed its name to CFAAR (Coalition for . . .) under threat of a suit by the animal liberation group AFAAR, which ironically pursues alternatives in scientific education and research. In addition to letter writing and public talks, CFAAR held a "Celebration of Life and Health Day" in April 1988, the same day as an animal rights protest. Within a year, CFAAR had 350 members, making it the second largest campus group. Chapters began to form at universities around the country.[51]

The California Biomedical Research Association (CBRA) formed in April 1983, the same time as the first Lab Animals Week. By then, several universities already saw animal rights as a controversy that would not be quickly resolved. Rather than dealing with each issue in an ad hoc way, it made sense to pool resources. From its handful of founding members, including Stanford, Berkeley, the University of Southern California, and the Heart Association, CBRA membership has grown to include forty-four research institutions. With a budget of several hundred thousand dollars, it collects and disseminates information, provides public speakers, organizes exhibitions in libraries, and even sponsors a high school essay contest on "Why are animals used in biomedical research?" It avoids political lobbying, even that allowed under tax-exemption rules. It focuses entirely on the use of animals, ignoring—in spite of its name—other issues in biomedical research. Eighteen other states have followed the California example and established organizations to counter the influence of the animal rights movement on public opinion.

At a national level, the Foundation for Biomedical Research (FBR), created in 1979, publicizes the medical results of animal research, lobbies state and federal legislatures, and circulates pamphlets and newsletters. It provides state-level organizations with information and pamphlets, and they in turn help support FBR (for example, CBRA contributed $50,000 in 1988). Playing the same game as animal groups, FBR trots out well-known celebrities such as Helen Hayes, and famous transplant surgeons, such as Michael DeBakey, who display patients aided by research with animal models.

FBR has also entered the battle of emotional images. In early 1989, it produced three glossy and witty posters, also run as newspaper ads. One shows a picture of animal protestors, with a large headline, "Thanks to animal research, they'll be able to protest 20.8 years longer." Another has enlarged photos of diseased tissue showing heart disease, cancer, and AIDS, and a headline "If we stop animal research, who will stop the real killers?" But in a third, full-color poster, FBR hit home with an emotional symbol to match the pained, grotesque animal photographs displayed by activists. A sweet child with a teddy bear peers calmly from her hospital bed: "It's the animals you don't see that really helped her recover."[52] In a similar vein, FBR has produced a videotape entitled, "Will I Be All Right Doctor?" featuring children whose lives have been saved with techniques developed through animal studies.

There is nothing that can match a living symbol. Biomedical societies have helped organize chapters of a group called the Incurably Ill for Animal Research (iiFAR) which now has over twenty chapters and several thousand members, perhaps 15 percent of them scientists. This group brings wheelchair-bound patients to public hearings. Like Stanford's heart recipients and NYU's sick child, iiFAR's members symbolize medical progress as effectively as animals symbolize its abuses. But iiFAR can convey more eloquent messages, for its representatives speak human languages.

Protests have broadly affected scientific practices, the awareness of scientists, and the costs of research; but only rarely have they actually stopped experiments. In 1985, Senator Robert Dole successfully sponsored amendments to the Animal Welfare Act, tightening the standards for the care of lab animals. And after the University of Pennsylvania publicity, NIH emphasized that responsibility for proper animal care must rest with universities. Along with the U.S. Public Health Service, NIH requires Animal Care and Use Committees to evaluate the necessity of proposed experiments and the humaneness of the research design, and to monitor the treatment of animals once the project is funded. They also provide training and advice about animal handling, anesthesia, painkillers, and euthanasia. The committees must include a nonscientist not affiliated with the institution, and in a few cases this has been an animal rights activist.

Scientific research has grown more costly. Some of the increase, caused directly by the protests, has little effect on animal care, as delays, equipment replacement costs, and security measures do not change the research itself. Delays in construction of the animal research facility at Stanford, for instance, cost the university about

$1.3 million. Other labs, besides reinforcing locks and barriers, hire security consultants, employ full-time security guards, and require employees to wear badges to control access. Security advisors have recommended that laboratories do psychological tests and background checks on the work histories and even on the private lives of potential employees. Vegetarians are especially suspect.[53]

Other new costs reflect the regulations intended to improve laboratory conditions and both the physical and "psychological well-being" of research animals. The University of Maryland claims that meeting such regulations cost $1.1 million initially and $50,000 each year. One researcher observed that the annual cost of meeting regulations was enough to support two graduate students and one post-doctoral fellow just at a time when the number of fellowships was declining: "Instead, it is going to the dogs."[54] While hardly embracing animal rights demands to abolish all use of animals, scientists have significantly reduced the number they use.

Animal rights fundamentalists reject regulation as the solution, for it does little toward abolishing animal use. When Senator Dole proposed his amendments to the Animal Welfare Act, most animal protection groups actively supported the bill, but the Society Against Vivisection from California contended that: "Those who are for the 'regulation' of animal experimentation either don't understand what vivisection is all about or worse yet, have a vested interest in keeping it going while pretending that they care." They argued that the Dole bill would in the end "permit the torture of even more innocent animals."[55]

Some activists contend that the Animal Welfare Act is poorly enforced, and that Institutional Animal Care and Use Committees are composed of scientists biased toward the research: "The foxes guard the chickens." They are "rubber stamp committees" that simply approve each other's proposals. During the many demonstrations and legal actions against California laboratories in 1987 and 1988, activists demanded that representatives of animal rights groups have unscheduled access to research facilities and participate in the meetings to plan animal experiments. "We want to make the universities accountable to the public."[56]

Andrew Rowan argues that "critics should see what is going on in the committees," for he feels they would be reassured.[57] Most committee members take their role very seriously, questioning procedures in detail and reducing the use of animals in the research projects they examine. Mostly scientists themselves, they can say what anesthetics or painkillers can be used without interfering with test results, or what mice are inappropriate for certain tests. Rowan, along with many others who have served on such committees, feel that there have been significant reforms in institutional practices.[58]

One effect of the movement has been to increase scientists'— especially younger scientists'—awareness of the suffering of their research subjects. Some laboratories train scientists in humane laboratory techniques. Bioethicist Arthur Caplan perceives "changes in the mindset of the research community with respect to the use of animals. . . . Many bench scientists have begun to think that they have a strong obligation to assure competent handling of their animals."[59]

Endocrinologists at the University of Houston have devised high technology radio monitors to use on monkeys in place of restraining chairs. At the University of California at San Diego, a scientist designed stainless steel tanks simulating a pond for a colony of frogs. A reporter described this locale as a "small-scale Malibu," with a deep-water swimming tank, a sunning beach, and live crickets—"the T-bone steak to amphibian gourmets."[60]

Sociologist Arnold Arluke has argued that research scientists have retained the traditional dualistic attitudes toward animals, treating their animal subjects both as beings to be nurtured and as resources to be exploited.[61] Pressure from the animal rights movement appears to be shifting this balance, resulting in fewer abuses of lab animals. There has also been renewed debate over the validity of much animal research,[62] and an increasing number of articles on improving animal welfare appear in scientific journals.[63]

Within the movement, the issue of animal experimentation has exacerbated tensions between fundamentalists and pragmatists. In 1986, John McArdle, HSUS Director of laboratory animal welfare, pointed to the radicalization of moderate protectionist groups: "The HSUS is definitely shifting in the direction of animal rights faster than anyone would realize from our literature."[64] He explained that the official position of HSUS was more tempered because the abolitionist demands implied by the notion of rights were too uncompromising to appeal to many HSUS constituents, especially its wealthy patrons. HSUS president John Hoyt soon dismissed McArdle, claiming that McArdle's statements reflected personal opinion, not organizational policy: "The HSUS is not an anti-vivisection society. We accept as inevitable some laboratory use of animals, given science's historical reliance on animals and its current state of knowledge."[65]

In contrast, fundamentalists such as Tom Regan want abolition of all research: "In reforming child labor people would say, 'Okay, not fourteen hours, but ten hours,' when in fact, what was needed was to abolish the whole practice. The modern movement is abolitionist."[66] This stance encourages an extremely defensive reaction by scientists, who then portray the movement as Luddites and terrorists. Extreme positions encourage like responses.

As with substance testing, pragmatists in the animal rights movement have had a significant impact on the practice of science through negotiation and legislation. Fundamentalists have drawn media attention through their shocking images and dramatic events, but their unwillingness to negotiate over reforms has left them little to show for their efforts. The fundamentalist position on science has been especially controversial; for the public, while ambivalent about science, ultimately perceives links between vivisection, scientific progress, and improved public health. Thus abolition, unlike reform, seems to directly pit human interests against those of animals, and few are willing to accept the extreme implications of this position. In unequivocally attacking all animal research, the fundamentalists have stepped beyond common moral intuitions, so that this remains the most sensitive and polarizing issue in the animal rights controversy. As a result, many rights groups, although still seeking the abolition of research, have shifted much of their attention to issues they hope will be less difficult.

TEN

Animals as Commodities

The day after Thanksgiving, the heaviest shopping day of the year, is "Fur-Free Friday" in many cities throughout the country. Trans-Species Unlimited promoted the first Fur-Free Friday in New York and twenty other cities in 1985 with the slogan, "If you don't want to see animals trapped, gassed, strangled, or electrocuted, don't wear fur." By 1990, Fur-Free Friday demonstrations targeted selected fur stores and played on consumer conscience in 101 cities. Christmas shoppers entering department stores and fur boutiques passed hundreds of activists carrying posters with such slogans as "Trapped by Greed," "It took 50 mother minks to make mother's fur coat," "How would you feel if I wore the skin on your back?" and "These babies miss their mother: is she on your back?"

In a parallel moral mission, the Farm Animal Reform Movement takes its cue from antismoking campaigns and sponsors an annual Great American Meat-out, intended to alert people to the destructive impact of factory farming practices on animal welfare, natural resources, and human health. The event includes information tables (called "steak-outs") at shopping centers, neighborhood festivals, and exhibits. Its targets are factory farms that involve "the confinement, crowding, deprivation, mutilation, and other gross abuse and slaughter of nearly six billion feeling, innocent animals," but also consumers, who are urged to sign a meat-out pledge: "I pledge to kick the meat habit on March 20th (first day of Spring), and to explore a less violent, more wholesome diet."

In 1990, Tim Carter participated enthusiastically in both events.[1] Raised in a wealthy section of the suburban sprawl of northern New Jersey, he now lives in the less affluent but gentrifying town of Hoboken, across the Hudson from Manhattan. He became active in environmental groups—especially those involved in recycling efforts—when he went to college in the mid-1970s, and has remained engaged ever since. His work programming computers allows him to devote five to ten hours each week to protests and volunteer activities. By 1990, he had belonged to Trans-Species Unlimited for two years, convinced of the links between animal rights and ecology. He is critical of fundamentalist rhetoric in animal rights, and hopes for more coalition building.

Furs and factory farming were his main animal issues. A vegetarian since the 1970s for environmental reasons, he sees these issues as linking animal rights and environmental concerns. He views meat-eating as a waste of water, grain, and land—a poor way to get protein (he speaks in bare utilitarian terms, as though humans were input-output machines). Trapping is an abomination, although fur ranching is not much better. He also despises fur coats out of disgust with the conspicuous consumption of the rich. He has no pets, which he feels only farmers should have.

Activists like Tim are increasingly turning their attention to the mass production of animals as commodities—fur coats and T-bone steaks—believed to be frivolous, immoral, and unnecessary. Factory farming and fur companies represent "Big Industry," and these issues tend to join fundamentalists, pragmatists, and sometimes welfarists in common cause. While some pragmatists have doubts about abolishing all animal experimentation in biomedical research, none support the use of animals for furs. And while many welfarists are not vegetarians, they generally join rights activists (almost all of whom are vegetarians) in opposing the cruelty in factory farms.

Neither issue is new: protests against conditions in the transport and slaughter of farm animals began with the nineteenth-century efforts of several groups appalled by the suffering and unnecessary wastage of animals. The fur trade galvanized the attention of the Fund for Animals in the early 1970s because of concerns about the cruelty of trapping. In recent years, however, the rhetoric of activists opposing the fur and food industries' use of animals has expanded beyond the question of cruelty to include a moral critique of the materialism of a consumer society and a political critique of an economic system that encourages profits at the expense of animals. Activists simultaneously target the suppliers of food and furs and the consumers who demand them.

Many pragmatists seek regulation of the production of fur and meat, hoping through these reforms to make life better for the animals used. But a full animal rights platform calls for abolishing all commercial use of animals, and this entails changing the private consumption choices of millions of people. In contrast to substance testing and scientific research, where animals are used in the production of something else (cosmetics, drugs, medical knowledge), factory farming and fur ranching turn animals themselves into the commodity. Cosmetics can be made without the use of animals; pork chops cannot. The object then becomes to change consumer taste so that these products are no longer desired. Like so many other moral crusades, the animal rights movement hopes eventually to achieve the moral transformation of society through individual conversions.

In 1906, American humane societies helped to promulgate the so-called twenty-eight-hour law regulating the confinement, feeding, and watering of animals in transit from farms to packing houses, but they failed to win legislation regulating conditions in slaughterhouses. Many European countries had begun to regulate animal slaughter in the late nineteenth century and have continued to develop progressive legislation requiring space, cleanliness, ventilation, and even consideration of animal stress. But it was not until 1958 that the United States, influenced by resurgent animal welfare groups, passed the Humane Slaughter Act requiring that animals be rendered insensible to pain by rapid mechanical, electrical or chemical means before being shackled, hoisted, or cut. This law excluded poultry and kosher-killed animals, and it pertained only to packers who sold their meat to the government. Others were subject to various state laws, effective in twenty-eight states. Thus the continued abuses of factory farming were a natural preoccupation for the new animal protection groups of the 1980s.

Farms themselves have changed in recent decades. In 1964, British writer Ruth Harrison coined the term "Factory Farming" in her book *Animal Machines*.[2] Describing the highly regimented conditions of slaughterhouses and the transport of animals by meat packing companies, she questioned the right of humans to place economic criteria over ethical considerations in the use of animals for food. Efficiency rules today's large farm. Chickens, which Americans consume at the rate of several billion a year, spend their lives in window-less buildings. They are subjected to intense light when they are young, because that stimulates rapid growth. They are kept in increasing darkness later in their seven-week lives, because this reduces their fighting with each other. Their beaks are cut off soon after they are born, so that they will do less damage to each other as they grow and fight. Each broiler chicken has about one half a square foot of space. Laying hens have the same space, but live longer, up to eighteen months, at which time they are sent to be slaughtered. Not just chickens, but pigs, veal calves, turkeys, and most other food animals are confined in small areas, often in darkness. Beef cattle spend their first six months in pastures, but are then shipped to cramped feedlots. These techniques have made American agriculture extremely efficient.

Following Ruth Harrison's and Peter Singer's lead (scientific research and factory farming were the two foci of *Animal Liberation*), both pragmatists and fundamentalists recognized that food production abused and consumed more animals than all other uses combined—several billion a year in the United States. This concern spawned specialized groups such as the Farm Animal Reform Movement (FARM) in 1981, the Food Animal Concerns Trust (FACT) in 1982, and the Humane Farming Association (HFA) in 1984. Some organizations focused on specific animals, such as Chickens Lib and Humans Against Rabbit Exploitation (HARE). Several groups, quixotically, even formed sanctuaries to offer refuge for liberated farm animals. Some vegetarian organizations joined the animal rights cause and conveyed information about the movement in their own literature.

The activities and rhetoric of these groups vary with their moral position. One set of moral arguments plays on compassion: production of animal food involves practices that are unnecessarily painful and therefore immoral. Other arguments derive from utilitarian principles: eating pork chops is a trivial pleasure compared to the profound suffering of those animals. A third kind of argument comes from the belief that animals have rights: it is immoral for humans to use animals—sentient beings—as resources for our own ends. The first position implies reform; the second, reduction; the third, immediate abolition. Animal welfare groups, hoping to reduce the cruelty of existing practices, work for legislative measures to regulate the industry. They seek to expand federal legislation to include poultry and kosher-killed animals, to ban the use of antibiotics in animal feed, to assure adequate space, bedding and ventilation for animals, and to require proper veterinary care.[3] They supply information about factory farming to their constituents, encouraging them to write to legislators.

Those who believe in the rights of animals as sentient beings support modest reforms, but only as a temporary measure, for their ultimate goal is to abolish altogether the production and consumption of meat. These groups have organized demonstrations and boycotts, picketed restaurants on Mother's Day, attacked turkey farms on Thanksgiving, and liberated restaurant lobsters. The ALF has gone further, leaving butchers and slaughterhouses with broken windows and graffiti. Even remote ranches have had water systems broken, fences cut, and equipment damaged.[4]

Both abolitionist and reformist organizations document the immorality of factory farming in brochures and magazines filled with gruesome photographs and ghoulish descriptions of cruelty in slaughterhouses and farms. These documents show contorted hens living their entire lives confined in wire cages so cramped that their toes grow around the wire. They show animals so closely confined that they need antibiotics to stay well. They describe the stressful conditions that cause pecking and cannibalism. Bulls are branded and castrated. Rabbits are "living machines" forced to produce eight to ten litters each year. Animals are crammed into trucks and shipped long distances to packing plants.

To highlight the immorality of industrial practices, the animal rights literature describes animals about to be killed for food or fun in human terms. Easily personified, veal calves are a favorite target of activists. Babies with large eyes, they are separated from their mothers ("yanked from their mothers' sides"), confined in stalls ("crated and tortured"), and kept anemic to produce lighter meat. Even lobsters are anthropomorphized: "They have a long childhood and an awkward adolescence. . . . They flirt. Their pregnancies last nine months and they can live to be over one hundred years old." They also have feelings and scramble frantically to escape the pot, "much the way I suppose I would sound were I popped into a pot and boiled alive."[5] In a story about Lucie, "our pet rooster [sic]," a writer for PETA claims that "All chickens have potential most of us don't know." Lucie has many human qualities; she likes to cuddle, greets her human companion when he gets home, and suffers from "an awkward adolescent rebellion."[6]

Pigs are a frequent subject of endearing articles. Susie is a paper trained piglet; Priscilla a family pet. John Robbins—author of *Diet for a New America,* heir to the Baskin Robbins Ice Cream Company, and the president of Earthsave—eulogizes pigs in "The Joy and Tragedy of Pigs," noting their high IQs, superior problem-solving abilities, and "sophisticated and subtle relationships with their human companions." They are "virtual gourmets who profoundly enjoy their victuals."[7] Capable of training and intelligence, even of being tragic heroes, pigs deserve, in the eyes of activists, to live out rich lives, not to be sliced up as bacon.

Sue Coe, a political artist with a flair for caricature, depicts the political and economic violence of the meat industry in an exhibit of paintings and graphics called "Porkopolis." She depicts the horrors of pork production in what she terms "a visually graphic story of the life of one pig today—from sperm selling, patenting, feeding, through every day of the pig's life, beyond death to profit. It's all in economic terms. It will end up with Wall Street 'making a killing.'"[8] In her paintings, workers blend into the ugly grays and browns of the factories, stripped of dignity just like the animals. Blood—symbol of violence and death—provides the only bright color. Her graphics illustrate an ideological refrain common to the movement.

Animal activists direct their moral outrage primarily against large corporations. Their rhetoric is couched in terms of *we* and *they,* two sides separated by a vast moral chasm. Fur and meat producers are depicted as villains, profiteering without regard to pain, and willing to place economic over moral value. Agribusiness thrives "on the backs of the least empowered groups in our social structure: farm workers, future generations, and, of course, farm animals." Animal activists exploit a long tradition of rhetoric against capitalism and the factory system to link animal rights with other social and political issues like exploitation and deprivation for profit.

A Trans-Species brochure describes "New MacDonald's Farm" as a full-scale factory in which animals are enslaved, becoming machines to produce meat. Having described the human qualities of pigs, John Robbins naturally criticizes "pork production engineers," who treat pigs like "machines." He quotes a trade journal, *Hog Farm Management:* "Forget the pig is an animal. Treat him just like a machine in a factory. Schedule treatment like you would lubrication. Breeding season like the first step in an assembly line. And marketing like the delivery of finished goods."[9] The critique of factory farms, in which machines dominate the production process with no regard for animals, follows Karl Marx's nineteenth-century attack on the

treatment of human labor in factories. Factory life turns living beings—humans or animals—into cogs in a relentless machine.

Anti-meat activists have readily linked their critiques to the politics of agribusiness and the decline of family farms. It is the former
whose mechanized, large-scale production has forced the closure of
many small farms. This image of the big bully who destroys others
accords with the activists' sentiments, and the linkage has brought
moderate animal protectionists—mostly welfarists and some pragmatists—into occasional alliance with small farmers and their organizations. Though clearly not inclined to support the abolition of all
animal breeding and consumption, these farm groups concur with
the moral objections to breeding conditions in large corporate farms.
"I eat meat . . . I don't intend to live on broccoli," writes a guest
editorialist for *Farm Journal*. "Having said that, allow me to say a
good word for animal rightists." As a threat to large livestock breeding, he argues, they will do the average farmer more good than harm.
Some small farmers thus see the movement as supporting their economic objections to the rise of agribusiness. "Which is more a threat
to your independent business as a family livestock farmer: animal
rights or animal megafactories? Think about it." Yet the coalition is
clearly one of convenience, as the farmer characterizes his proposed
allies as "diet dillies, organic nuts, and Bambi lovers."[10]

The alliance with small farmers is evident in debates over the
genetic engineering of farm animals. Agricultural scientists have been
creating transgenic animals: pigs with low cholesterol meat, dairy
cows with high yields, and chickens immune to certain viruses. In
1987, the U.S. Patent Office's decision to allow the patenting of
transgenic animals added a new item to the animal rights agenda.
Activists responded to the decision by anticipating the future horrors
of factory farming as industrial farmers could be expected to exploit
science to fulfill their corporate greed. In a strange alliance, animal
liberationists appeared in public hearings with the National Farmers
Union, the National Farmers Organization, the Coalition to Save the
Family Farm, and the League of Rural Voters—all concerned about
the consequences of genetic engineering for traditional breeding techniques, for continued concentration of the industry, and for the future of family farming. Animal protectionists could now attack animal breeding without seeming to assault that venerable American
symbol, the family farm.

In a 1984 lawsuit against the U.S. Department of Agriculture,
Jeremy Rifkin, a persistent critic of biotechnology, and Michael Fox

of HSUS claimed that genetic breeding practices were creating obese animals with skeletal abnormalities and unable to mate. More than simply cruel, these techniques violated the rights of animals by "robbing them of their unique genetic make up."[11] Genetic engineering has allowed activists to apply their critique of science to factory farming. The Humane Farming Association described "Super Pig No. 6707 was meant to be super fast growing . . . a breakthrough for genetic engineering. He was born with the human growth gene. He turned out a super-cripple. Excessively hairy, lethargic, riddled with arthritis and apparently impotent, he rarely gets up—the wretched product of a science without ethics."[12]

The advocates of genetic engineering see such experiments as eventually leading to genetically lean and disease-resistant animals, providing healthier meat to consumers than the fattier livestock injected with antibiotics that is sold today. However, activists see genetic engineering as an extreme instance of the evils of instrumentalism. The creation and patenting of animals will reduce "the entire animal kingdom of this planet to the lowly status of a commercial commodity, a technological product indistinguishable from electric toasters, automobiles, tennis balls, or any other patented product." HSUS President John Hoyt elaborates: ". . . the patenting of animals reflects a human arrogance towards other living creatures that is contrary to the concept of the inherent sanctity of every unique being. . . . It also reflects a dehumanistic and materialistic attitude towards living beings that precludes a proper regard for their intrinsic nature."[13] For animal rightists, animals must neither be reduced to tools, nor created simply to exist as tools. But for the agricultural industry, supported by the American Medical Association and other health associations, genetic engineering of animals was critical to medical as well as agricultural innovation.

The factory farming campaign also tries to convince businesses to change their practices on the basis of their own self-interest. Just as animal rights groups buttress their critique of animal experiments with technical arguments about their validity, so they gather economic evidence to undermine the assumptions of corporate farming. FACT, for example, compiled data to show that the abolition of factory farming would have no significant effect on the cost of food production, that the cost of raising food animals was essentially the same whether the animals were raised in confinement or in yards. Similarly, a report from the Center for Rural Affairs claims that "free enterprise has little to do with the development of today's gigantic hog factories,"[14] that humane husbandry systems are, in fact, more economical for pork production. The report also claims that humanely raised calves have fewer health problems; 22 percent require veterinary attention compared to 55 percent in the crate system. While admitting that free-range egg production is more costly, FACT says that these eggs are nonetheless in demand because they are tastier and more nutritious. Yet virtually all layer hens are raised in total confinement systems. Although a few farms—especially small ones—see a market for "humane" produce, most have not changed their practices under the onslaught of animal rights criticism.

Implementing the moral vision of animal rights requires raising the consciousness of consumers about the implications of their choices, not simply attacking corporate practices. Since most people do not share animal rights beliefs, effective arguments to change eating habits must be couched in more moderate welfarist and pragmatic language. Activists, trying to arouse feelings of guilt and responsibility toward animals, find cruelty their most effective theme.

Thanksgiving provides an opportunity for reaching consumers ready to roast their turkeys. Is all the torture, simply "to please our palates," worth the price? Lorrie Bauston, who runs a sanctuary for farm animals, organized a turkey adoption campaign, asking people to adopt turkeys to sit at, not on, the Thanksgiving table. Henry Spira's Animal Rights International, moving from cosmetics to factory farming, has placed large ads in newspapers attacking Frank Perdue (the poultry producer who claims his animals live in a "chicken heaven") for "Violence, Mutilation, Electrocution, Greed . . ." "If you're planning to celebrate any of these this Thanksgiving, maybe you should do it with a Perdue Turkey." The ad claims that "Mr Perdue is not really a farmer. His main business is slaughter and marketing." And after describing the disturbing treatment of animals, it goes on to say that "Mr Perdue appears to be equally callous to his workers," with high rates of worker injury.[15]

Thanksgiving is a tough symbolic target, connoting family, companionship, abundance, feasting, and generosity. No other holiday is so associated with a single food, so that renouncing turkey seems to be the rejection of all these positive values. Popular impressions of turkeys do not help, either. Seen as the canniest of birds in the wild, they not only challenge the hunter but place him in a venerable American tradition: Benjamin Franklin had once proposed that this indigenous creature be made the national bird. Such attitudes preclude much sympathy for Spira's efforts and suggest the difficulties of changing deeply rooted consumption habits.

Animal rightists themselves are commonly vegans: strict vegetarians who avoid not just meat but any products from animals. (One commentator was even shocked to learn that animal bones are used to process most sugar.)[16] Vegetarianism is a model of engaged, concerned consumption, precisely the goal of the animal protection movement, so that a natural alliance has formed between these two movements. In its long history, vegetarianism has been associated with spiritual values. The Greek mystic, Pythagoras, argued that brutalizing animals for food jeopardized the spirituality of man, and Eastern mystics have long associated vegetarian diets with a spiritual life. The notion of "Ahimsa" shared by Buddhists, Jainists, and Hindus, rejects the practice of injuring or killing conscious beings, and associates vegetarianism with purity and nonviolence. In a paper reprinted by animal groups, the contemporary Hindu mystic, Sant Darshan Singh, traces out the philosophy underlying these religious traditions: "If we wish to follow the path of nonviolence and love for all creation, then we will adhere to a strict vegetarian diet."[17] Buddhists Concerned for Animals, a San Francisco group, has mobilized those with interests in Buddhism to stop factory farming by encouraging vegetarianism.[18]

Vegetarianism surfaced occasionally in the seventeenth and eighteenth centuries, sometimes linked with the growing enlightened concern about cruelty toward humans and by extension toward animals. Thomas Tryon gave up meat in the 1680s, and a chapter in his book, *The Way to Health,* was called "The voice of the dumb; or the complaints of the Creatures expostulating with Man, touching the cruel Usages they suffer from him."[19] During the nineteenth century, the humanitarian arguments in the vegetarian literature were pervaded by religious messages and a vision of moral living associated with a precapitalist "natural" order. Percy Bysshe Shelley felt that animal food was the root of all evil, a cause of vice. Vegetarianism was natural and pure. Throughout the nineteenth century, small vegetarian communities flourished as utopian experiments in the United States.[20] And Henry Salt, the British grandfather of animal rights, combined the two causes in his Humanitarian League in the late nineteenth century.

Contemporary vegetarianism expanded in the 1960s, along with the growing interest in Eastern philosophy and alternative lifestyles. Estimates of the number of vegetarians in the United States today range from about 6 million to 14 million. Articles in their journals suggest their sympathy and support for the animal rights cause—especially on the issue of factory farming. And they clearly live in accordance with this major animal rights goal.

The campaign against meat brings out the profound gap between the symbolic worlds of animal rightists and most of the rest of society: to animal rightists, eating meat is a form of cannibalism—a compelling argument for those who blur the moral boundaries between humans and other animals, but meaningless for others. As Mary Midgley says, "The symbolism of meat-eating is never neutral. To himself, the meat-eater seems to be eating life. To the vegetarian, he seems to be eating death."[21] Especially in societies where it is scarce, meat connotes prosperity, power, and success. And it is sometimes thought to increase virility. Among affluent people who take prosperity for granted, however, meat eating has little symbolic value. Norbert Elias contrasts contemporary practices of meat-eating with those of medieval courts, where whole animals were carved at the table, and fowl were served with the feathers on: "People in the course of the civilizing process, seek to suppress in themselves every characteristic they feel to be 'animal.' They likewise suppress such characteristics in their food."[22] Vegetarians seem to follow this historical trajectory of increasing disgust when reminded of the animal origins of food, to the point of eliminating it altogether.

Though most people are not vegetarians, many are concerned about the health risks associated with the production and consumption of meat. Factory farming requires animals to be treated with hormones to regulate their growth and antibiotics to control disease, both potentially harmful to consumers. A sign at an animal rights demonstration reads, "Antibiotics for Dinner." Activists present government studies and nutritional guidelines associating a fatty diet with heart disease and cancer. Consider, says a FARM brochure, "that every minute of every hour of every day, three Americans suffer a painful death from meat-induced heart disease, stroke, or cancer." A PETA brochure adds arthritis, osteoporosis, and diabetes. A Trans-Species pamphlet informs its readers that "Each year billions of cows, pigs, and chickens are enslaved in factory farms and their lives are snuffed out to turn their bodies into meat, a product which directly contributes to the destruction of human health." To support these arguments, animal rights publications cite studies indicating that Americans consume more fat than necessary, and offer their readers vegetarian recipes and diet advice. Americans' recent concern for their diet makes them vulnerable to such appeals. A campaign may backfire, however, as when HARE (Humans Against Rabbit Exploitation) predicted that the preoccupation with cholesterol would enhance the appeal of rabbit, a low cholesterol meat. "Bunny burgers" would replace Big Macs. Reformist goals can be traps as well as tactical opportunities.

Food industry representatives have defended existing practices in instrumental terms, as a means to maintain low consumer prices. They scorn the movement's anthropomorphic view of animals as nonscientific. While activists see similarities between animals and humans, farmers see rigid boundaries, and freely treat animals like machines.

Yet the meat and food industry has inadvertently contributed to the anthropomorphic intuitions that drive animal protection demands. At least since Charlie the Tuna, food commercials have thoroughly personified their own products. In one commercial, two anthropomorphic cows shoot at a Lea and Perrins bottle, "the steak sauce only a cow could hate." The only speaking parts in an ad for Roy Rogers' chicken club sandwich belong to two fast-talking goldfish. Talking chickens, fish, and other animals seem clever, but they also remind sensitive viewers of the origins of their food.

A large majority of Americans eat meat, and so far, they do not seem inclined to change their habits. Animal activists believe that mass conversion to vegetarianism would mark the ultimate success of their crusade. But neither their appeals to compassion nor their critiques of industrial practices have had much influence on consumer taste. Surveys show that American beef consumption has drifted slowly downward from a peak of over ninety pounds per person in 1976 to eighty pounds in 1986. By 1990, consumption was below seventy pounds. However, the shift is certainly due to health concerns more than to animal activism.[23]

The campaign against furs has had far greater impact—especially on the attitudes of consumers. In 1989, a New York City lawyer tells a reporter that she feels "very conflicted" about owning a fur, as her own son tells her she is doing something immoral. A fashion agent has no desire to wear her mink coat, for "it's asking for trouble." A travel consultant says she is "a little nervous about walking down a street and being pelted with eggs or paint." A business executive says that when she bought her mink coat it did not occur to her to think about how animals are bred or killed. "Now I am aware of the brutality of trapping an animal, and I would not wear a trapped fur."[24]

Environmentalists and animal protectionists had once attacked the fur industry primarily because of the cruelty involved in trapping wild animals. This view still dominated their discourse in 1979, when the Animal Welfare Institute published and widely distributed an exposé, *Facts on Furs,* that focused on leg-hold traps. But animal rightists equally condemn the ranching of fur animals, which now accounts for roughly 80 percent of furs sold. Although most ranched animals die from gas or lethal injection, critics claim that many foxes are still electrocuted by means of a clip on their lip and a probe in their anus.[25] Such practices are seen as brutal and unwarranted, a blight on civilized society.

Anti-fur activists hurl venom at large fur-ranching operations, linking the cruelty of fur farming to pressures from foreign competition and the need to exploit labor. They attack foreign companies which, using cheap labor, import lower-cost furs into the United States. Targeting Jindo, a Korean fur giant, PETA says: "Behind the colorful culture, tradition, and beauty of Korea lies a hidden world of animal suffering." The goal of this firm, according to PETA, is to "cut fur prices so low that anyone can afford a fur coat. Its secret: low cost Korean 'slave' labor. Its dream: to become 'the McDonalds of fur.'"[26]

In response, the fur industry cannot appeal to public health and safety; at best, it can argue that consumers demand their product. Spokespersons also claim that the way of life of the Inuit and other indigenous peoples depends on money earned from pelts, though this claim is not convincing when most furs are farmed rather than trapped. The industry, acting through its trade association, the Fur Retailers Information Council, has mainly emphasized the violence of the animal protection movement—not surprisingly, since fur retailers claim to be victims of broken windows and ugly graffiti, including anti-Semitic slogans.

Furriers routinely label all animal activists as terrorists. Even the audience at a "Rock Against Fur" concert were "supporting terrorism." When Beauty Without Cruelty published ads with a list of celebrities under the caption, "Say NO to furs—They did," the Fur Retailers Council wrote to each person listed. It implied they were being used by terrorist groups, and warned them to "review the enclosed material recently sent to police chiefs and sheriffs throughout the U.S. calling attention to violence and revenue-producing campaigns that often have very little relationship to animal care."[27] The materials included lists of break-ins and animal thefts. Labeling the movement the "Animal Rights Protection Industry," the Council also provided information on the net worth of various organizations such as Greenpeace and the ASPCA.[28] Both animal rightists and their opponents denounce each other as large, powerful, and ruthless.

Like scientists, furriers and trappers regard animals as resources. In a 1979 commentary on Canada's seal hunt, the Newfoundland minister of mines and energy said, "I see little difference between someone in Florida harvesting oranges and someone in northeast Newfoundland engaging in the seal hunt."[29] The fur industry scoffs at the sentimental view of animal activists. Sometimes the industry even justifies itself by describing animals as evil. The Missouri state government defines a predator—including foxes, bears, bobcats—as "any creature that has beaten you to another creature you wanted for yourself."[30] Then there is the advertisement placed in the *Milwaukee Journal* by Littman's Fur Factory. It argues that, "Animals can be: DANGEROUS: If you are bitten by a rabid animal, you can be killed . . . DESTRUCTIVE: Uncontrolled animals destroy farmers' crops and land, and their dirty hair and droppings can be found in the vegetables you eat . . . DEADLY: Many wild animals are vicious and will attack you and try to kill you . . . DISEASE CARRIERS: Lyme disease spread by deer and other wild animals is causing an epidemic in this country . . . ASK YOUR DOCTOR." Wild animals are such a health menace that, "More than 81,000 farmers in Wisconsin say, 'Bless the people who wear fur and bless the furrier who can take our wild, destructive animals and turn them into something desirable and help us financially.'"[31]

Perhaps because protestors have had little success with ranchers, current anti-fur campaigns are aimed at those who wear furs more than at trappers, making department stores and fur salons the sites of protest. In 1987, Bob Barker, a popular television game show host, publicly refused to participate in a Miss U.S.A. pageant in which the women were to parade out in furs and remove them to reveal swim suits. One prize was to be a fur coat. The following year Barker attracted further media attention at the head of the Fur-Free Friday march in New York; he seemed to encourage demonstrators to spit on passersby wearing furs by saying that this tactic had been effective in changing public attitudes toward fur in Europe. Demonstrations spread gradually: forty cities in 1987, sixty-seven in 1988, ninety-four in 1989; and one hundred-one in 1990. According to organizers, nearly four thousand people marched in New York City in 1989—the largest anti-fur protest in history. Tanned and silver-haired, Bob Barker again led the march, receiving wild applause when he said, "For fur, the price is never right."[32]

Demonstrators have picketed, spray painted, and smashed the windows of fur stores, distributed the names and home addresses of furriers, harassed women by shouting or spitting on them, placed advertisements on subways and city buses, and sponsored fashion shows with the message "Real People Wear Fake Furs" and "Fake People Wear Real Furs." They have organized rock concerts, liberated beavers from fur farms, and held public memorial services for animals killed for furs. Graphic slogans provide effective moral shocks: "Somewhere There Are Animals Missing Their Paws," and "Wear the Bloody Side Out!" Like the anti-meat crusade, anti-fur films and photos dwell on the cruelty and pain inflicted on vulnerable and sensitive beings. A photograph of a rack of pelts is captioned: "A few moments ago, these were live, vulnerable beings capable of fear, happiness, hope, and pain." A sign on a New York City bus encourages empathy by portraying a trapped animal: "Get a Feel for Fur. Slam your hand in a car door." Some activists even oppose the wearing of wool, combining arguments based on pain (sheep may be nicked during shearing or may be cold once shorn) with rights talk (sheep should not be used for human ends).

These images win considerable media attention. Articles in newspapers dwell on the changes in fashion brought about by the animal rights movement. Television programs have shown anti-fur films; the fur protest even became the subject of episodes in *L.A. Law* and *Designing Women,* both of which portrayed the issue as reasonable but the protestors as kooky, suggesting more sympathy for the movement's goals than for its tactics.

Cruelty is key for anti-fur campaigns just as it was for anti-meat efforts. "Wearing their fur is as glamorous as drinking their blood," says a card slipped into the pockets of fur coats on store racks. As in the protest against cosmetic testing, the rhetoric about fur coats often seems to reflect a puritan suspicion that luxury is not only frivolous, it is a sin. The symbolic value of fur coats is far from neutral: some people see wealth, beauty, and warmth; animal activists see "fifty dead animals." The campaign against furs speaks to the social and political aspirations of modern women by linking furs to sexism. Males, some argue, use furs to manipulate women:

The script is crammed with male-developed values: wealth, power, domination, elitism—all in a cocoon of haughty, external beauty. . . . Women's bodies (in particular) have been used throughout history as an enticement to secure power or financial advantage. So why get upset about the latest furriers' campaigns? For one reason: they use beautiful females and the appeal of 'glamour' to block from view the ghastly horror that underpins the fur business.[33]

The article suggests that the fur industry helps to maintain patriarchy, suppressing female virtues of compassion and gentleness.

Arguments to target consumers are reinforced by intimidation. Steve Siegel, formerly of Trans-Species, believed that appeals to compassion were not sufficient to deter fur buyers; consumer harassment was necessary to create sufficient pressures to force change. He told his members: "Let's make wearing a fur coat a miserable experience," something saliva and spray paint do quite effectively. In a newspaper interview, he described his strategy as public embarrassment: "By embarrassing them publicly, we're giving selfish people a selfish reason to stop wearing fur coats, even if they don't give a damn about the animal."[34] At Fur-Free Friday in New York, one placard tried a more modest appeal to self-interest: "Fur Makes You Look Fat."

Furriers launched a multi-million-dollar campaign against the animal protection movement. The movement has had even greater influence in European countries, where fur sales have drastically declined (fur sales have dropped 90 percent in the Netherlands, 75 percent in Britain and Switzerland since the early eighties), and Harrods, once boasting it sold every existing product, has abandoned its sale of fur coats.[35] The industry defends itself as catering to consumer choice and protecting fundamental freedoms. A radio commercial by the fur industry asks the listener to imagine enjoying a steak dinner in a nice restaurant: "Suddenly there's a commotion. People are around your table jostling you. Shouting. Pointing at your steak and screaming that you are a killer."[36] Ads in major newspapers proclaim, "Today fur. Tomorrow Leather. Then wool. Then meat . . ." The American Fur Industry/Fur Information Council of America ends with an appeal to American individualism: "The decision to wear fur is a personal one. We support the freedom of individuals to buy and wear fur. This freedom is not just a fur industry issue—it's everybody's issue."[37] This defense of consumer choice as a fundamental freedom is as close to the high moral ground as the fur industry can come.

Furs are a relatively easy target. Few people wear them, and fashions are flexible (fake furs are now in style). Consumer rights arguments lack strong moral conviction. In addition, fur coat owners are concentrated in the same urban areas as animal rights activists—one-third of United States fur sales occur in New York City alone. No doubt many fur owners have friends involved in animal protection. American fur coat sales, after nearly tripling from 1980 to 1986, have declined slightly in recent years; many of the large furriers have posted losses and several have filed for bankruptcy. Sandy Parker, who edits two fur industry magazines, said in late 1989 that fur prices were at their lowest levels in twenty years.[38] Though furriers blame warm winters and a bad economy for lack of demand, and overproduction for the low price of pelts, animal rightists have clearly had an effect.

Targeting consumers and reforming large companies are very different strategies. Procedures within large factory farms can be made more humane, and, as in the case of cosmetic testing and scientific research, negotiation and appeals to self-interest may effectively produce change. But changing the tastes of individual consumers is more tricky. Some, who share the values of animal rightists, are ripe for conversion. Others simply do not share the sentiments of the animal protection movement and can be reached only by moderate appeals to compassion.

Pragmatic efforts to reform the practices of large corporations are more likely to succeed than is moral outrage. The ALF cannot liberate billions of chickens and hundreds of thousands of hogs; nor can PETA persuade many consumers to become vegetarians on the grounds animals have rights. Thus Spira's pragmatic, negotiating style may be the only one that could improve the conditions of factory farming. Yet to moral extremists negotiation can only compromise their abolitionist goals. While Peter Singer estimates that Spira's quiet efforts to develop alternatives for substance testing have saved millions of animals from pain and suffering, Ingrid Newkirk of PETA criticizes Spira for "hobnobbing in the halls with our enemy."[39]

The campaigns against reducing animals to commodities are still taking shape, and there are many strategic quarrels, but pragmatists as well as fundamentalists believe that in the long run meat eating and fur wearing must end. Even in the reformist strategy of the three R's—Refinement, Reduction, Replacement—reduction and replacement are clearly a move toward vegetarianism, as a way ultimately to replace meat with "beans, tofu, and nuts."[40] Unlike stopping research, changing consumer preferences to stop the commodification of animals raises few dilemmas for activists. It is a goal widely accepted in the animal rights movement. But it is also a goal with revolutionary implications for daily habits that are likely to meet wide-scale resistance and indignation about interference in personal lives.

ELEVEN

Animals
on Display

If activists see furs and cosmetics as consumer frills, then
it follows that they see the use of animals for entertainment as certain
exploitation of life for a trivial purpose. Animals appear in traveling
road shows, rodeos, carnivals and circuses, film and television programs and, of course, zoos. There are jumping frogs and dancing
bears, boxing kangaroos and diving mules. There are cockfights and
dog fights, horse races and dog races, pig chases and turtle races.
Though these events vary in the cruelty imposed on animals, for animal protectionists they are all flagrant abuse because they seem frivolous. Like many moral crusaders, most animal rightists are deadly
serious about their subject, their writing shows little humor, and they
look askance at human pleasures that employ animals. But the response from those who use animals in entertainment is equally vocif-
erous, for they are convinced of their right to do so; and, in the case
of zoos and shows, they defend the public benefits of animals on
display.

It was the "sports" of bear and bull baiting that first mobilized
British humane groups in the nineteenth century. Welfarists still
worry about cruelty to carriage horses (though it is hardly the problem it was in the nineteenth century). However, in recent years, the
exploitation of animals for human enjoyment has also engaged the
more radical animal rights organizations. Indeed, to fundamentalists
in the movement, this use of animals is the most outrageous because
it seems the least necessary.

Animals had been a source of entertainment long before the ancient Romans started to build their numerous circuses as the stage for various animal spectacles. The circus, a circle or ring, was the site of chariot races, trained animal shows, brutal battles between gladiators and animals, and animal sacrifices. In 55 B.C., some 500 lions and leopards were butchered to amuse the public. Roman conquerors had brought these wild animals back from their military expeditions; some were slaughtered in public arenas, others were kept on display as objects of curiosity as well as symbols of power, status, and military domination. In nineteenth-century Europe, animal spectacles—most often zoos—similarly served not only educational purposes but as an endorsement of colonial expansion, visibly displaying the power and prestige of conquering nations and the subservient status of their colonies.

Since the gladiatorial struggles in the Roman arenas, the use of animals in competitive situations—in races or in actual fights—has been a continuous form of entertainment. Animal baiting, dogfights, and cockfights persist in the United States, even when outlawed. Activists are appalled by the cruelty. Richard Avanzina, president of the San Francisco SPCA, wrote a pamphlet denouncing the use of cats, rabbits, and small animals as bait in training pit bulls. He observed that a single pit bull can kill as many as ninety animals while in training. Yet, ironically, whenever the courts have insisted on killing pit bulls that maul people, the same animal advocates object: the problem, they say, lies in the sadism of owners who have trained these gentle animals to attack. Cockfighting is another target, often described as an Hispanic sport, part of the "quest for Machismo," reflecting a "sadistic mentality." It continues despite prohibition in forty-four states. HSUS associates the practice with prostitution, rape, and violence, projecting the view, similar to that of nineteenth-century humane societies, that cruelty to animals causes people to be callous and cruel to each other.

Animal activists oppose racing sports as trivial and cruel. They object to dog racing because of the brutal training of the dogs, and because live animals occasionally still serve (especially when dogs are being trained) as the bait to be chased. Critics add a further lurid dimension, claiming that racing dogs, once retired, may be shipped to medical schools as research subjects. Horse racing is another target, since horses are frequently administered drugs and pain killers to keep them going despite injuries. Animal protectionists question the morality of using animals to satisfy "the craving for parimutuel gambling." Yet despite frequent exposés in their magazines, racing has not yet generated much active protest.[2]

Worse, in the eyes of animal protectionists, are sports that pit humans against animals. As in the case of hunting, such contests are never evenly matched, and are thought to encourage brutal attitudes in the men and women who participate. Live bird shoots, for example, continue in several American states, a kind of gory target practice most often using pigeons or doves. To animal defenders, the only difference between shooting clay pigeons and live birds is the perverse satisfaction of killing a living creature. The shoots take place as part of family outings and picnics, raising questions about the humane education of children, who are often deployed to collect the dead and wounded birds. Because of the link with children, bird shoots are a classic humane society cause. In testifying against an annual Labor Day shoot in Hegins, Pennsylvania, an HSUS spokesman described the "trapper boys":

> . . . local teenagers paid $28 for the day . . . employed a variety of techniques that apparently pass for mercy killing in Hegins. Some trapper boys bent a bird's neck back against its body and squeezed until bones crack, some preferred to repeatedly bash wounded birds against the ground until they succumb, there were boys who broke a bird's neck over the rim of a metal barrel while still others held a bird by the head and swiveled its body until the neck dislocated.[2]

Such activities hardly seem to offer a humane education for the young.

Rodeos are another sporting event in which humans systematically dominate animals, even if the humans themselves often take a beating in the process. One thousand official rodeos occur annually in the United States, primarily in the Western states.[3] Standard programs include bronco riding and even bull riding, calf and steer roping, steer wrestling, and barrel racing. To devotees, rodeos, like hunting, are part of American myth, relics of how the continent was conquered by rugged individuals. Animal protectors counter that it is a past that should stay buried, observing that rodeos feature all the implements of sadism and domination: whips and spurs, leather and branding irons. However, animal rights demonstrations are rare, usually occurring when a rodeo is brought to a large city. There are not many activists in the rodeo belt, and rough-and-ready cowboys respond to protestors differently than do wealthy ladies in fur coats. Indeed, as activists embedded in an urban culture confront these rural practices, they meet a hostile response, and sometimes even religious or patriotic defenses. A rodeo announcer and former cowboy defends his business with the argument that: "I think the Lord put animals on this earth for men."[4] One way to argue against one moral vision is to counter it with another, and to those who believe that the Bible commands the use of animals for human purposes, it is animal rightists who are sinful and destructive of the American way.

Making little headway against American sports, activists have occasionally turned to practices taking place outside the United States. Brian Davies' International Fund for Animal Welfare published a brochure describing brutal practices it claims take place at the more than 2,000 fiestas each year in Spain. Geese, cockerels, and chickens are strung up and beheaded, sometimes from horseback, sometimes by passing boats, even by swimmers. Bulls are slowly tormented and killed by means of poles, thrown bottles, and small knives. In one case, the brochure reports that crowds blow darts at bulls, hoping for a literal "bull's-eye." Pigeons, squirrels, and the occasional kitten or puppy are placed in clay pots and then knocked off tall poles.[5] Because they cannot respond and defend themselves, foreigners can be inflated into symbols of horrendous animal abuse, providing American animal groups with powerful rhetoric for their fundraising.

Many uses of animals for entertainment are less aggressive than animal fights and rodeos. As an example, consider the circus. In 1785, a British stunt rider built an amphitheater in Philadelphia, where he organized the first American circus. Thirty years later, two entrepreneurs set up the first big top—a traveling circus show. Barnum and Bailey formed their three ring circus in 1881. Bought by the Ringling Brothers, it has remained the preeminent American circus, playing today in ninety-two cities before about 12 million people each year. Several dozen smaller circuses also tour the country. Animal shows, featuring trained elephants, lions, and other wild and domestic animals, are a major attraction, and a major target for animal rights groups. While the shows themselves do not feature competition or violence between animals, protectionists find cruelty in the training behind the scenes.[6]

The humane societies led the attack on animal abuse in circuses, largely because of the brutal training thought necessary to make the animals perform. Each year, animal welfare activists follow the circus to assure the proper treatment of animals. Sue Pressman of the HSUS traveled incognito with circuses. Working as a clean-up person, she documented overcrowded conditions, insufficient water supplies, and extensive abuse of animals that perform out of fear of punishment.

In 1984, the ASPCA called for a boycott of Ringling Brothers after it tried to pass off four goats with horns surgically implanted in their skulls as "living unicorns." In Takoma Park, Maryland, the city council voted to ban the Moscow circus because of its abuse of animals. Apparently, one council member had been alerted to problems by the complaints of his fourteen-year-old daughter.[7] In 1987, the Coalition to End Animal Suffering in Experiments (CEASE) made a widely publicized attack on a Ringling Brothers show in Boston. Through heavy leafletting and work with the media, activists painted "The Greatest Show on Earth" as "The Cruelest Show on Earth." The tactics of their protest, however, attracted the most publicity. Dressed as clowns, protestors appeared in front of the circus entrance asking children if they wanted to smoke a reefer. And someone (CEASE denied it was involved) plastered circus advertisements with large stickers saying the circus had been canceled and instructing ticket holders to call a toll-free number for a refund. The number reached a Michigan pig breeding firm, which was soon besieged with phone calls at its own expense.

Local fairs and carnivals have long given away animals as prizes, a practice now under attack because recipients receive animals they may not want or will not care for properly. In 1990, an Arkansas detective complained about ducks being used as prizes at the state fair, for at least one had been tossed off the Ferris wheel, and another drowned in a cup of beer. The fair switched to stuffed bears.[8] Publicity about the fate of circus animals has darkened the traditional perception of the circus as a place of fun and games. Instead, it has become another arena for the struggle over animal rights.

Exposing examples of cruelty to animals, a writer for the *Animals' Agenda* claims the circus has been "caught with its tents down." But, he continues, even if conditions were perfect, and animals were treated royally, the very practice of removing animals from their natural habitat to be exploited for the benefit of humans is morally wrong. His moral outrage is clear as he describes the fate of retired circus animals, sometimes sent to game ranches to be "shot 'on safari'—often at point blank range—by some cholesterol-ridden, slack bellied desk jockey who can then return to brag of his sporting prowess to his wife, kids, and mistress."[9]

As PETA grew and adopted new targets, it turned the rhetoric of rights to animal shows. PETA focused not only on vicious training practices, but on the immorality of using animals at all. In 1989, PETA targeted the Bobby Berosini Show at the Stardust Casino in Las Vegas. Berosini uses orangutans in a popular animal act. That fact itself, PETA writes, is immoral: "At first glance, perhaps, Berosini's act, in which these naturally dignified and intelligent Great Apes make obscene gestures and blow kisses, looks harmless. But surely these Sumatran 'people of the forest' should be entitled to a life of their own, high up in the treetops, unmolested, and far away from the noise, neon lights, and cigarette smoke."[10] Borrowing tactics from its earlier exposés of research laboratories, PETA convinced one of the dancers in the Berosini show to conceal a video camera in the training room to document Berosini's techniques. PETA then used the video to persuade a local judge to issue a constraining order against the animal act on grounds of cruelty. The show was temporarily stopped, and Berosini sued PETA and its collaborators. While PETA's experts insisted there were signs of abuse, inspectors from both the United States Department of Agriculture and the South Nevada Humane Society examined the animals and reported that they looked healthy. Berosini went back on stage, and was awarded $4.2 million for defamation.

Animals must be trained extensively for films as well as for circuses and animal shows. In 1984, former trainer Pat Derby founded the Performing Animal Welfare Society (PAWS) to expose the treatment of entertainment animals and to lobby for change. Reporting on behind-the-scenes practices and eliciting random confessions from animal trainers, PAWS claims that the philosophy of animal training is "beat'em-into-obedience."[11] Organizations call attention to scenes that are especially abusive: kittens dumped into a pie shell in the film "Young Einstein," rats submerged in liquid oxygen in "Abyss," mice decapitated in "Mondo New York," horses tripped in many Westerns. The organizations sponsor letter writing campaigns to film critics, circulate lists of films to be boycotted, and urge their members—if they do see the films—to hiss and heckle during the animal scenes.

Animal rightists' concern does not stop with physical abuse. Feminist writer Carol Adams recounts the case of a stripping chimpanzee named Deena. For one hundred dollars, a person planning a party could hire Deena and her trainer, and the small animal would go through a striptease act. What was appalling to Adams, who links the exploitation of animals to that of women, was that the animal was being stripped of its dignity as well as its clothes. Performing for humans without knowing what it is doing, in an act that would be tawdry if performed by a woman, violates the chimp's inherent worth. No physical cruelty need be involved.[12] Rights cover dignity and liberty as well as simple existence.

Horses have lived in human communities for thousands—perhaps tens of thousands—of years, making them, along with dogs, the most familiar and beloved animals.[13] For some, they symbolize the empathic bond between animals and humans, as horse and rider think and act as one; for others, they represent aristocratic leisure and status, a world of jodhpurs and fox hunts. Their association with cowboys implies adventure, freedom, and individualism; their appearance in "equestrian" statues links them to a nobler form of warfare than that of the atomic age. Horses have also been the primary source of power on farms and for transportation: even today we measure work energy in horsepower. Horses represent not just strength, but strength combined with beauty and grace. In the nostalgia of urban America, we see in horses a reassuringly simple, older way of life, a slower pattern, a rural pace.[14]

More Americans ride horses today (nearly 30 million) than ever before, almost solely for pleasure.[15] In a Mary Robison short story the narrator finds comfort in riding, and says, "I was grateful, because my marriage and most of the rest of me had recently splintered."[16] Horses, like other animals, appeal in part because they offer simple, manageable emotional bonds in a world where relationships between humans are complex and difficult. And, as in the case of pets, American culture has a clear image of how horses should be treated. This makes it especially egregious when they are treated poorly.

Horse-drawn carriages, once a primary means of transportation, are now a tourist attraction in places like midtown Manhattan, where they are a romantic memento of the old city. Winter and summer, the colorful carriages move through Central Park and the heavy traffic in the streets south of the park. The treatment of carriage horses was the issue that had prompted Henry Bergh to form the ASPCA in the 1860s. At that time, the humane societies associated the mistreatment of animals with the poor moral standards of the lower classes who usually drove the carriages. When the animal rights movement renewed their attack on the carriages in the 1980s, activists once again associated cruelty to animals with the dubious morals of the carriage drivers: "They drink and take drugs. They don't take care of their equipment, and they often don't even speak English," complained a guest speaker at one Trans-Species Unlimited meeting.

Activists called media attention to abuses by focusing on particular dramatic incidents. For example, in the summer of 1988, a carriage horse called "Whitey" collapsed from heat exposure.[17] Animal rights groups held a vigil for the horse, using the occasion to attack the whole carriage horse trade. They criticized the extremes of weather in which the horses worked, the fumes from the city streets, the over-taxation of the horses, as well as the general use of horses for an unnecessary—and what activists considered trivial—human pleasure. They launched a campaign to prevent carriages from using New York streets, but in response Mayor Koch vetoed proposed restrictions, suggesting instead that horses wear hats in the sun. A year later, however, the City Council overrode Koch's veto, restricting the hours and routes of the carriages and requiring periodic rests.[18] Rights groups have supported these reforms as better than nothing, though they want to abolish the trade entirely so that horses need never pull carriages.

Carriage horses are only one example of a worldwide industry based on the use of animals for tourism. Burros carry visitors up mountains; camels take them across North African sands. And, of course, hunting and fishing are major tourist lures. The most striking use of animals, though, may be the introduction of dolphins into swimming pools. Since 1985, a handful of such programs have appeared in resort hotels. Although the capture of wild dolphins is carefully regulated, the National Marine Fisheries Service lacks specific rules about this new use of dolphins. Promoters claim that swimming with dolphins is a way to increase public appreciation of the animals, but animal advocates see only the trivial abuse, and are sure that dolphins could not enjoy such play.[19]

Entertainment and education are sometimes hard to distinguish. We watch nature shows and visit zoos to be entertained, but also to learn something about the animals. Animal dissection, intended for education, can be a fascination, satisfying our curiosity to see under the skin of another creature. The subjective line between education and entertainment is an issue for moral debate among animal protectionists.

Objections to animal shows, races, and rides concentrate on cruelty and abuse, and activists can portray crowded cages and brutal treatment to arouse compassion and activate protest. But zoos somehow seem different. Many zoos seek to replicate the natural habitat of animals, and their explicit purpose is to educate as well as entertain. They serve to protect endangered species, to study wildlife diseases, and to give people a chance to increase their appreciation and compassion for animals. And they can be a sanctuary for certain beasts. Most zoos have given up many practices that now appear questionable, such as posed photographs, rides for children, and cramped cages lacking adequate shelter. Although children loved riding the elephants at the Denver Zoo, a zoo official insisted it was a matter of dignity: ". . . the question was this: 'Was this a dignified way to present the elephant?' No, it really was not."[20]

Despite reforms, many animal rights groups vociferously oppose zoos. Michael W. Fox describes his favorite zoo exhibit: a large mirror behind some bars with the caption, "*Homo Sapiens,* a dangerous predatorial tool- and weapon-making primate. Status: endangered by its own doing."[21] Fox and others argue that the educational function of zoos could be better met with documentary films, that zoos do more harm than good because they create diseased and frustrated animals. He describes the behavior of caged animals, for instance their relentless pacing, as neurotically repetitive compulsions resulting from captivity and stress. Other critics attack zoo conditions, finding overcrowded cages, dirty environments, or improper food. Since most zoos are careful about their animals, critics object mainly to the very notion of captivity as intrinsically immoral. Wild animals, they say, have the right to be free. And what happens to the baby animals from children's zoos when they are no longer cute? To animals no longer needed for display? Critics claim they are sold to research laboratories, circuses, or hunting preserves. Better to abolish zoos all together.

Other uses of animals, clearly intended for education, are also controversial. Take that ritual of high school biology classes, the dissection. Six million animals, some live and some pickled in formaldehyde, are dissected in American schools each year, half of them frogs.[22] Animal fundamentalists and pragmatists both argue that dissections are not educationally essential, that there are good alternatives, and that dissections continue only because teachers themselves were trained that way. Like the tuna boycott, protests against dissection have been a children's crusade, primarily involving girls. Teachers and principals often dismiss their objections to dissection as merely squeamish. But once the issue was framed as one of animal rights and publicized by organized groups, the children's objections were taken more seriously. In some cases, classroom practices have changed.

The most famous dispute over dissection involved Jenifer Graham, subject of a CBS television special entitled "Frog Girl." This was the nickname classmates gave her when, in 1987, she sued her California school district for penalizing her for refusing to dissect a frog.[23] Graham wished to use a model instead, but, interestingly, the school said such models would give her an unfair advantage over other students. Apple Computer took up this argument and made a commercial featuring Graham in order to demonstrate the educational advantages of its computer simulation of a frog.[24] Graham's suit was dismissed when the school allowed her to view photographs of a frog dead from natural causes (rather than killed specifically for dissection). Although this was still not satisfactory to the child and her attorneys, her case and her testimony helped persuade the California legislature to rule that students must not be penalized for refusing to dissect animals. Massachusetts has passed a similar law.

The movement against dissection has grown rapidly, with broad results. Supported by PETA, Jenifer Graham's mother now operates a "vivisection hotline" providing information on alternatives to dissection, and she receives over a thousand calls per month. Students have also begun to sue universities for not offering alternatives to dissection in biology courses. Veterinary and medical schools have begun offering substitutes to their students. Of the ninety-two medical schools that have dissection or live experimentation, sixty-one of them provide students alternatives, with 5 percent to 10 percent of students choosing them.[25] Even the annual Westinghouse Science Talent Search for high school students now excludes experiments on live vertebrates.

The use of animals for entertainment involves practices that range from abusive to benign. Yet all these practices have outraged both moderates and extremists in the animal protection movement. Welfarists generate arguments for compassion, pointing to the abuses in training animals and the poor conditions in which show animals work. But fundamentalists insist that animals (these "people of the forest") must be treated with dignity and have lives of their own. Their moral objections are strengthened because entertainment, like furs and cosmetics, appears frivolous and unnecessary. Such practices also reinforce a view, held by some activists, that people are basically callous, brutal, and cruel. Michael W. Fox sees zoos and animal shows as an emblem of capitalist industrial technology. Exploiting such techniques as behavioral monitoring and genetic engineering, public spectacles of performing animals are a ritual enactment of human control over nature. They "serve to perpetuate the righteousness of humankind's domination over animals and nature as well as the myth of human superiority."[26] They reflect, he feels, a desire for power and control. The need for human mastery of the beast and its wild instincts, claims Fox, represents a puritanical fear of our own impulsive nature, of our own "beastly" passions. Similarly, a writer for *Animals' Voice* describes the "horror shows promoting animal slavery," and sees the greatest horror in the fact "that many find nothing wrong with the events."[27] And others express nativist biases by associating such horrors with the uncivilized attitudes of immigrants or the practices of foreigners.

The animal protection movement has drawn attention to some of the abuses that take place in using animals for entertainment, and brought about reforms like alternatives to dissection practices in the schools and improved conditions in circuses and zoos. These successes, however, are due less to an acceptance of animal rights arguments than to the sympathetic individuals who operate zoos, or to the availability of alternatives such as computer-aided advances in science education. The movement has had the least effect where the use of animals is deeply rooted in popular tradition and nonurban culture. Races and rodeos are supported by people who are deeply resistant to change. Their moral sentiments, often buttressed by various Christian theologies, do not lead them to anthropomorphize animals very readily. popular events such as circuses are unlikely to give up their animal shows, for these are viewed as central to their audience appeal. And zoos, with their many educational and protective as well as entertainment purposes, are willing to improve conditions, but they are unlikely to close. Some uses of animals have potential educational benefits; some are tenaciously rooted in local traditions; others are broadly popular with many Americans. By refusing to consider such differences, the movement frustrates popular understanding and limits its own public support.

TWELVE

The Limits of a Moral Crusade

In June 1990, almost 30,000 activists came to Washington, D.C. to participate in a "March For the Animals." It was the first united mobilization of the animal rights movement, and its largest rally, attracting people from across the United States. Both militant and moderate animal rights groups were represented at the demonstration, and the leading animal rights activists were there: Peter Singer, Tom Regan, Ingrid Newkirk, George Cave, Alex Pacheco, and Michael Fox.[1] Their speeches, conveying a strong anticorporate message, denounced "corporate oligopolies" and the "big business interests of vivisection." It was the "S & L rascals" who should be put into cages. Feminists also spoke to the crowd, observing the sympathy of women who "know it is not a very comfortable thing to be a piece of meat." Responding to government officials who had labeled animal rights tactics "terrorist," many demonstrators wore paper badges boasting: "I am an animal rights terrorist."

After a series of speakers had celebrated "the decade of animal rights," actor Christopher Reeve addressed the crowd, urging moderation rather than confrontation. This, he advised, was strategically wise for changing public opinion and affecting public policy: "The worst thing that can happen to you is to be identified as the fringe." The audience booed him off the stage. Engaged in a moral crusade, the animal rights activists were certain they knew good and evil. They were hardly inclined to accept advice for moderation.

The animal protection movement, staid promoter of compassion for more than a century, had been radicalized in less than two decades. In the late 1970s, in the wake of a series of social and political protests all directed toward extending the concept of rights, new animal rights groups such as the Fund for Animals began to form—with more inclusive demands than those of the welfare tradition. Their goals were to reform the widespread institutional uses of animals for food, testing, dress, entertainment, and research. Some groups, such as the American Fund for Alternatives to Animal Research and the Scientists' Center for Animal Welfare, were founded in the late 1970s to rethink laboratory procedures. The actions of this period, such as the protests against the Museum of Natural History and the companies using the Draize test, went after institutional practices rather than individual aberrations.

At first, the events of the 1970s seemed to be only the latest of the welfare movement's occasional bursts of activism since World War II. They drew on the same social practices and moral intuitions driving the compassionate tradition: the increasingly urban life which provided few contacts with animals except as pets, the neutralization and romanticization of nature, the emotional intensity of domesticity and family life, and the resulting anthropomorphic sentimentalization of pets and other animals. But the resurgent activities also reflected a new set of social forces and ideas. Peter Singer's critique of scientific research resonated with a growing ambivalence, even skepticism, about increasingly complex and sophisticated developments in science and technology that created potential risks or that appeared to be morally questionable. It captured a widespread disaffection with the growing influence of professional expertise and the domination of modern life by large bureaucratic organizations. The 1970s had seen many public controversies—over nuclear power, recombinant DNA research, the teaching of evolution, and research on the human fetus—all reflecting the public's ambivalence towards science and technology. The critiques of animal research picked up many of the same themes.

Similarly, Singer's attacks on factory farming captured the growing concerns about instrumentalism and consumerism. He targeted the concentration of agribusiness which had changed the face of rural America. And he warned against the dangers of animals raised on antibiotics in crowded conditions—profitable for companies but a risk to consumers. Calling for major institutional changes, Singer provided a powerful ideology for the new animal protection groups.

Though revitalized by a current and dynamic ideology, the groups that formed in the 1970s continued to appeal primarily to popular sympathies for animals and to pragmatic, reformist strategies of dialogue and compromise. Through negotiation, these pragmatic groups succeeded in winning many reforms in the use of animals by strategically targeting large organizations, such as cosmetic companies, which had sufficient resources and incentives to change their practices.

However, in the early 1980s, new groups such as PETA and Trans-Species Unlimited began to form, committed to the belief that there are no significant boundaries between humans and other animals, so that animals deserve extensive rights and should never be used as instruments for human goals. Militant in their moral convictions, these groups skillfully adopted the radical strategies of Greenpeace, one of the more militant environmental organizations that combined memorable direct actions with extensive fundraising through direct mail. Attracting media attention with their unconventional demonstrations, these radical groups came to dominate the ideas of the emerging animal rights movement, and to capture its sympathizers. Their orientation and organization began to affect the rhetoric and goals of the pragmatic organizations that had formed in the 1970s, and even affected the traditional welfare groups.

The radicals' broad, uncompromising vision and dramatic strategies have found an enthusiastic following. Unlike the extremists in most social movements, they have been successful as fundraisers. Their sense of urgency, their direct actions, and their radical demands have held considerable appeal to many members of the older humane societies like the HSUS. These were people who had become frustrated with the limits of normal political channels, and felt that years of legislative lobbying had yielded only minimal advances in animal protection. Their societies have had to adopt aspects of the new fundamentalist rhetoric in order to maintain the commitment of their contributors. Because of the renewed attention to animal protection, the more pragmatic animal protection groups also gained ground in their negotiations; in some cases their targets responded out of fear of direct action or negative public opinion. However, the pragmatists were less successful in their direct mail campaigns than were the fundamentalist groups, driven by their sense of moral mission.

The broad appeal of these animal rights groups rests on the deep emotional resonance animals have for many people. With their rich symbolic associations, animals can easily become lightning rods for a variety of political causes and moral issues. This fact may help to explain the animal protection movement's remarkable growth and radicalization in the last decade. The organizations of the 1980s attracted people with strong convictions about the value of animals and, at the same time, grave suspicions about society's major institutions. Their leaders have linked philosophical arguments about the exploitation of animals to prevailing social concerns: the mistrust of science and medicine, the disaffection with big business and commodity culture, the disillusionment with bureaucracy and expertise, and the resistance to domination so important in feminist critiques. These issues have shaped the movement's rhetoric and its choice of targets. The campaign against factory farming plays on specific concerns about the health effects of cholesterol and residual antibiotics in meat. The campaign against vivisection builds on ambivalence about the American medical establishment and its preference for costly technologies rather than prevention of disease. The attack on furs and cosmetic testing captures cynicism about consumerism as well as social class resentment against the small fraction of the population who can afford fur coats.

Because of its wide social, political, and cultural references, and the emotional currency from the multi-layered meaning of animals in the lives of contemporary urban dwellers, the movement has attracted the support of people not often allied in concern and activism. Young punks dressed in voguish black demonstrate alongside the elderly matron with a poodle; conservatives (common in animal welfare organizations) march next to radical feminists. For all these men and women, animals are an important part of their social and environmental community.

For some, however, the animal rights cause involves a turning away from the increasingly visible problems of American urban life. The slashing of funds for public housing and welfare subsidies in the 1980s created problems in American cities that often appear intractable. Although movement leaders argue that the degradation of humans and of animals is linked, providing sanctuaries for animals seems simpler than providing for the homeless and the poor. Moreover, some people identify more easily with animals in distress than with troubled people. With their vulnerability and dependence on humans and unquestioning gratitude, animals needing help inspire some people to bold rhetoric and extreme actions.

The moral language of rights has helped to radicalize animal protection. Because rights are dichotomous—one either has full rights or none at all—the very concept establishes a broad moral imperative.

Applying the concept of rights to animals generated demands for the abolition of all uses of animals, increasingly disruptive tactics, and the inclusion of more and more species in the animal rights agenda. Although the movement's philosophers distinguish between species more or less deserving of protection, the crusade itself continually pushes beyond any such limits.

But the fundamentalist impulse of the movement, its absolutist and uncompromising position, runs the risk of going too far, losing contact with the very sentiments that inspired its rapid growth. Most Americans sympathize with some relaxing of the strict boundaries between humans and other species, especially in the case of dogs and cats, but they resist when activists deny any relevant distinctions between species. Bees, snakes, and banana slugs simply do not arouse much compassion. And potential supporters of animal rights are especially alienated when activists deny moral distinctions between human and animal life by rhetorically comparing Holocaust victims to chickens, or Downs Syndrome children to chimps.

The animal rights movement also appears to outdistance popular sentiment when it fails to distinguish between domestic and wild animals. Asserting that all animals have inherent rights, many activists "would return domestic animals to their wild origins, free to pursue their destinies without human interference."[2] But this defies common sense, for domestic animals are tamed and bred to live with humans, and are inevitably dependent on human care. What, indeed, would dachshunds and dairy cows do if left to their own devices? The animal rights movement might be more effective if it embraced the environmentalist perspective on animals in the wild, and focused solely on helping domestic ones.

The movement goes beyond common understanding when it fails to distinguish different abuses and uses of animals, some abuses being more cruel than others, some uses having more obvious benefits for people than others. Activists criticize the efforts of environmentalists to save a species by thinning out a herd. They dismiss the claim that in zoos and other contexts animals may be useful to people while not subjected to pain. And they reject the human benefits of medical research and education as a justification for the use of animals. Yet most Americans are willing to sacrifice animal lives to gain these benefits.

Some people question the priorities of those who organize to help animals rather than needy humans. Not only do they ask if activists care as much for people as for animals; they also wonder why, with so many problems in our society, animals should come first. Many observers see deep ironies in the funding of opulent animal sanctuaries while so many people live on the street, insisting that homeless humans should be attended before homeless dogs. Animal protection groups respond that human suffering and animal suffering have common sources. Rather than diverting attention from pressing human problems, they feel that they are raising fundamental questions about American society.

To those who blur the boundaries of humans and animals, the issues of human and animal rights are connected. But others are appalled when animal rightists draw comparisons between human and animal suffering, believing such comparisons denigrate human beings. A scientist, speaking at a news conference, expressed a common view of such comparisons. Displaying an animal rights poster that portrayed a chained slave and a restrained dog as if they represented the same problem, he remarked: "If we blur the distinction between humans and animals, we begin to lose some of our moral sensitivity about human rights."[3]

The extreme tactics of some animal rights activists violate the political tastes of many Americans. The tactics of moral urgency include not merely civil disobedience but laboratory break-ins, vandalism, threats of personal violence, and the liberation of animals. For those who see the exploitation of animals as inherently outrageous, such tactics seem appropriate, even necessary. Yet most Americans hold private property as inviolable. Other recent social movements, even while encouraging civil disobedience, have dissuaded their members from sabotage and property destruction. But because protest movements are loose collections of diverse organizations and individuals, they cannot always control the face they present to the public. The leaders of many animal rights groups are anxious to distance themselves from the actions of the ALF, fearing that destruction and the threat of violence will undermine the credibility of the movement and provide ammunition to critics who wish to paint animal protectionists as terrorists. Many leaders condemn and would like to suppress the anti-Semitic, racist, and xenophobic sentiments that certain individual members openly express in the hate mail they send to researchers and other targets. They see the potential backlash arising from such ugly feelings. Yet the statements of the most radical activists, in fact, encourage misanthropic expressions. And the badges worn by marchers at the June demonstration suggest that many activists are pleased to be labeled "terrorists." At its extreme, animal rights fundamentalism encourages intolerance and tactics of violence and intimidation.

Radical strategies and extreme demands have undeniably put animal protection on the political agenda, capturing media attention, spurring extensive public debate about the treatment of animals, and recruiting new members to the cause. Though often extending beyond accepted sentiments, fundamentalist tendencies have changed the orientation of the whole animal protection movement. Even welfarists now criticize factory farming, scientific research, and zoos; attacks on substance testing have become central to their fundraising appeals. Through their ability to intimidate, fundamentalists have also strengthened the position of the more moderate activists as they negotiate with institutions to bring about reforms.

In the last ten years, the animal rights movement has had a broad impact on the treatment of animals in many American institutions. In contrast to the humane education efforts of the nineteenth century, recent reforms have occurred primarily in large organizations hidden from public view. Researchers, subject to stricter oversight from animal care and use committees, have improved laboratory conditions, using larger cages, better air circulation, and more careful monitoring of anesthesia to avoid unnecessary pain. Cosmetics companies have reduced or discontinued their use of animals, relying on cell and tissue cultures instead of rabbit's eyes to test their products. School districts offer students alternatives to dissection. Tuna companies use fishing methods that do not harm dolphins. Zoos have eliminated many practices that are undignified or may cause harm to animals.

Some changes would perhaps have occurred in any case. The increasing cost of some research animals was limiting their use in the laboratory. The series of warm winters in the late 1980s was inevitably hurting the sales of fur coats. But animal rightists have been a critical factor in the changing use of animals, especially when they have succeeded in influencing public opinion. The extent of public support for animal rights causes has been suggested by various state and local referenda. A 1988 initiative in Massachusetts asked voters to ban several painful factory farming practices, including the confinement of veal calves in crates. In 1990, the question of banning fur sales was put to the voters of Aspen, Colorado. In both cases, animal rightist lost the referenda, but they managed to win one-third of the vote, despite heavy media campaigning by the meat and fur industries.[4] These initiatives as well as public attitude surveys suggest there is a large minority supporting animal protection measures.

Nevertheless the movement, even when supported by moralistic rhetoric, has had only limited influence on the routine behavior and basic preferences of most individuals. As long as they see a link between healthy children and vivisection, most Americans will view animal rightists as essentially misanthropic, valuing animals over people. While many see cosmetic testing as an abuse of animals for frivolous purposes, some fear that this will shift the burden of risk on to consumers. While many Americans are giving up furs, relatively few are willing to give up chicken or meat. Factory farming may well be the central animal rights issue of the 1990s. It will test the honesty of the fundamentalists, who have often gone after easy targets that help them raise funds, rather than after the practice that consumes—by far—the most animals. It will test the ability of pragmatists to negotiate a solution with an industry that is far less image-conscious than cosmetics, and is located, not in urban but in rural areas, where sympathy for animal rights is low. And it will challenge the movement to convert large numbers of people to vegetarianism if they are to go beyond the minor reforms of existing farm practices.

The radicalization of the animal protection movement has had its costs. As in so many other protest movements, stridency, denunciation, and demonization of enemies have often precluded communication, negotiation, and resolution. Historian Robert Wiebe characterized the polarization between populists and their enemies in the 1890s: "In place of communication, antagonists confronted each other behind sets of stereotypes, frozen images that were specifically intended to exclude discussion. Reinforcing the faithful's feeling of separateness, the rhetoric of antithetical absolutes denied even the desirability of any interchange."[5] Similar dynamics characterize the animal rights controversy today.

To animal rights activists, those who exploit animals are brutal, cruel, and self-serving torturers; to the targeted groups, the animal rightists are ignorant fanatics, fascist in their sweeping demands. Each side portrays the other as wealthy, powerful, and dangerous. Each side relies on emotional visual appeals, and accuses the other of cheap emotionalism and surreptitious infiltration. There are moderates on both sides of the animal protection debate. But they are usually ignored, as the extremists, driven by fundamentalist visions, become the most visible actors in the controversy.

Political philosophers often write about democracy as a kind of conversation among those who disagree, yet in the modern world disagreements are often stark. Alasdair MacIntyre has argued that Western societies have lost the ability to ground moral arguments in convincing ways that elicit consensus.[6] Debates like those over nuclear power, equal opportunity, abortion, and animal rights go on and on without resolution, for there are no moral principles acceptable to all. Disturbed by moral relativism, political activists are continually tempted to retreat to fundamentalism, reifying their own principles as ultimate Truth. Most often they rely on religion—in movements as diverse as the Moral Majority, creationism, and the worldwide resurgence of Islamic fundamentalism. Yet even secular movements find it convenient to insist on a particular truth: that abortion is murder, that corporations are evil, that America is inherently racist or patriarchal.

Such certainties are reassuring to those who hold them. Amidst the moral confusions of contemporary culture, animal rightists offer a clear position based on a set of compelling principles. They offer moral engagement and commitment in a secular society with few opportunities to sort out one's values, appealing especially to those who reject organized religion as a source of moral tenets. Animals are a perfect outlet for moral impulses, for—unlike people—they seem incapable of duplicity, infidelity, or betrayal. Like children, they are innocent victims, unable to fight for their own interests. Thus, protecting animals sometimes inspires the shrill tone, the sense of urgency, and the single-minded obsession of a fundamentalist crusade. Its members become missionaries, defining the world in terms of the treatment of animals. They see the world as good or evil, and the villain—the person who exploits animals—becomes a model of malice. The animal rights literature is obsessed with sadistic details that purge the enemy of every admirable quality. Seeking conversions, special significance is attached to the renegade from the enemy camp—the scientist who defects from "scientism," the person who converts to the cause. Convinced of the truth of their moral mission, many animal rights activists feel justified in using radical tactics as well as revolutionary rhetoric to serve their cause of abolishing all animal exploitation. Ironically, fundamentalists in the movement elevate animals from the status of means to that of ends, but reduce their enemies from the status of rational actors to be persuaded through argument to that of objects to be manipulated and bullied.

Extreme stances can effectively call attention to an issue and achieve quick results. But in the long run, radical positions may be counterproductive. Fundamentalist tactics undermine the ability to engage those with competing visions in the democratic conversation necessary to develop acceptable policies. Strident rhetoric—designed to appeal to direct mail constituents—precludes dialogue with opponents, who tend to respond with matching fervor. Moralistic positions thus polarize debate.

Animal rights is but one of many controversies that have grown out of a clash of basic moral values, of competing world views. Unlike conflicts based on interests, such controversies cannot be fully resolved. Yet, raising basic questions that reflect widespread social and political concerns, moral crusades can never be dismissed. To stubbornly defend current practices is to encourage further polarization. To denounce the movement as irrational, kooky, or terrorist is to miss the popular appeal of its moral intuitions and political beliefs. If a solution is possible in such rancorous conflict, it will require good faith from both sides to ensure the dialogue and compromise basic to a democratic conversation.

Appendix

Paperback Sales of Singer's *Animal Liberation,* 1977–1988 (in thousands)

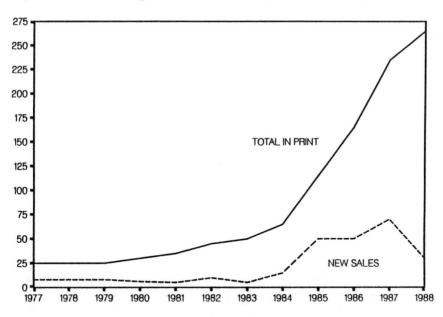

Since almost all animal rights activists have a copy of Peter Singer's book, Animal
Liberation, *its distribution seems a good indicator of the growth of the movement
in the 1970s and 1980s. The graph's top line shows a cumulative total of all copies
in print, while the bottom line shows the number of new copies printed and distributed each year. (We have used the number of copies printed rather than copies sold,
since those figures were more precise.) The take-off in numbers begins in 1985. We
think the numbers began to drop in 1988 because the movement began to slow in
its growth and the publisher stopped printing new copies in anticipation of a new,
revised edition of the book that appeared in 1990.*

Types of Contemporary Animal Protectionists

	Beliefs About Animals	*Major Goals*	*Primary Strategies*
Welfarists	Objects of compassion, deserving of protection. Clear boundaries between species.	Avoid cruelty; limit unwanted animal populations.	Protective legislation, humane education, shelters.
Pragmatists	Deserve moral consideration; balance between human and animal interests. Some hierarchy of animals.	Eliminate all unnecessary suffering; reduce, refine, and replace uses of animals.	Public protests, but pragmatic cooperation, negotiation, and acceptance of short-term compromises.
Fundamentalists	Have absolute moral rights to full lives without human interference. Equal rights across many species.	Total and immediate elimination of all animal exploitation.	Moralist rhetoric and condemnation. Direct action and civil disobedience. Animal sanctuaries.

Notes

Chapter 1   A Moral Crusade (pages 1–10)

1. Quoted in "Animals in Testing. How the CPI Is Handling a Hot Issue," *Chemical Week* 135, 23 (December 5, 1984): 38.
2. Quoted in Richard J. Brenneman, "Animal 'liberator' promises more raids on labs," *Sacramento Bee,* July 2, 1984, p. B1.
3. James Rachels, *Created from Animals* (New York: Oxford University Press, 1990).

Chapter 2   Moral Sentiments (pages 11–25)

1. We use the terms moral sentiments and moral intuitions interchangeably to get at what Raymond Williams called structures of feeling. "Sentiment" hints at feelings and emotions, while "intuition" indicates implicit understandings and assumptions. We believe the emotional and cognitive aspects to be inseparable and equally important.
2. Our phrase is meant to parallel Edward Shorter's discussion of the sentimentalization of the modern family, in *The Making of the Modern Family* (New York: Basic Books, 1975). Viviana Zelizer, *Pricing the Priceless Child* (New York: Basic Books, 1985), describes the parallel process by which children came to be valued independently of their economic potential.
3. From *The Principles of Morals and Legislation,* 1789. Quoted in Tom Regan and Peter Singer, ed., *Animal Rights and Human Obligations* (Englewood Cliffs, N.J.: Prentice-Hall, 1976), 129.
4. "A life . . ." comes from a Philadelphia activist quoted on *48 Hours;* "A rat . . ." from Ingrid Newkirk, as quoted in Katie McCabe, "Who Will Live and Who Will Die?" *Washingtonian,* August 1986, 114; and "it is obvious . . ." from George P. Cave, "Vivisection and Misanthropy," *International Journal for the Study of Animal Problems* 4, 1 (January–March 1983): 22.
5. John Berger, "Why Look At Animals?" in *About Looking* (New York: Pantheon, 1980), 5. Other works on the history of relationships between humans and animals include James A. Serpell, *In the Company of Animals* (New York: Basil

Blackwell, 1986); Andrew N. Rowan, ed., *Animals and People Sharing the World* (Hanover, N.H.: Tufts University/University Press of New England, 1988); R. J. Hoage, ed., *Perceptions of Animals in American Culture* (Washington, D.C.: Smithsonian Institution Press, 1989); Alan M. Beck and Aaron H. Katcher, *Between Pets and People* (New York: Putnam Pub. Group, 1983); Yi-Fu Tuan, *Dominance and Affection: The Making of Pets* (New Haven: Yale University Press, 1984); and Harriet Ritvo, *The Animal Estate* (Cambridge: Harvard University Press, 1987).

6. Gordon M. Burghardt and Harold A. Herzog, Jr., "Beyond Conspecifics: Is Brer Rabbit Our Brother?" *BioScience* 30, 11 (1980): 763–768. The same authors discuss these themes in "Animals, Evolution, and Ethics," in Hoage, *Perceptions of Animals,* 129–151, and in "Attitudes Toward Animals: Origins and Diversity," in Rowan, *Animals and People,* 75–94.

7. The best analyses of these changes include Norbert Elias, *The Civilizing Process,* vol. 1: *The History of Manners* (New York: Pantheon, 1978; first published, 1939); Philippe Ariès, *Centuries of Childhood* (New York: Vintage, 1962); and Yi-Fu Tuan, *Segmented Worlds and Self* (Minneapolis: University of Minnesota Press, 1982).

8. Keith V. Thomas, *Man and the Natural World* (New York: Pantheon, 1983), ch. 3, describes the growing fondness for pets in early modern England. He says, "But it was in the sixteenth and seventeenth centuries that pets seemed to have really established themselves as a normal feature of the middle-class household, especially in the towns, where animals were less likely to be functional necessities and where an increasing number of people could afford to support creatures lacking any productive value," 110. Alan Macfarlane, *The Culture of Capitalism* (Oxford: Blackwell, 1987), ch. 4, claims that England was especially prone to nature worship, since it had conquered its own wild areas much earlier than other countries; with less to fear, the English could see the beauty and interest in animals, plants, and landscapes.

9. Robert Darnton, *The Great Cat Massacre* (New York: Basic Books, 1983), ch. 2.

10. Quoted in Keith Thomas, *Man and the Natural World* (New York: Pantheon, 1983), 173–174.

11. James Rachels, *Created From Animals: The Moral Implications of Darwinism* (Oxford: Oxford University Press, 1990). On the reception of Darwin's ideas, see David L. Hull, *Darwin and His Critics* (Cambridge: Harvard University Press, 1973), and Alvar Ellegård, *Darwin and the General Reader* (Chicago: University of Chicago Press, 1990).

12. Ralph H. Lutts, *The Nature Fakers* (Golden, Colo.: Fulcrum, 1990) provides an account of the outlandish claims made in the United States around 1900 concerning animals in the wild, including beavers' bandaging their own legs, and porcupines rolling down hills to escape predators. Barbara Novak, *Nature and Culture: American Landscape and Painting, 1825–1875* (New York: Oxford University Press, 1980) recounts the growing popularity of landscape painting. Several good sources on the expansion of suburbs in the United States are Kenneth T. Jackson, *Crabgrass Frontier: The Suburbanization of the United States* (New York: Oxford University Press, 1985); Henry C. Binford, *The First Suburbs: Residential Communities on The Boston Periphery, 1815–1860* (Chi-

cago: University of Chicago Press, 1985); Robert Fishman, *Bourgeois Utopias: The Rise and Fall of Suburbia* (New York: Basic Books, 1987); John R. Stilgoe, *Borderland: Origins of the American Suburb, 1820–1939* (New Haven: Yale University Press, 1988). Peter J. Schmitt describes the cult of nature at the turn of the century in *Back to Nature: The Arcadian Myth in Urban America* (New York: Oxford University Press, 1969).

13. On the importance of compassion, family relations, and animals in Victorian Britain and the United States, see F. M. L. Thompson, *The Rise of Respectable Society* (Cambridge: Harvard University Press, 1988); Christopher Lasch, *Haven in a Heartless World* (New York: Basic Books, 1977); Harriet Ritvo, *The Animal Estate* (Cambridge: Harvard University Press, 1987); Ernest S. Turner, *All Heaven in a Rage* (New York: St. Martin's Press, 1964); James Turner, *Reckoning with the Beast* (Baltimore, Md.: Johns Hopkins University Press, 1980).

14. These figures come from the *Statistical Abstract of the United States* (Washington, D.C.: Government Printing Office, 1982–1983). Of these, 26.3 percent lived in places of fewer than 2,500 residents (table 23), and 2.7 percent of those employed were in agriculture (table 648).

15. Dr. Monique Maniet, quoted in "For Fido, Broccoli And Yogurt," *New York Times*, April 16, 1989, p. 47.

16. Stephen Kellert has examined a range of sentimental and utilitarian attitudes toward animals. He presents his findings in "American Attitudes Toward and Knowledge of Animals: An Update," *International Journal for the Study of Animal Problems* 1, 2 (1980): 87–119, and (with Miriam O. Westervelt) in "Historical Trends in American Animal Use and Perception," *International Journal for the Study of Animal Problems* 4, 2 (1983): 133–146. They are also summarized in "Perceptions of Animals in America," in Hoage, *Perceptions of Animals*, 5–24, and "Human-Animal Interactions," in Rowan, *Animals and People*, 137–176. Kellert's work is based primarily on interviews done in 1978 with 3,100 randomly sampled Americans.

17. Jack C. Horn and Jeff Meer, "The Pleasure of Their Company," *Psychology Today*, August 1984, 52–58. Although this was a readers' survey rather than a scientific, randomly sampled poll, the results are comparable to those from other surveys of pet owners.

18. Serpell, *In the Company of Animals*, 23. Marc Shell presents a psychoanalytic interpretation of contemporary pet owning in "The Family Pet," *Representations* 15 (Summer 1986): 121–153. Also see E. K. Rynearson, "Pets as Family Members: An Illustrative Case History," *International Journal of Family Psychiatry* 1, 2 (1980): 263–68.

19. Some of this research is presented in Boris M. Levinson, *Pets and Human Development* (Springfield, Ill.: Charles C. Thomas, 1972); Erika Friedmann et al., "Pet Ownership and Coronary Heart Disease: Patient Survival," *Circulation* 58 (1978): 11–168; Phil Arkow, *"Pet Therapy": A Study of the Use of Companion Animals in Selected Therapies* (Colorado Springs, Colo.: Humane Society of the Pikes Peak Region, 1982); Alan M. Beck and Aaron H. Katcher, *Between Pets and People* (New York: Putnam, 1983); Aaron H. Katcher and Alan M. Beck, eds., *New Perspectives on our Lives with Companion Animals* (Philadelphia: University of Pennsylvania Press, 1983); and the Center to Study Human–

Animal Relationships and Environments, *The Pet Connection: Its Influence on our Health and Quality of Life* (Minneapolis: University of Minnesota Press, 1984).

20. Marian Breland Bailey, "Every Animal Is the Smartest: Intelligence and the Ecological Niche," in a useful collection for the lay reader, R. J. Hoage and Larry Goldman, eds., *Animal Intelligence* (Washington, D.C.: Smithsonian Institution Press, 1986). Also see, Stephen F. Walker, *Animal Thought* (London: Routledge and Kegan Paul, 1983); Donald R. Griffin, *Animal Thinking* (Cambridge: Harvard University Press, 1984); Eugene Linden, *Apes, Men, and Language* (New York: Saturday Review Press, 1974); and *Silent Partners: The Legacy of the Ape Language Experiments* (New York: Times Books, 1986). Animal activists readily promote these works, as in Phil Maggitti, "Animal Thinking," *Animals' Agenda* 10 (April 1990): 24–29, 46.

21. Susan Sperling, *Animal Liberators* (Berkeley, University of California Press, 1988), 165.

22. Interviewed on WXRK radio in New York: April 21, 1990.

23. Amy Hempel, "At the Gates of the Animal Kingdom," in *At the Gates of the Animal Kingdom* (New York: Alfred A. Knopf, 1990), 85–96.

24. Desmond Stewart, "The Limits of Trooghaft," in Tom Regan and Peter Singer, eds., *Animal Rights and Human Obligations,* 2d ed. (Englewood Cliffs, N.J.: Prentice Hall, 1989), 273–280. The editors are two animal rights philosophers who see the importance of extreme anthropomorphism in promulgating pro-animal sentiments.

25. The main exponent of this view is Ronald Inglehart, *The Silent Revolution* (Princeton: Princeton University Press, 1977). While Inglehart's survey questions artificially force respondents to choose between material and postmaterial values, we find his general argument convincing. He has expanded and updated his argument in *Culture Shift in Advanced Industrial Society* (Princeton: Princeton University Press, 1990).

26. Robert J. Levine, *Ethics and Regulation of Clinical Research,* 2d ed. (Baltimore: Urban and Schwarzenberg, 1986).

27. Montye Rivera, "Are Animals Slaves?" (letter) *New Age Journal* (July-August 1989): 10.

28. Hermann Göring, August 28, 1933, in *The Political Testament of Hermann Göring,* arr. and trans. by H. W. Blood-Ryan (New York: A.M.S. Press, 1972), 70–71, 73.

29. William E. Seidelman, "Animal Experiments in Nazi Germany," the *Lancet,* May 24, 1986, p. 1214; see also *Journal of the American Medical Association* 101, 14 (September 30, 1933): 1087.

30. See Larry Horton, "A Look at the Politics of Research With Animals: Regaining Lost Perspective," *The Physiologist* 31, 3 (1988): 41–44, and "The Enduring Animal Issue," *Journal of the National Cancer Institute* 81, 10 (1989): 736. Animal protection responses include Roberta Kalechofsky, "Pro-Vivisection Propaganda and the Nazi Lie," *Animals' Agenda* (July–August 1989): 54; and Merritt Clifton, "Ecology Fakes and Facts," *Animals' Agenda* 10(June 1990): 53. Boria Sax provides a serious analysis of the German context in the early twentieth century in "Abuse of a Good Cause," *Anthrozoös,* forthcoming, which should discourage facile comparisons to the present situation.

31. Yaron Ezrahi, *The Descent of Icarus* (Cambridge: Harvard University Press, 1990), 288.
32. Doug McAdam, *Political Process and the Development of Black Insurgency 1930–1970* (Chicago: University of Chicago Press, 1982), 91. McAdam mentions the importance of urban churches in a discussion that otherwise concentrates on new opportunities for political action. Benjamin Mays and Joseph W. Nicholson, *The Negro's Church* (New York: Arno Press, 1969), and Aldon Morris, *The Origins of the Civil Rights Movement* (New York: Free Press, 1984), also discuss the importance of the urban black churches, although Morris stresses their resources as much as their moral message.
33. On the effects of *Brown,* see Irwin Gerber, "The Effects of the Supreme Court's Desegregation Decision on the Group Cohesion of New York City's Negroes," *Journal of Social Psychology* 58 (1962): 295–303. While Brown was primarily important for giving hope that change was possible, it also encouraged an integrationist moral vision.

Chapter 3   The Birth of a Movement (pages 26–41)

1. Spira, "Fighting to Win," in Peter Singer, ed., *In Defense of Animals* (New York: Harper and Row, 1985), 195, 196. Also Spira, "Fighting for Animal Rights: Issues and Strategies," in Harlan B. Miller and William H. Williams, eds., *Ethics and Animals* (Clifton, N.J.: Humana Press, 1983); Jane Gregory, "Science, and Research: Doing Unto Animals," *Los Angeles Times View,* December 9, 1979; Kevin L. Morrissey, "Henry Spira: An Animal Activist Who Gets Things Done," *Animal Crackers,* Fall 1979; and Jonathan Weiner, "Animal Liberation," *Cosmopolitan,* July 1980. For a comparison of this campaign with battles against Cornell and New York University in the late 1980s, see James M. Jasper, Dorothy Nelkin, and Jane Poulsen, "When Do Social Movements Win? Three Campaigns Against Animal Experiments," Paper presented at the American Sociological Association annual meeting, 1990.
2. Nicholas Wade, "Animal Rights: NIH Cat Sex Study Brings Grief to New York Museum," *Science* 194, October 8, 1976, 162.
3. Henry Spira, "Animals Suffer for Science," *Our Town,* July 1976, 26–27.
4. Nicholas Wade, "Animal Rights: NIH Cat Sex Study Brings Grief to New York Museum," *Science* 194, October 8, 1976, 162.
5. Kevin Morrissey, "Henry Spira," 4.
6. Cited in John F. Burns, "American Museum Pinched for Funds," *New York Times,* February 16, 1976, p. 23.
7. Roger Simon, "Cutting Up Cats to Study Sex—What Fun!" *Chicago Sun Times,* July 25, 1976.
8. Quoted in Jane Gregory, "Science and Research."
9. Spira, "Fighting to Win," 200.
10. Ingrid Newkirk, "One Person's Efforts," *Between the Species* 1, 4 (Fall 1985): 45. On PETA, also see Harry Minetree with Diane Guernsey, "Animal Rights—And Wrongs," *Town and Country,* May 1988, 158–161, 230.
11. Pacheco tells his story in "The Choice of a Lifetime," *Between the Species* 6, 1 (Winter 1990): 36–39.

12. Alex Pacheco with Anna Francione, "The Silver Spring Monkeys," in Peter Singer, ed., *In Defense of Animals,* 136.

13. *PETA Annual Review,* December 1989. According to a reporter, one former accountant has alleged that large donations were never recorded, available for purposes not allowed in PETA's charter, including aiding and perhaps controlling other animal organizations, and paying the legal fees and fine of an ALF member. This unnamed former employee is cited in Katie McCabe, "Beyond Cruelty," *The Washingtonian,* February 1990, pp. 186–187. PETA is suing McCabe for her article, which has been widely distributed by the scientific community.

14. 1989 assets, spending, and salaries for the major animal organizations are reported in Merritt Clifton, "Who Gets the Money?" *Animals' Agenda* 11 (March 1991): 33–35.

15. Entitled "Fact Sheet on PETA."

16. Personal interview, August 1989.

17. Telephone interview, December 1990.

18. Personal interview with Roy Henrickson, August 1989.

19. Personal interview, August 1989.

20. Michael Munzell, "Birth of a Celebration," *San Francisco Focus,* November 1988, p. 68. Katz is also discussed in David Darlington, "Animal Rights (and Wrongs)," *East Bay Express,* October 19, 1984; and Marshall Krantz, "Jewish Activists Pushing Animal Rights," *Northern California Jewish Bulletin* 134, June 14, 1985.

21. Personal interview, August 1989.

22. Personal interview, August 1989.

23. Telephone interview, December 1990.

24. Telephone interview with Elliot Katz, September 1989.

25. Cole McFarland, "Portrait of a 'Terrorist'," *Animals' Voice* 3, 1: 40–41.

26. Quoted in "Animal Rights Violence Skyrockets," *San Francisco Chronicle,* January 4, 1988.

27. Reprinted in Berke Breathed, *The Night of the Mary Kay Commandos* (Boston: Little, Brown and Company, 1989). Breathed managed to spread information about testing through his strips.

28. Joyce S. Tischler, "Rights for Nonhuman Animals: A Guardianship Model for Dogs and Cats," *San Diego Law Review* 14 (1977): 484–506.

29. Personal interview with Joyce Tischler, August 1989. She has also described the history of the ALDF in "Tracing the Birth of an Organization—The Animal Legal Defense Fund," *Mainstream* (Spring 1988): 11, 43. The ALDF also publishes the quarterly *Animals' Advocate.*

30. Telephone interview, March 1991.

31. Our estimates come in part from *Animal Organizations and Services Directory, 1988–1989,* 3d ed., compiled by Kathleen A. Reece (Huntington Beach, Calif: Animal Stories). We have included updates through 8. This is hardly a comprehensive list, and it is biased toward national organizations, but we feel it reasonably indicates the pattern of group formation over time.

32. In early 1990, the Animal Rights Information and Education Service had almost 600 groups on the list it compiles, although not all were rights groups.

33. A private industry survey; the information was provided by Andrew Rowan.

34. So many people in the movement speak of reading Singer's book that it seems a good approximation of movement growth. The appendix provides a chart showing both the total in print and the new copies distributed each year.

35. Andrew Rowan, "The Development of the Animal Protection Movement," *The Journal of NIH Research* 1 (November–December 1989): 97–100.

36. Telephone interview with Scott Van Valkanbeurg, February 1990.

37. We surveyed protestors at a Manhattan rally sponsored by Trans-Species Unlimited on World Laboratory Animal Day, April 1988, against drug addiction experiments being conducted at New York University. This was a nonrandom sample in which 270 protestors out of a crowd of around 1,000 completed surveys. The same week, we surveyed a smaller crowd at the University of California at Berkeley, where 35 out of roughly 100 protestors completed questionnaires. See James M. Jasper and Jane Poulsen, "Animal Rights and Antinuclear Protest: Condensing Symbols and the Critique of Instrumental Reason," paper presented at the American Sociological Association annual meeting, 1989.

38. Patrice Greanville and Doug Moss, "The Emerging Face of the Movement," *Animals' Agenda* 5, 2 (March/April 1985): 10.

39. These are the same characteristics Kellert found to be associated with more sentimental and less instrumental attitudes toward animals in his surveys.

40. Karen Martinez, interviewed on *Channel 2 News,* April 23, 1988.

41. Francesca Cancian, *Love in America* (Cambridge: Cambridge University Press, 1987), 4; Irene H. Frieze, Jacquelynne E. Parsons, Paula B. Johnson, Diane N. Ruble, and Gail L. Zellman, *Women and Sex Roles* (New York: W. W. Norton, 1978), ch. 4.

42. "Youth Can Build Anew," *Coordinator's Report,* the Coalition to Abolish the LD_{50}, June 1983, p. 3.

43. In the 1983 *Agenda* survey, 7 percent labeled themselves conservative and 22 percent middle of the road; in our survey, 11 percent claimed to be conservative and 13 percent middle of the road. See "What Sort of Person Reads AGENDA," *Animals' Agenda* 4 (May/June 1983): 26.

44. The political blinders of animal rights advocates surfaced in France when advocate Brigitte Bardot, in a far right French newspaper, condemned the ritual slaughter practices of Islamic immigrants, playing directly into anti-Arab politics. In response to criticism, Bardot said: "I do not do any politics." *New York Times,* August 1, 1990.

Chapter 4   Moral Militancy (pages 42–55)

1. George Cave, "Will He Know Peace on Earth?" Trans-Species Unlimited fund raising brochure, Winter 1985.

2. George Cave, "Up from the Roots," *Between the Species* 4, 3 (Summer 1988): 225.

3. Patrice Greanville, "The Greening of Animal Rights," *Animals' Agenda* 8 (September/October 1988): 36.

4. The *Animals' Voice* specializes in glossy photographs of both happy and tormented animals.

5. In her study of anti-abortion activists, Kristin Luker found that 80 percent were not recruited by the movement, but learned something that upset them enough

to search out an organization. *Abortion and the Politics of Motherhood* (Berkeley: University of California Press, 1984), 150.
6. This figure is from our own survey of April 1988.
7. At a forum convened to discuss the Off Broadway play, "Better People," February 1, 1990, at the Theatre for a New City.
8. "Six million," quoted in Chip Brown, "She's a Portrait of Zealotry in Plastic Shoes," *Washington Post,* November 13, 1983, pp. B1, B10. This quote, p. B10.
9. Marjorie Spiegel, *The Dreaded Comparison* (Philadelphia, Pa.: New Society Publishers, 1988).
10. Quoted in Jack Rosenberger, "Animal Rites," *The Village Voice,* March 6, 1990, p. 30.
11. Beginning in late 1989, a rift developed between the national office of Trans-Species and its New York chapter, in part due to the growing charisma of the New York president. Since he was removed and the position was downgraded, women have filled it. In 1990, Trans-Species became Animal Rights Mobilization. Its acronym (ARM), written in the style of spray-painted graffiti, emphasizes its radicalism, presumably to enhance its direct-mail appeal. In 1991, the New York chapter closed.
12. Quoted in Howard Goodman, "Medical Ethics and Animals," *Inside* (Fall 1987): 98.
13. Carl Cohen, "The Case for the Use of Animals in Biomedical Research," *New England Journal of Medicine* 315 (October 2, 1986): 865–870.
14. The authors disagree in their assessments of the frequency of anti-Semitism in the animal rights movement. Jasper considers it rare, while Nelkin believes it to be quite common.
15. Anonymous interview, June 1990.
16. Jeremy Cherfas, "Two Bomb Attacks on Scientists in the U.K.," *Science* 248, June 22, 1990, p. 1485.
17. Interviewed on KRON–TV4, of San Francisco, February 6, 1989.
18. For details of Trutt's case, see Gary Indiana, "All Things Cruel and Profitable," *The Village Voice,* December 13, 1988, pp. 37–38; John Motavalli, "Dog Soldier," *7 Days,* October 4, 1989, 16–23; Tom Regan, "Misplaced Trust," *The Animals' Voice* 3, 1 (1990): 18–25; and *New York Times,* "Animal-Rights Fighter Is Sentenced to Prison," July 17, 1990, p. B2.
19. Quoted in Kirk Johnson, "Arrest Points Up Split in Animal-Rights Movement," *New York Times,* November 13, 1988, p. A40.
20. "Rattlesnake Round-Up," *Animals International* 10 (Spring 1990): 5.
21. *PETA News,* July–August 1989, 4–5.
22. *The ARIES Newsletter* 2, 7, July 1990, 1.
23. Jane Gross, "Courage Is an Ingredient At Banana Slug Festival," *New York Times,* March 22, 1989, p. A16.
24. George Cave, "Up From the Roots," 224. For a similar argument about the domination in pet owning, see Yi-Fu Tuan, *Dominance and Affection: The Making of Pets* (New Haven: Yale University Press, 1984).
25. Jim Mason, "For the Pleasure of Their Company," *The Animals' Voice* 3, 2 (1990): 25, 27.
26. Patrice Greanville and Doug Moss, "The Emerging Face of the Movement," *The Animals' Agenda* 5 (March–April 1985): 11.

27. Animal Rights Mobilization, "What Can I Do For Animals?" n.d.
28. Patrice Greanville, "The Greening of Animal Rights," and Merritt Clifton, "To Life!" *Animals' Agenda* 10 (April 1990) 15–20, 57.
29. Speaking at the conference on "Animals, Ethics, and Social Policy," Berkeley, California, February 16, 1990.
30. J. Baird Callicott, *In Defense of the Land Ethic*, 1 (Albany, N.Y.: State University of New York Press, 1989); Roderick Nash, *The Rights of Nature* (Madison, Wisc.: University of Wisconsin Press, 1989).
31. "Animal Rights Is a Feminist Issue," brochure.
32. John Sanbonmatsu, "Animal Liberation: Should the Left Care?" *Zeta Magazine*, October 1989; quotations, 101, 108, and 109.
33. Jean Bethke Elshtain, "Why Worry About the Animals?" *The Progressive*, March 1990, 23.
34. Speaker at the Berkeley, California, conference, February 16, 1990.
35. Colleen McGuire, letter to *Z Magazine*, September 1990, 8.
36. Jane J. Mansbridge found similar dynamics in the movement for the Equal Rights Amendment: *Why We Lost the ERA* (Chicago: University of Chicago Press, 1986), 191. In *Risk and Culture* (Berkeley: University of California Press, 1982), Mary Douglas and Aaron Wildavsky similarly describe organizational pressures leading protest groups to use an extreme, moralistic language.

Chapter 5   The Compassionate Tradition (pages 56–70)

1. Statement by Leonard Eaton to the American Humane Association, 12th Annual Report, from annual meeting, October 17–19, 1888 (Brooklyn: Eagle Book Company, 1889), 22.
2. On British humane and anti-vivisection societies, see James Turner, *Reckoning with the Beast* (Baltimore: Johns Hopkins University Press, 1980); Antony Brown, *Who Cares for Animals? 150 Years of the RSPCA* (London: Heinemann, 1974); Harriet Ritvo, *The Animal Estate* (Cambridge: Harvard University Press, 1987), ch. 3; Richard D. French, *Antivivisection and Medical Science in Victorian Society* (Princeton: Princeton University Press, 1975); and Nicolaas Rupke, ed., *Vivisection in Historical Perspective* (New York: Croom Helm, 1987).
3. See Roswell C. McCrea, *The Humane Movement* (New York: Columbia University Press, 1910); William J. Shultz, *The Humane Movement in the United States, 1910–1922* (New York: Columbia University Press, 1924); and Sidney H. Coleman, *Humane Society Leaders in America* (Albany, N.Y.: American Humane Society, 1924).
4. As editor of the *Lady's Book,* Hale felt that women were to be the moral saviors of society, civilizing men and drawing them from their crass, violent, and money-grubbing ways. See Ruth E. Finley, *The Lady of Godey's: Sarah Josepha Hale* (Philadelphia: J. B. Lippincott, 1931); Ann Douglas, *The Feminization of American Culture* (New York: Avon, 1977), ch. 2; and David Leverenz, *Manhood and the American Renaissance* (Ithaca, N.Y.: Cornell University Press, 1989), ch. 5.
5. Coleman, *Humane Society Leaders in America,* 177. Several commentators have explained the pressures on middle-class women of the time to be moral

and spiritual exemplars, to perfect their domestic skills, and to enter the public arena only when needed to give it moral direction (an expectation that provided surprising scope for political activity): Ann Douglas, *The Feminization of American Culture;* Carl N. Degler, *At Odds: Women and the Family in America from the Revolution to the Present* (New York: Oxford University Press, 1980); Mary P. Ryan *Women in Public* (Baltimore: Johns Hopkins University Press, 1990); and Barbara Welter, "The Cult of True Womanhood," *American Quarterly* (Summer 1966): 151–174.

6. Resolution adopted by AHA, Philadelphia, October 1892, in H. S. Salt, *Animal Rights* (New York: MacMillan, 1894), 176.

7. The relative silence of anti-vivisection groups was broken in the 1930s by William Randolph Hearst's support for anti-vivisection through his extensive newspaper chain.

8. Charles D. Niven, *History of the Humane Movement* (New York: Transatlantic Press, 1967), 110.

9. Patrick B. Parkes and Jacques V. Sichel, *Twenty-five Years of Growth and Achievement* (Washington, D.C.: The Humane Society of the United States, 1979), p. 3.

10. U.S. Congress, House Committee on Agriculture, Subcommittee on Livestock and Feed Grains, 89th Cong., March 7–8, 1966, H. Rept.

11. In the early 1980s seven states—Illinois, Minnesota, South Dakota, Utah, Iowa, Oklahoma, and North Carolina—required pounds to yield or sell animals to labs, while eight—New Hampshire, Connecticut, New Jersey, Pennsylvania, Rhode Island, Maine, Hawaii, and Massachusetts—prohibited this action. See Daniel S. Moretti, *Animal Rights and the Law* (London and New York: Oceana, 1984). In 1973, nine states required the release of pound animals for research, while only three states prohibited it, according to Andrew N. Rowan, *Of Mice, Models, and Men* (Albany, N.Y.: State University of New York Press, 1984), 151.

12. Recreated, to be precise. In 1892, an idiosyncratic Englishman named Henry Salt had articulated many of the themes reworked by the philosophers discussed in this chapter, and even used the term "animal rights." The Humanitarian League, which he founded, pursued a range of issues—vegetarianism, anti-vivisection, animal rights—reminiscent of the contemporary movement. But his ideas, like his League, were lost to most people and had to be reinvented. See Salt, *Animals' Rights Considered in Relation to Social Progress* (London: George Bell and Sons, 1892); and George Hendrick and Willene Hendrick, eds., *The Savour of Salt: A Henry Salt Anthology* (Fontwell, U.K.: Centaur Press, 1989).

13. Quoted in Jeffrey M. Berry, *Lobbying for the People* (Princeton: Princeton University Press, 1977), 111. We depend here on Berry's useful description of the fund, in ch. 5.

14. Demonstrating the old saw that revolutions consume their own offspring, Amory came under increasing fire in 1989 and 1990 from more radical activists angry that the manager of the Black Beauty Ranch also raised and sold livestock. To avoid hurting the credibility of the movement, they kept their criticism private, but the man was fired.

15. John C. Petricciani and Ethel Thurston, "Regulation, Abolition, or Alternative Research?" *The California Veterinarian,* January 1983, 82.

16. Arizona activist quoted in Patty A. Finch, "The Crucial Role of Humane Education," *Animals' Agenda* (May 1988): 18.
17. Merritt Clifton, "Who Gets the Money?" *Animals' Agenda* 11 (March 1991): 33–35 and (July/August 1991): 34–35.
18. Ibid.
19. "Animal Rights and Human Obligations," Humane Society of the United States, brochure, 1981.
20. John Hoyt, address to the 1979 annual conference, in Parkes and Sichel, *Twenty-five Years of Growth and Achievement*, 38, 44.
21. Speaker at the Berkeley conference on "Animals, Ethics, and Social Policy," February 17, 1990.
22. Speaker at the Berkeley conference; see preceding note.
23. John Dorschner, "See Spot Die," *The Animals' Voice* 3, 2 (1990): 36.
24. See Leo Grillo, "Feral Cats . . . and How to Save Them," *The Animals' Voice* 3, 2 (1990): 45.
25. Quoted in Lisa W. Foderaro, "400 Animals in Small Shelter: Kind or Cruel?" *New York Times,* June 19 1990, pp. B1, B3. This quotation, p. B3.
26. Theresa Corrigan, "The Elephant-Hearted Woman: An Interview with Pat Derby," in Theresa Corrigan and Stephanie Hoppe, eds., *With a Fly's Eye, Whale's Wit, and Woman's Heart: Animals and Women* (San Francisco: Cleis Press, 1989), 78–97. These quotations, 83, 86, 92, 94, and 96. Brackets in original.
27. See Clayborne Carson, *In Struggle: SNCC and the Black Awakening of the 1960's* (Cambridge: Harvard University Press, 1981); and Herbert H. Haines, *Black Radicals and the Civil Rights Mainstream, 1954–1970* (Knoxville, Tenn.: University of Tennessee Press, 1988). Although Doug McAdam, "Tactical Innovation and the Pace of Insurgency," *American Sociological Review* 48 (1983): 735–754, analyzes the effect of tactical innovation on the pace of insurgency, he ignores the importance of new recruits, especially college students, as a source of tactical innovation.
28. See James M. Jasper, *Nuclear Politics* (Princeton: Princeton University Press, 1990), 120–124.

Chapter 6   Animals in the Wild (pages 71–89)

1. Davies described his efforts in *Savage Luxury* (New York: Ballantine Books, 1970). This quotation, 12. Farley Mowat has documented the history of seal (and other) hunts in eastern Canada in *Sea of Slaughter* (Boston: Atlantic Monthly Press, 1984).
2. *Savage Luxury,* 20.
3. From a fundraising letter sent by the International Fund for Animal Welfare, March 1989, over Davies' signature.
4. *Silent Spring* (Greenwich, Conn.: Fawcett Crest Books, 1962). H. Patricia Hynes has written about this book and its impact in *The Recurring Silent Spring* (New York: Pergamon, 1989). Histories of the American environmental movement include Joseph M. Petulla, *American Environmentalism* (College Station, Tex.: Texas A & M University Press, 1980); Samuel P. Hays, *Beauty, Health and Permanence* (Cambridge: Cambridge University Press, 1987); and Walter

A. Rosenbaum, *The Politics of Environmental Concern* (New York: Praeger, 1973). For an intellectual history, see Roderick Nash, *The Rights of Nature* (Madison, Wis.: University of Wisconsin Press, 1989).

5. Christopher D. Stone, *Should Trees Have Standing?* (Los Altos, Calif.: William Kaufmann, 1974). Joyce Tischler of the Animals Legal Defense Fund says this work heavily influenced her thinking about the rights of animals.

6. Personal interview, August 1989.

7. Civil disobedience—breaking a law one considers immoral—and direct action—taking matters into one's own hands rather than going through normal channels—are two forms of exemplary action with deep roots in American Protestantism. They were widely used by abolitionists, and Henry David Thoreau defended his own civil disobedience protesting the war with Mexico in his 1849 essay "Resistance to Civil Government." See David R. Weber, ed., *Civil Disobedience in America* (Ithaca, N.Y.: Cornell University Press, 1978); Robert Cooney, ed., *The Power of the People: Active Nonviolence in the United States* (Philadelphia, Pa.: New Society Publishers, 1987); and Ronald Dworkin, *A Matter of Principle* (Cambridge: Harvard University Press, 1985), ch. 4.

8. On the implications of direct mail fundraising and recruitment, see Larry J. Sabato, *The Rise of Political Consultants* (New York: Basic Books, 1981), ch. 4, and "Political Consultants and the New Campaign Technology," in Allan J. Cigler and Burdett A. Loomis, eds., *Interest Group Politics* (Washington, D.C.: Congressional Quarterly Press, 1983); and R. Kenneth Godwin and Robert Cameron Mitchell, "The Implications of Direct Mail for Political Organizations," *Social Science Quarterly* 65, 3 (1984): 829–839.

9. John D. McCarthy and Mayer N. Zald pointed out the professionalization of social movement organizations in 1973 in *The Trend of Social Movements in America: Professionalization and Resource Mobilization* (Morristown, N.J.: General Learning Press), although they emphasized staff careers and organizational longevity rather than who carried out direct action.

10. William Cronon, *Changes in the Land* (New York: Hill and Wang, 1983), examines the conflict between Native American attitudes toward the land and the new, instrumental vision of European settlers. In *The Death of Nature* (San Francisco: Harper & Row, 1980), and *Ecological Revolutions* (Chapel Hill: University of North Carolina Press, 1989), Carolyn Merchant traces instrumental views of nature back to the rise of modern science beginning in the sixteenth and seventeenth centuries. Similar ecological perspectives include Bill Devall and George Sessions, *Deep Ecology* (Salt Lake City, Utah: G. M. Smith, 1985); Christopher D. Stone, *Should Trees Have Standing?* and *Earth and Other Ethics* (New York: Harper and Row, 1987). Lester W. Milbrath compares environmental and mainstream values and beliefs in *Environmentalists, Vanguard for a New Society* (Albany, N.Y.: State University of New York Press, 1984).

11. Personal interview with Joyce Tischler, August 1989.

12. "And STILL the Slaughter Goes On . . . Baby Seals are Hacked to Death—21 Years after We First Shocked the World," *Daily Mirror,* February 6, 1989, p. 5.

13. Lilly's books include *Man and Dolphin* (Garden City, N.Y.: Doubleday, 1961); *The Mind of the Dolphin: A Nonhuman Intelligence* (Garden City, N.Y.: Doubleday, 1967); and *Communication Between Man and Dolphin* (New York: Crown Publishers, 1978).

14. Quoted in Edward J. Linehan, "The Trouble With Dolphins," *National Geographic,* April 1979, 538–539. For a debunking of claims for the intelligence of dolphins, see Margaret Klinowska, "Are Cetaceans Especially Smart?" *New Scientist* 29 (October 1988), 46–47. On the other hand, a careful review by Susan Wintsch in the National Science Foundation's *Mosaic,* "You'd Think You Were Thinking," 21, 3 (Fall 1990), 34–48, presents impressive, if ultimately inconclusive, evidence for dolphin capacities.

15. See Andrew Davis, "The Slaughter of Dolphins," *The Nation,* November 14, 1988, 486–488; Kenneth Brower, "The Destruction of Dolphins," *The Atlantic,* July 1989, 35–58; Timothy Egan, "New Evidence of Ecological Damage Brings a Call to Ban Drift-Net Fishing," *New York Times,* November 14, 1989, p. A24; and *New York Times,* "Tokyo Is to Ban Fish Nets Early," July 18, 1990, p. A12.

16. Philip Shabecoff, "3 Companies to Stop Selling Tuna Netted With Dolphins," *New York Times,* April 13, 1990, p. A1; Anthony Ramirez, "'Epic Debate' Led to Heinz Tuna Plan," *New York Times,* April 16, 1990, p. D1; Trish Hall, "How Youths Rallied To Dolphins' Cause," *New York Times,* April 18, 1990, p. C1.

17. "Navy Suspends a Plan to Use Dolphins as Guards," *New York Times* July 24, 1990, p. A16.

18. Michael M'Gonigle, "Short-Term Economics vs. The Environment," *Greenpeace Examiner,* Spring 1981, 3.

19. The project brochure describes many whales, some with photographs, and promises to "keep you posted on the activities and whereabouts [of the whale you adopt] in future issues of *Whalewatch*." Descriptions include not only physical characteristics but social ties—other whales they are often seen with—and sexual proclivities: "An active whale, we expect to see another calf in future years."

20. John Gulland, a whale researcher and scientific advisor to the International Whaling Commission, estimates increases in whale populations, and feels that current whaling poses no threat to most species of whales, in "The End of Whaling?" *New Scientist,* October 29, 1988, 42–47. *Moby Dick* notwithstanding, the peak year for world whaling was 1962, when 66,000 were killed.

21. Tom Rose recounts this event in *Freeing the Whales: How the Media Created the World's Greatest Non-Event* (New York: Carol Publishing Group, 1989).

22. Jane Perlez, "Ivory Trading Ban Said to Force Factories to Shut," *New York Times,* May 22, 1990, p. A14.

23. In addition to the newsletters of both organizations, see Patricia Curtis, "If a Gibbon Bangs His Head, It's Best to Bang Yours, Too," *Smithsonian* 14, 12 (March 1984): 119–125.

24. See Nelson Bryant, "Red Wolf Fighting for Survival," *New York Times,* May 20, 1979, p. V13; Boyce Rensberger, "The Wolf Gets a Better Image with Biologist's Help," *New York Times,* February 16, 1977 p. Il1; L. David Mech, "Where Can the Wolf Survive?" *National Geographic,* October 1977, 518–537; Marc Bekoff and Michael C. Wells, "The Social Ecology of Coyotes," *Scientific American,* April 1980, 130–148.

25. *New York Times,* "Curb on Shrimp Nets Urged to Protect Turtles," May 20, 1990, p. A33.

26. Reported in *Animals International,* the WSPA's newsmagazine, Summer 1989, 11.
27. Michael Satchell, "The American Hunter Under Fire," *U.S. News and World Report,* February 5, 1990, 30–36.
28. Wayne Pacelle, "Saviors or Sellouts?" *Animals' Agenda* (July–August 1988): 6–9.
29. Jolene R. Marion, "Whose Wildlife Is It Anyway?," *Pace Environmental Law Review* 4 (1987): 401–438; Ron Baker, *The American Hunting Myth* (New York: Vantage Press, 1985); "Taking Aim at Fish and Game Boards," *The Animals' Advocate,* ALDF newsletter, Winter 1990.
30. Jeffrey Schmalz, "Florida Hunting Weekend Prompts Questions About Children and Guns," *New York Times,* October 17, 1988, p. A14.
31. Richard Slotkin explores some of these myths in *Regeneration Through Violence: The Mythology of the American Frontier, 1600–1860* (Middletown, Conn.: Wesleyan University Press, 1973).
32. In Berke Breathed, *Night of the Mary Kay Commandos* (Boston: Little, Brown and Company, 1989).
33. George Michaels, "The Dead Zone: Disaster in Alaska," *Animals' Agenda* 9 (September 1989): 23–25.
34. The *Agenda* articles were Larry M. Brown, "Should Fish Be Exempt From Human Consideration?" 8 (September–October 1988): 38–39, and Victoria Moran, "A Little Fish Now and Then," 9 (March 1989): page 49. In the *Voice* appeared Cole McFarland, "Tranquil Seas, Deadly Waters," *Animals' Voice* 2, 1 (1989): 19–21, 106–107.
35. Statement of John W. Grandy, Vice President for Wildlife, Humane Society of the United States, testimony before the House Subcommittee on Health and the Environment of the Committee on Energy and Commerce, House of Representatives, in *Health and the Environment, Miscellaneous, part 7* (Washington, D.C.: U.S. Government Printing Office, August 3, 1984), 352.
36. Jeanie Kasindorf, "The Fur Flies," *New York,* January 15, 1990, 32.
37. This figure apparently came from a U.S. Department of Commerce study from 1966. Argus Archives, *Traps and Trapping, Furs and Fashion* (New York: 1971, rev. 1977), 34.
38. Testimony of Susan Russell, vice president, Friends of Animals, before the House Subcommittee on Health and the Environment of the Committee on Energy and Commerce, August 3, 1984 (in *Health and the Environment, Miscellaneous, part 7),* 419.
39. Testimony before the House Subcommittee on Health and the Environment of the Committee on Energy and Commerce, August 3, 1984, 478–479.
40. Testimony of Vivian Pryor, Georgia's delegate to the National Wildlife Federation, to the House Subcommittee on Health and the Environment of the Committee on Energy and Commerce, August 3, 1984, 607–616. These quotations, 613, 611.
41. See Mark Linenthal, "A Green Who Hunts," *Green Letter,* Spring 1989, 24; and Billy Ray Boyd, "Beyond the Hunt: An Ex-hunter Responds," *Green Letter,* Summer 1989, 14.
42. Talk at Berkeley, California, conference on "Animals, Ethics, and Social Policy," February 17, 1990.

43. *Animals' Agenda* (March 1989): 2.

44. Participant at Berkeley, California, conference, February 17, 1990.

45. J. Baird Callicott, *In Defense of the Land Ethic* (Albany, N.Y.: State University of New York Press, 1989), 57; his italics and ellipsis.

46. Michael Blumenthal, "Human, All Too Human," *New York Times,* July 23, 1989, p. E25.

47. "A Helping Hand for Injured Wildlife," the *New York Times,* September 30, 1982, p. C13. Ecologist Ralph H. Lutts comments, "Wildlife rehabilitation is of little or no ecological benefit and it rarely has any impact upon the survival of a species . . . if it makes you feel good, then you might as well do it, if you can do it properly. If done improperly, wildlife rehabilitation can amount to little more than torture, despite the best intentions." *The Nature Fakers: Wildlife, Science and Sentiment* (Golden, Colo.: Fulcrum, 1990), 197.

48. In the tradition of Carlos Castaneda, *The Teachings of Don Juan: A Yaqui Way of Knowledge* (Berkeley: University of California Press, 1968), recent examples include Andrée Collard with Joyce Contrucci, *Rape of the Wild* (Bloomington, Ind.: Indiana University Press, 1989), 22–24; D. M. Dooling and Paul Jordan-Smith, eds., *I Become Part Of It* (New York: Parabola Books, 1989); and Carolyn Merchant, *Ecological Revolutions* (Chapel Hill: University of North Carolina Press, 1989).

49. Brochure entitled "Indigenous Survival International. Indigenous Peoples and Sustainable Development," n.d.

50. *New York Times,* "Pride in Fur Is Promoted By Alaskans," March 20, 1990, p. A20.

51. Anonymous interview, March 1990.

Chapter 7   Philosophers as Midwives (pages 90–102)

1. Peter Singer, *Democracy and Disobedience* (Oxford: Clarendon Press, 1973), v. Singer has expanded his applied ethics, for example examining birth control, test-tube babies, and the treatment of handicapped children. See *Practical Ethics* (Cambridge: Cambridge University Press, 1979); *The Expanding Circle* (New York: Farrar, Straus & Giroux, 1981); *Test-Tube Babies* (with William A. W. Walters; New York: Oxford University Press, 1982); and *Should the Baby Live?* (with Helga Kuhse; New York: Oxford University Press, 1985).

2. Singer and others who apply philosophy to practical affairs are bucking the trend of modern philosophy since the seventeenth century toward abstract theorizing about universal truths. Stephen Toulmin portrays this tendency as "so deep and long-lasting that the revival of practical philosophy in our day has taken many people by surprise," *Cosmopolis* (New York: Free Press, 1990), 34.

3. Quoted in Singer, *Animal Liberation* (New York: Avon, 1977), 7–8. Italics in original.

4. Singer describes his own intellectual history in "Animal Liberation: A Personal View," *Between the Species* 2, 3 (Summer 1986): 148–154. The *New York Review of Books* essay was "Animal Liberation," April 5, 1973, a review of Stanley Godlovitch, Roslind Godlovitch, and John Harris, eds., *Animals, Men and Morals: An Enquiry into the Maltreatment of Non-Humans* (New York: Taplinger, 1972), 17–21. Other essays by Singer dealing with animal liberation

include, "All Animals Are Equal," *Philosophical Exchange* 1, 5 (Summer 1974): 103–116; "Not for Humans Only: The Place of Nonhumans in Environmental Issues," in K. E. Goodpaster and K. M. Sayre, eds., *Ethics and Problems of the 21st Century* (Notre Dame, Ind.: University of Notre Dame Press, 1979); and the Prologue and Epilogue to Singer, ed., *In Defense of Animals* (New York: Harper and Row, 1985).

5. New York: New York Review of Books, 1975. A paperback edition appeared in 1977 (Avon), and a second edition by New York Review of Books appeared in 1990.

6. Richard Ryder first used the term "speciesism" in a privately printed 1970 pamphlet by that name, and later in the 1974 book, *Speciesism: The Ethics of Vivisection* (Edinburgh: Scottish Society for the Prevention of Cruelty to Animals), but Singer made it common usage.

7. Singer's italics. "The Significance of Animal Suffering," *Behavioral and Brain Sciences* 13, 1 (1990): 9–12. This quotation, 10. This issue contains a symposium on the welfare of laboratory animals, 1–61.

8. *Animal Liberation,* 180.

9. Some philosophers, like Frank Jackson, argue that Singer fails to provide any basis for criticizing the painless killing of animals. "Singer's Intermediate Conclusion," *Behavioral and Brain Sciences* 13, 1 (1990): 24–25. In his reply, "Ethics and Animals," 45–49, Singer does not refute the point, but says that, in a society of factory farms, there is much animal suffering that needs to be alleviated before we can worry about the ethics of eating animals that did not suffer (page 48). Here, Singer puts practical politics before philosophical argument.

10. Personal interview, August 1989.

11. Anonymous interview, January 1989.

12. Regan describes his conversion to animal rights in "The Bird in the Cage: A Glimpse of My Life," in *Between the Species* 2, (1): 42–49; (2): 90–99. This quotation (2): 93. "The Bird in the Cage" was later reprinted in Tom Regan, *The Struggle for Animal Rights* (Clarks Summit, Penn.: International Society for Animal Rights, 1987).

13. "The Search for a New Global Ethic," interview with Tom Regan by Patrice Greanville, The *Animals' Agenda* 6 (December 1986): 40.

14. Regan's writings include "The Moral Basis of Vegetarianism," *Canadian Journal of Philosophy* 5, 2 (1975): 181–214; "Exploring the Idea of Animal Rights," in David Paterson and Richard Ryder, eds., *Animals' Rights: A Symposium* (Fontwell, U.K.: Centaur Press, 1979); "Animal Rights, Human Wrongs," *Environmental Ethics* 2, 2 (1980): 99–120; *All that Dwell Therein: Animal Rights and Environmental Ethics* (Berkeley: University of California Press, 1982). Regan has also edited *Earthbound: New Introductory Essays in Environmental Ethics* (Philadelphia, Penn.: Temple University Press, 1984); and with Donald VanDeVeer, eds., *And Justice for All* (Totowa, N.J.: Rowman and Littlefield, 1982). For essays on Regan's philosophy, see the *Monist* 70, 1 (January 1987).

15. See Dale Jamieson and Tom Regan, "On the Ethics of the Use of Animals in Science," in Regan and VanDeVeer, eds., *And Justice for All,* 190.

16. Berkeley: University of California Press, 1983.

17. Regan defines anthropomorphism (page 6) as *falsely* attributing human characteristics to nonhumans. But in the many cases when one simply cannot know if the attribution is accurate or not, he relies on his own moral intuitions and suggests giving animals "the benefit of the doubt" (page 367).

18. Quotations from pages 367 and 384.
19. Page 367.
20. Page 374.
21. Page 363.
22. Mark Sagoff, "Animal Liberation and Environmental Ethics: Bad Marriage, Quick Divorce," *Osgoode Hall Law Journal* 22, (1984): 306.
23. Callicott, *In Defense of the Land Ethic,* 45.
24. Page 393.
25. "The Bird in the Cage," part 2, 94.
26. "The Bird in the Cage," part 2, 94–95.
27. See her article "Is 'Moral' A Dirty Word?" *Philosophy* 47, 181 (1972): 206–228.
28. Mary Midgley, *Animals and Why They Matter* (Athens, Ga.: University of Georgia Press, 1983).
29. *Animals and Why They Matter,* 98.
30. *Animals and Why They Matter,* 102.
31. *Animals and Why They Matter,* 119. For other arguments that humans may follow abstract moral principles yet still treat loved ones in special ways, see several of the contributions to *Behavioral and Brain Sciences* 13, 1 (1990). J. A. Gray, "In Defence of Speciesism," 22–23, uses the argument to claim that we can systematically treat humans better than animals. But Evalyn F. Segal, "Animal Well-Being: There Are Many Paths to Enlightenment," 36–37, says—as does Midgley—that many animals are close to us; we typically feel closer to our pets than to humans we have never met. And Steve F. Sapontzis, "The Meaning of Speciesism and the Forms of Animal Suffering," 35–36, points out that special treatment for loved ones does not allow us to violate the rights of strangers—any more than we must treat strangers as we treat loved ones.
32. Books include Stephen R. L. Clark, *The Moral Status of Animals* (Oxford: Clarendon Press, 1977); Mary Midgley, *Beast and Man* (Ithaca, N.Y.: Cornell University Press, 1978) and *Animals and Why They Matter* (Athens: University of Georgia Press, 1983); Bernard E. Rollin, *Animal Rights and Human Morality* (Buffalo, N.Y.: Prometheus Books, 1981).

Articles responding to Singer include James Rachels, "Do Animals Have A Right to Liberty?" in Tom Regan and Peter Singer, eds., *Animal Rights and Human Obligations* (Englewood Cliffs, N.J.: 1976), 205–223; Christine Pierce, "Can Animals Be Liberated?" *Philosophical Studies* 36, 1 (July 1979): 69–75; David Lamb, "Animal Rights and Liberation Movements," *Environmental Ethics* 4, 3 (Fall 1982): 215–233; and—for a review of the debates—T. L. S. Sprigge, "Philosophers and Antivivisectionism," *Alternatives to Laboratory Animals* 13, 2 (December 1985): 99–106.

Among other philosophical works are Richard Knowles Morris and Michael W. Fox, eds., *On the Fifth Day: Animal Rights and Human Ethics* (Washington, D.C.: Acropolis Books, 1978); David Paterson and Richard Ryder, eds., *Animals Rights: A Symposium* (Fontwell, U.K.: Centaur Press, 1979): Harlan B. Miller and William H. Williams, eds., *Ethics and Animals* (Clifton, N.J.: Humana Press, 1983). Regan and Singer compiled a series of statements by contemporaries and important historical figures in philosophy, *Animal Rights and Human Obligations* (Englewood Cliffs, N.J.: Prentice-Hall, 1976).
33. Telephone interview, June 1990.

34. Steve F. Sapontzis, *Morals, Reason, and Animals* (Philadelphia: Temple University Press, 1987).

35. Telephone interview, June 1990.

36. George Cave, "Rational Egoism, Animal Rights, and the Academic Connection," *Between the Species* 1, 2 (Spring 1985): 26.

37. Dale Jamieson and George Cave, "Discussion: Jamieson and Cave," *Between the Species* 1, 4 (Fall 1985): 48.

38. Telephone interview, June 1990.

39. Tom Regan, *The Struggle for Animal Rights* (Clarks Summit, Penn.: International Society for Animal Rights, 1987).

40. Mary Anne Warren, "Difficulties With the Strong Animal Rights Position," *Between the Species* 2, 4 (Fall 1986): 170–171. See also Evelyn Pluhar, "Speciesism: A Form of Bigotry or a Justified View?" *Between the Species* 4, 2 (Spring 1988): 83–96, and the essays in the *Monist* 70, 1 (January 1987).

41. Josephine Donovan, "Animal Rights and Feminist Theory," *Signs* 15, 2 (1990), 372. Other theoretical efforts to link feminism and animal rights include Carol J. Adams, *The Sexual Politics of Meat: A Feminist-Vegetarian Critical Theory* (New York: Continuum, 1990), Constantina Salamone, "The Prevalence of the Natural Law Within Women: Women and Animal Rights," in Pam McAllister, ed., *Reweaving the Web of Life* (Philadelphia: New Society, 1982); Andrée Collard with Joyce Contrucci, *Rape of the Wild: Man's Violence Against Animals and the Earth* (Bloomington, Ind.: Indiana University Press, 1989); and Jean Bethke Elshtain, "Why Worry About the Animals?" *The Progressive,* March 1990, 17–23.

42. Gilligan's controversial argument can be found in *In a Different Voice* (Cambridge: Harvard University Press, 1982), while useful responses and criticisms are in Eva F. Kittay and Diana T. Meyers, eds., *Women and Moral Theory* (Totowa, N.J.: Rowman & Littlefield, 1987) and a special issue of *Social Research* 50, 3 (1983).

Chapter 8   From Rabbits to Petri Dishes (pages 103–114)

1. Letter dated November 2, 1987 from Peggy E. Kunzer, Consumer Affairs Coordinator of Beecham Cosmetics, to Michael Simmons.

2. The LD_{50} test finds the amount of a substance that will kill 50 percent of a test population of animals.

3. Marjorie Sun, "Lots of Talk About LD_{50}," *Science* 222, December 9, 1983, 1106; Henry Spira, "How to Save 4 Million Animals from LD_{50}," *Our Town,* October 2, 1983; Leonard Rack and Henry Spira, "Update: LD_{50}," *The Unicorn,* January 1984.

4. Described in Marjorie Sun, "Lots of Talk About LD_{50}."

5. Letter dated March 30, 1987, from Frank E. Young, Commissioner of Food and Drugs, to Kenneth H. Masters, Maryland state legislator from Baltimore, responding to the question, "Is the use of these animal tests, such as the Draize eye irritancy test, necessary to establish the safety of cosmetic products under the regulatory control of the FDA?"

6. Letter to Harry Jerpeer of New York.

7. Anita Roddick, quoted in Douglas C. McGill, "Cosmetics Companies Quietly Ending Animal Tests," *New York Times,* August 2, 1989, p. D22.

8. "Dear Abby," *San Francisco Chronicle,* September 28, 1988.

9. In some cases, notably thalidomide, the drugs were not *adequately* tested on animals. These arguments often rely on the dubious works of Hans Ruesch, a Swiss anti-vivisectionist whose books, *Naked Empress or The Great Medical Fraud* (Zurich: Civis Publications, 1982), and *Slaughter of the Innocent* (New York: Bantam, 1978) circulated widely in the early 1980s. Written as blatant exposés, Ruesch sees animal research as the central rite in "the Religion of Modern Medicine."

10. Eben Shapiro, "Drug Companies Leave Cosmetics," *New York Times,* December 28, 1989, p. D2.

11. Constance Holden traces some of the concern with finding alternatives to animal tests to the 1976 Toxic Substances Control Act, which required that new chemicals be tested before entering the market. Previously, only existing chemicals had been tested for toxicity, so that the industry was not anxious to facilitate testing. Holden, "New Focus on Replacing Animals in the Lab," *Science* 215, January 1, 1982, 35–38.

12. Philip Shabecoff, "Industry Fights Use of Animal Tests to Assess Cancer Risk," *New York Times,* July 25, 1989, p. C4.

13. Natalie Angier, "The Electronic Guinea Pig," *Discover* 4, 9, September 1983, 77.

14. *Feminists for Animal Rights Newsletter,* Spring–Summer, 1989.

15. "Alternatives to Animals," *The Economist,* December 2, 1989, 97.

16. Spira, *Coordinator's Report '86,* Animal Rights International. See the *Science* article: Constance Holden, "A Pivotal Year for Lab Animal Welfare," *Science* 232, April 11, 1986, 147–150.

17. Myra Alperson, "More Bark, More Bite," Council on Economic Priorities, Research Report, July–August 1988, 2.

18. Letter from Lynn Baron, Consumer Information Center, to Julie Van Ness, December 14, 1984.

19. Telephone interview with Elaine Benvenuto, from Avon's public affairs office, November 16, 1990.

20. Constance Holden, "Cosmetics Firms Drop Draize Test," *Science* 245, July 14, 1989, 125.

21. Barnaby J. Feder, "Noxell Replaces Rabbits In Tests of Cosmetics," *New York Times,* January 10, 1989.

22. U.S. Congress Office of Technology Assessment, *Alternatives to Animal Research in Research Testing and Education* (Washington D.C., 1986). See also, Animal Rights International, *Coordinator's Report '88.* Also, M. A. Mehlman, ed., *Benchmarks: Alternative Methods in Toxicology* (Princeton, N.J., Princeton Scientific Publishing Company, 1989).

23. Natalie Angier, "The Electronic Guinea Pig," 76–80.

24. To name a few: *Toxicology and Industrial Health* has been published since 1985; *In-Vitro Toxicology* since 1986; *Toxicology in Vitro* since 1987; and *Molecular Toxicology* since 1987.

25. Spira, "Fighting to Win," 206.

26. Quoted in Helen Mathews Smith, "Would You Shoot This Dog?" *MD,* March 1984, 94–100.

27. Quoted in Myra Alperson, "More Bark, More Bite," Council on Economic Priorities, Research Report, July–August 1988, 3.
28. Quoted in *International Society for Animal Rights Report,* March–April, 1988, 2. See also Barnaby J. Feder, "Beyond White Rats and Rabbits," and "The Protestors Shift Gears," *New York Times,* February 28, 1988, pp. C1, C8.
29. E. Edward Kavanaugh, quoted in Elizabeth Venant and David Treadwell, "Biting Back," *Los Angeles Times,* April 12, 1990, p. E12.
30. Spira, "Alternatives Edge Toward Center Stream," *Newsletter* of the Johns Hopkins Center for Alternatives to Animal Testing 6, 1, Winter 1988, 7.

Chapter 9   Test Tubes with Legs (pages 115–137)

1. Some postwar anti-vivisectionists embraced marginal causes such as eugenics, explicitly criticizing the sacrifice of healthy animals to save unhealthy people. A 1967 book, for example, states that the cruelty of the laboratory is ruining the human race.

   > Until we completely revise our ideas on the sanctity of human life . . . until we accept the discipline of a code of eugenics we cannot stop the present trend of breeding more and more disease into our already decadent and degenerate populations; until that is arrested, more and more sickness will turn up with the need for more and more animals being sacrificed in the laboratories. . . . The abolition of all cruelty in the laboratory may be the practical step in stopping the breeding of a diseased and degenerate human race.

   Charles D. Niven, *History of the Humane Movement* (New York: Transatlantic Arts, 1967), 164–165, 167.
2. The Hastings Center for the study of bioethics formed in 1969 and initiated a journal, *The Hastings Center Report,* airing the ethical problems generated by scientific and technological advances in medicine.
3. See, for example, Paul K. Feyerabend, *Against Method* (London: Verso, 1978) and "How to Defend Society Against Science," in Ian Hacking, ed., *Scientific Revolutions* (Oxford: Oxford University Press, 1981); Jürgen Habermas, *Knowledge and Human Interests* (Boston: Beacon Press, 1971) and "Technology and Science as 'Ideology,'" *Toward a Rational Society* (Boston: Beacon Press, 1970), ch. 6.
4. Special Issue on "Limits of Scientific Inquiry," *Daedalus* 107, 2 (Spring 1978).
5. Yaron Ezrahi traces the changing image of science from an embodiment of uncontroversial knowledge to a source of ethical dilemmas in *The Descent of Icarus* (Cambridge: Harvard University Press, 1990). For applications to animals, see Harlan B. Miller and William H. Williams, eds., *Ethics and Animals* (Clifton, N.J.: Humana Press, 1983).
6. In the Tuskegee Syphilis Study, the Centers for Disease Control had knowingly denied treatment to a group of research subjects—elderly, rural black males—who had been part of a study to determine the natural course of untreated syphilis. See James H. Jones, *Bad Blood* (New York: Free Press, 1981).
7. Hans Reusch, *Slaughter of the Innocent* (Swain, N.Y.: Civitas, 1983).

8. Meredith D. McGuire, *Ritual Healing in Suburban America* (New Brunswick, N.J.: Rutgers University Press, 1988).
9. Evelyn Fox Keller, *A Feeling for the Organism* (New York: Freeman, 1983) and "Feminism and Science," *Signs* 7, 3 (1980): 589–602.
10. Part of the empathy of these researchers is rather anthropomorphic, as when Jane Goodall speaks of returning to "Gombe—back home. Many old chimp friends were there. . . . Melissa and her 7-year-old daughter, Gremlin, were enjoying their last meal of the day, the yellow blossoms of the *msiloti* tree. Nearby sat my old friend Fifi. I had known her as an infant: Now she was mother of two . . ." in "Life and Death at Gombe," *National Geographic* (May 1979), 592–621. Also see Jane Goodall, *In The Shadow of Man* (Boston: Houghton Mifflin, 1971), *The Chimpanzees of Gombe* (Cambridge: Harvard University Press, Belknap, 1986), and *Through a Window* (Boston: Houghton Mifflin, 1990); and Dian Fossey, *Gorillas in the Mist* (Boston: Houghton Mifflin, 1983). Donna Jeanne Haraway provides an interesting interpretation of how these women mediate between gender, culture, and nature in *Primate Visions* (New York: Routledge, 1989), ch. 7. Josephine Donovan explicitly presents them as a model for science in "Animal Rights and Feminist Theory," *Signs* 15, 2 1990: 373.
11. Kathy Beauchamp and Lesley Lafferty, quoted in *Rochester Democrat and Chronicle,* May 29, 1983.
12. Rick Kraus, "The Arguments Against Vivisection," *UCLA Daily Bruin,* July 19, 1984.
13. Javier B. Burgos, "Let's Abolish Dissection of Animals in our Schools! The Case Against Dissection," distributed by SUPRESS. SUPRESS does not define itself as an animal rights group, spurning moral and philosophical arguments in favor of technical critiques of science.
14. "Point/Counterpoint: Responses to Typical pro-Vivisection Arguments," distributed by AAVS, 7.
15. Steve Rauh, at the conference "Animals, Ethics and Social Policy," the Pacific School of Religion, Berkeley, Calif., February 17, 1990.
16. United Action for Animals, "Animal Experimentation, Science or Savagery?" brochure.
17. Kerry Luft, "Animal Lovers, Doctors at Odds Over Experiments," New Orleans *Times-Picayune,* August 29, 1983, p. E3.
18. Robert Kanigel, "Lab Specimen No. 1913: A Rat's Brief Life in the Service of Science," *San Francisco Chronicle,* March 8, 1987, p. 13.
19. Mary T. Phillips, "Constructing Laboratory Animals: An Ethnographic Study in the Sociology of Science," Ph.D. diss. New York University, December 1990.
20. Aubry Hampton, "Guest Editorial," *ARIES Newsletter* 2, 7, July 1990, 1.
21. Kerry W. Buckley, *Mechanical Man* (New York: Guilford, 1989), and *John Broadus Watson and the Beginnings of Behaviorism* (New York: Guilford, 1989).
22. John McArdle, "Psychological Experimentation on Animals: Not Necessary, Not Valid," *Humane Society News,* Spring 1984, 21.
23. Coalition to End Animal Suffering in Experiments (CEASE), no title, n.d.
24. "Some of the Abuses Our Taxes Support," Leaflet distributed by PETA.
25. This type of argument is characteristic in social movements that attack science.

For example, the creationists point to disagreements among evolutionary biologists to discredit the entire field. Dorothy Nelkin, *The Creation Controversy* (New York: W. W. Norton, 1984).

26. Chimpanzees infected with the HIV virus do not get precisely the same disease. Some of these arguments even appear in the gay press. See *Gay Community News,* January 29, 1989.

27. Lawrence K. Altman, "Is the Artificial Heart Bad for the Brain?" *New York Times,* September 29, 1985, p. IV7. The heart was too large to test in primates, but the blood of calves, sheep, and goats—the animals that were used in testing—does not clot the same way that human blood does.

28. Michael W. Fox, quoted in *M.D.,* March, 1984, 99.

29. "Neomorts: A New Alternative in the Laboratory," *Animals' Agenda* 7 (March 1987): 20–21.

30. In Richard H. Schwarz, "Animal Research: A Position Statement," *Science* 244, 1128 (letter).

31. Quoted in Linda Goldston, "Animal Groups Rally to Save Two Laboratory Monkeys," *San Jose Mercury,* July 24, 1983.

32. Roberta Kalechofsky, intro. to John Vyvyan, *The Dark Face of Science* (Marblehead, Mass.: Micah Publications, 1989), 5.

33. Jimmy, "Do Scientists Cheat?" in SUPRESS's New Year 1989 pamphlet.

34. Dorothy Nelkin, ed., *Controversy: The Politics of Technical Decisions* (Beverly Hills, Calif.: Sage Publications, 1984).

35. Gary Fong, "Ends and Means in the Laboratory," *San Francisco Chronicle,* March 9, 1986, p. 18.

36. Fong, "Ends and Means."

37. Personal communication from Charles McCarthy, June 1989.

38. Dick Pothier, "Animal-Rights Groups Vs. Scientists: No Middle Ground," *Philadelphia Inquirer,* June 10, 1984.

39. David O'Reilly, "She Would Empty All the Cages," *Philadelphia Inquirer,* August 28, 1984.

40. "Animal Research," *San Francisco Chronicle,* January 5, 1988, p. A18.

41. For a fuller analysis comparing the Cornell, New York University, and American Museum of Natural History campaigns, see James M. Jasper, Dorothy Nelkin, and Jane Poulsen, "When Do Social Movement Campaigns Win? Three Campaigns against Animal Experiments," paper presented at the American Sociological Association annual meeting, 1990.

42. Quoted in Sarah Lyall, "Pressed on Animal Rights, Researcher Gives Up Grant," *New York Times,* November 22, 1988, pp. B1, B5.

43. Colin Norman, "Cat Study Halted Amid Protests," *Science* 242, November 18, 1988, 1001.

44. Colin Norman, "Cat Study Halted Amid Protests," 1001–1002.

45. These letters were made available to the authors through the generosity of John Burness.

46. Personal interview, August 1989.

47. *AMA Animal Research Action Plan* (brochure) (Chicago: June 1989), 2.

48. New York University press conference, April 21, 1989.

49. Dorothy Nelkin, *Selling Science* (New York: W. H. Freeman, 1987).

50. Interview with Roy Henrickson, April 1988.

51. On CFAAR, see Charles S. Nicoll, "Organization Committed to Direct Action Supporting Animal Research Formed at Berkeley," *The Physiologist* 31, 6 (December 1988): 153ff.; and Charles S. Nicoll and Sharon M. Russell, "Animal Research vs. Animal Rights," *The FASEB Journal* 3 (1989): 1668–1671; on CLEAR see Rex Dalton, "Waging War On The Animal Rights Lobby," *The Scientist* 3, 3 (February 6, 1989): 4.

52. Richard W. Stevenson, "Advertising: A Campaign for Research on Animals," *New York Times,* January 20, 1989, p. D5.

53. Tabitha M. Powledge, "Locking Up the Lab," AAAS Observer, January 6th, 1989, pp. 1,6,7.

54. Stanton Glantz, "Letter to the Editor," *Science* 244, June 30, 1989, 1531.

55. "Telling It Like It Is," 3; and "Why We Oppose the Dole Bill S.657," SAV, Summer 1984, 7.

56. "Animal Rights Group Sues UC Over Meetings," *San Francisco Chronicle,* August 14, 1987. See also L. A. Chung, "Animal Rights Protest—Scores Arrested," *San Francisco Chronicle,* April 25, 1986.

57. Personal interview, July 1990.

58. Those who serve on care and use committees do not feel that they are merely rubber stamps. Joseph Spinelli, head of the committee at the University of California at San Francisco, recounts the case of a researcher who wished to administer electric shocks to monkeys, but claimed they would not be in pain. The committee suggested she be administered the shocks so that the committee could observe whether she appeared in pain. She dropped these research plans. (Recounted in Anne Mackay-Smith, "Animal-Rights Fight Against Pet Projects Worries Researchers," *Wall Street Journal,* November 30, 1983, pp. 1, 24.)

59. Quoted in Janet Else Basu, "Improving The Lot of The Laboratory Animal," *The Scientist* (January 9, 1989): 2.

60. Janet Else Basu, "Improving the Lot of the Laboratory Animal," 2.

61. Arnold Arluke, "Sacrificial Symbolism in Animal Experimentation: Object or Pet?" *Anthrozoös* 2 (1988): 98–117; and "The Significance of Seeking the Animal's Perspective," *Behavioral and Brain Sciences* 13, 1 (March 1990): 13–14.

62. See Gill Langley, ed., *Animal Experimentation: The Consensus Changes* (New York: Chapman and Hall, 1990). For an earlier assessment, see William Paton, *Man and Mouse: Animals in Medical Research* (Oxford and New York: Oxford University Press, 1984).

63. The increase, dating from 1982, is documented in Mary T. Phillips and Jeri A. Sechzer, *Animal Research and Ethical Conflict* (New York: Springer-Verlag, 1989), ch. 4.

64. Cited in Katie McCabe, "Who Will Live, Who Will Die?" *Washingtonian,* August 1986, p. 115.

65. Letter to the ed., *Science* 243, March 17, 1989, 1420.

66. Kirk Johnson "Arrest Points Up Split in Animal-Rights Movement," *New York Times,* November 13, 1988, p. 40.

Chapter 10   Animals as Commodities (pages 138–155)

1. Because he is not a public figure or official organizational leader, we have used a pseudonym.

2. Ruth Harrison, *Animal Machines* (New York: Ballantine Books, 1966). Harrison is often called the Rachel Carson of the British animal rights movement.
3. Alex Hershaft, "The Legislative Promise for Farm Animals," *Animals' Agenda* (December 1986): 16–19.
4. Yonkers *Herald Statesman,* "Meat is Murder, Militants Believe," November 19, 1989, p. A9.
5. "Lobster Liberation," *PETA News,* July–August 1989, pp. 3–5.
6. "Lucie's Story," *PETA News,* September–October 1988, p. 14.
7. *Animals' Agenda* (January 1989): 12.
8. Marly Cornell, "Sue Coe: Rebel With Many Causes," interview in *Animals' Agenda* (February 1989): 7–9. This quotation, 8.
9. John Robbins, "The Joy and Tragedy of Pigs," *Animals' Agenda* 9 (January 1989): 18.
10. Gene Logsdon, "Maybe the Animal Rights Movement Is Good for Us," *Farm Journal,* January 1989, p. 26–D.
11. Jeffrey L. Fox, "USDA Animal Research Under Fire," *BioScience* 35, 1 (January 1985).
12. *Agscene; Newsletter of Compassion in World Farming,* May 1988, 1.
13. "Patents and the Constitution: Transgenic Animals," Hearings Before the Subcommittee on Courts, Civil Liberties and the Administration of Justice of the House of Representatives, Committee on the Judiciary, 100th Congress, 1st session, 1987. See Betsy Hanson and Dorothy Nelkin, "Public Responses to Genetic Engineering," *Society* 27, 1 (November–December, 1989): 76–80.
14. Cited in the Animal Welfare Institute, *Factory Farming: An Experiment that Failed* (Washington, D.C.: Animal Welfare Institute, 1987), 52.
15. Advertisement in *The Village Voice,* November 21, 1989, p. 29.
16. The Animal Rights Education and Information Service *Newsletter* 2, 2, February 1990, 3, reprinted this tidbit from the *Vancouver Island Vegetarian Association Newsletter.*
17. Sant Darshan Singh, "Vegetarian Diet and the Spiritual Life," pamphlet, n.d., 5.
18. Buddhists Concerned for Animals, *Newsletter* 9, Winter 1985–1986.
19. Thomas Tryon, *The Way to Health, Long Life and Happiness* (London: A. Sowle, 1683).
20. See Stephen Nissenbaum, *Sex, Diet, and Debility in Jacksonian America* (Westport, Conn.: Greenwood Press, 1980).
21. Mary Midgley, *Animals and Why They Matter,* 27. Carol Adams also provides an extensive symbolic analysis of meat in *The Sexual Politics of Meat* (New York: Continuum, 1990).
22. Norbert Elias, *The Civilizing Process, 1; The History of Manners* (New York: Pantheon, 1978), 120.
23. Molly O'Neill, "An Icon of the Good Life Ends Up On a Crowded Planet's Hit Lists," *New York Times,* May 6, 1990, pp. E1, E4.
24. Carol Lawson, "As Women Pull Out Their Furs, Some Wonder Whether They're Asking for Trouble," *New York Times,* November 19, 1989, p. 50.
25. Jeanie Kasindorf, "The Fur Flies," *New York:* January 15, 1990, p. 31.
26. "Jindo: Exporting Cruelty," *Peta News,* September–October 1989, 3–5. These quotations, 3 and 4.

27. Letter from Thomas G. Riley to Jack Jones, dated October 18, 1988.

28. Flyer entitled "The Animal Rights Protest Industry," dated September 1, 1988.

29. Quoted in Laurie Johnston, "Newfoundland Seal Harvest In March Stirs Early Storm," *New York Times,* January 10, 1979, p. B6.

30. Quoted in John W. Grandy and Richard L. Randall, "Predator Control: A National Disaster," *Frontiers* (Philadelphia: Academy of National Sciences of Philadelphia, 1977).

31. Reprinted in *Harper's,* February 1990, p. 27.

32. The national Trans-Species (now ARM) office apparently discouraged participation by Barker in 1990, perhaps because he stole the spotlight from the organization itself.

33. Holly Jensen, "Lethal Glamour," *Animals' Agenda* (January–February, 1987): 12.

34. Marianne Yen, "Animal-Rights Groups Harass Fur Wearers," *Washington Post,* March 11 1989, p. A3.

35. See Jeanie Kasindorf, "The Fur Flies," *New York:* January 15, 1990, 27–33; Leonard Sloane, "The Price of a Fur Goes Down When It Should Be Going Up," *New York Times,* November 4, 1989, p. 50; and Dirk Johnson, "Some View Battle in Snow Country as Turning Point in War Over Fur," *New York Times,* February 12, 1990, p. A18.

36. Quoted in "Thumbs Up," *Mainstream* 21, 2 (Spring 1990); 5.

37. Versions of the advertisement vary slightly; for one example, see *New York Times,* November 26, 1989, p. 12.

38. Quoted in Stacey Burling, "Fur-Trapping Hard Hit by Low Prices, Rabies Upsurge," *The Harrisburg Patriot-News,* December 25, 1989, p. B8.

39. See Barnaby J. Feder, "Pressuring Perdue," *New York Times Magazine,* November 26, 1989, 60, for the Newkirk and Singer quotations.

40. Michael Fox, "Vegetarianism and Farm Animal Welfare," unpublished speech, Center for Respect of Life and Environment, Washington, D.C.; n.d.

Chapter 11   Animals on Display (pages 156–166)

1. Exposés include Nancy Perry, "Racing for their Lives," *Animals' Voice* 2, 5 (1989): 20–21; and Phil Maggitti, "They Shoot Up Horses, Don't They?" *Animals' Agenda* (November 1990): 19–24.

2. Guy R. Hodge, Testimony before the General Assembly of Pennsylvania on a Bill to Prohibit Live Pigeon Shoots, May 26, 1989.

3. See Douglas Kent Hall, *Rodeo* (New York: Ballantine Books, 1976); and Elizabeth A. Lawrence, *Rodeo: An Anthropologist Looks at the Wild and the Tame* (Knoxville, Tenn.: University of Tennessee Press, 1982).

4. Bob Teaff, quoted in DeNeen L. Brown, "Animal-Rights Activists Kick Up Some Dust as Rodeo Nears," *Washington Post,* March 2, 1990, p. C6.

5. International Fund for Animal Welfare, "Dossier of Horror," n.d.

6. For a history of the American circus, see John Culhane, *The American Circus* (New York: Henry Holt, 1990), and for an interpretation, Paul Bouissac, *Circus and Culture* (Bloomington, Ind.: Indiana University Press, 1976).

7. "Circus Cruelties," *PETA News,* May–June 1990, p. 11.

8. "Fair's Fair," *PETA News,* May–June 1990, p. 11.

9. Phil Maggitti, "Where the Unicorn Is King: A Look at the Circus," *Animals' Agenda* 9 (November 1989): 26.
10. "Berosini Busted!!" *PETA News,* November–December 1989, pp. 3–6. This quotation, 4.
11. Phil Maggitti, "Where the Unicorn Is King," 25.
12. Carol J. Adams, "'Deena'—The World's Only Stripping Chimp," *Animals' Voice* 3, (1): 72.
13. Stephen R. Kellert reports the most popular species in the United States as dogs, horses, swans, robins, and butterflies. See "Human-Animal Interactions," in Andrew N. Rowan, ed., *Animals and People Sharing the World* (Hanover, N.H.: University Press of New England, 1988), 158.
14. Anthropologist Elizabeth A. Lawrence has analyzed horses in American society in *Rodeo* and *Hoofbeats and Society* (Bloomington, Ind.: University Press, 1985).
15. A Department of the Interior survey from the late 1970s found that 27 million Americans rode at least once a year, and half of these rode quite regularly. In the United States, today over one million people own a total of six million horses. Reported in Jon Nordheimer, "Boots and Saddles For a New Breed," *New York Times,* July 25, 1990, pp. C1, C4.
16. Mary Robison, "In the Woods," in *Believe Them* (New York: Alfred A. Knopf, 1988), 56.
17. Mary Hoffman, "Is It Possible to Use Horses to Pull Carriages in New York City and Still Be Humane? We Say No," *Action Line* (FOA), November–December 1988, 10.
18. Donatella Lorch, "Horse-Carriage Drivers Call New Law's Reins Too Tight," *New York Times,* December 3, 1989, p. 58.
19. See Keith Schneider, "Swim Programs with Dolphins Drawing Fire," *New York Times,* August 11, 1989, pp. A1, A16, and Nancy Daves Hicks, "The Saga of the Golden Nugget," *Mainstream,* Fall 1989, 25–26.
20. Quoted in Dirk Johnson, "Zoo, Sadly: Elephants Are Not For Riding," *New York Times,* May 14, 1990, p. A12.
21. Michael W. Fox, "The Trouble with Zoos," *Animals' Agenda* 6 (June 1986) 8.
22. *The Economist,* "Animal Rights and Wrongs," November 25, 1989, 28–29.
23. "Frog Girl: The Jenifer Graham Story," CBS broadcast, October 17, 1989.
24. *New York Times,* "Student Who Sued School Isn't Required to Cut Frog," August 3, 1988, p. A8.
25. The survey, conducted by the Association of American Medical Colleges, is described in Constance Holden, "Animal Rights Activism Threatens Dissection," *Science* 250, November 9, 1990, 751.
26. Michael W. Fox, "Unnatural Acts," *Animals' Agenda* 6 (June 1986): 9.
27. Delilah Cooper, "Epilogue," *Animals' Voice* 2, (5): 37.

Chapter 12   The Limits of a Moral Crusade (pages 167–176)

1. John Sanbonmatsu, "Animal Rights Mobilization," *Z Magazine,* July–August 1990, 60–61.
2. Harriet Schleiffer, "Images of Death and Life: Food Animal Production and the

Vegetarian Option," in Peter Singer, ed., *In Defense of Animals* (New York: Harper and Row, 1985), 72.

3. Frederick Goodwin, speaking at New York University press conference, April 21, 1989.

4. Early surveys had shown majority support for the Massachusetts measure. Many animal activists claimed to be pleased with the outcome of the votes, perhaps correctly. In 1976, several state referenda to shut down nuclear power plants lost by roughly two-to-one votes; within five years, public opinion had been reversed. See *New York Times,* "Voters in Ski Resort Opt for Continued Fur Sales," February 15, 1990, p. A26; and Merritt Clifton, "Furriers on the Defensive," *Animals' Agenda* (April 1990): 39–40.

5. Robert H. Wiebe, *The Search For Order, 1877–1920* (New York: Hill and Wang, 1967), 96.

6. For a work at the center of recent debates over moral philosophy, see MacIntyre's *After Virtue* (Notre Dame, Ind.: Notre Dame University Press, 1981).

Index